CONTROL THEORY

CONTROL THEORY

A New Explanation of
How We Control Our Lives

WILLIAM GLASSER, M.D.

Originally published as *Take Effective Control of Your Life*

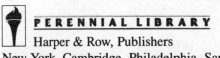

PERENNIAL LIBRARY
Harper & Row, Publishers
New York, Cambridge, Philadelphia, San Francisco
London, Mexico City, São Paulo, Singapore, Sydney

A hardcover edition of this book is published by Harper & Row, Publishers, Inc., under the title *Take Effective Control of Your Life*.

CONTROL THEORY. Copyright © 1984 by William Glasser, Inc. All rights reserved. Printed in the United States of America. No part of this book may be used or reproduced in any manner whatsoever without written permission except in the case of brief quotations embodied in critical articles and reviews. For information address Harper & Row, Publishers, Inc., 10 East 53rd Street, New York, N.Y. 10022. Published simultaneously in Canada by Fitzhenry & Whiteside Limited, Toronto.

First PERENNIAL LIBRARY edition published 1985.

Designer: Helene Berinsky

Library of Congress Cataloging in Publication Data

Glasser, William, 1925–
    Control theory.

    Previously published as: Take effective control of your life.
    Includes index.
    1. Control (Psychology) 2. Imagery (Psychology)—Therapeutic use. 3. Emotions.
4. Performance.
I. Title.
BF632.G55   1985   158'.1   84-47574
ISBN 0-06-091292-8 (pbk.)

    87 88 89 MPC 10 9 8 7 6

To my wife, Naomi, whose meticulous editing of the manuscript has added so much to the way it reads, and to my cousin, Bob Glasser, whose sound editing of my first four books contributed much to their success. I deeply appreciate both their patience with me and their total dedication to clarity. Through their efforts I have learned most of what I know about writing.

Contents

viii   CONTENTS

Acknowledgments

Since 1977, when I was introduced to control theory through William T. Powers' highly theoretical book *Behavior: The Control of Perception* (Chicago: Aldine, 1973), I have been fascinated with the possibilities of using this theory to add strength to our lives. This book is my attempt to put these possibilities into practice, but it is a book of ideas, not research.

There is, however, a small but growing body of psychological research that, though independent of my work, is completely supportive of my control theory ideas. I am grateful to Dr. Ellen J. Langer of Harvard University for compiling much of this corroborating research in her recent well-documented book, *The Psychology of Control* (Beverly Hills, Calif.: Sage Publications, 1983).

Author's Note

Much of this book is concerned with the behaviors we choose as we attempt to control our lives. As I will explain in great detail, all behavior is made up of three components: what we do, what we think, and what we feel. Doing and thinking are always expressed as verbs, like running or meditating, but feelings are usually expressed as adjectives, like depressed, or nouns, like depression. For example, we are used to hearing a man who has just lost a good job complain that he is depressed, or hearing his friends describe him as suffering from depression.

To say the man is depressed would be to infer that the depression happened to him. What I will explain in this book is that it is a behavior he is choosing in order to deal with the difficulty of losing his job. To describe accurately what this man is feeling as a behavior and also be grammatically correct, I would have to say that he is depressing or choosing to depress.

Therefore, throughout this book, verbs rather than nouns and adjectives will be used when they refer to feelings. For example, *headache* will become *headaching*, *phobia* will become *phobicking*, and *anxiety* will become *anxieting*.

While this new and accurate usage may seem strange at first, as you read you will understand why I could not use the familiar adjectives and nouns to describe feelings and remain faithful to the theme of this book—control theory. Language is not insignificant. It is the main vehicle by which we communicate. The more we use it correctly, the farther it will take us in the direction we want to go.

Preface

Our genes, which are the building blocks of our lives, are nothing more than a series of instructions that we must follow if we are to survive and prosper. We become aware of many of these instructions as pictures in our heads—pictures that must be satisfied through the way we live our lives. Driven by our genes, we are captive to these pictures, but what we need to learn is that we are not captive to how we attempt to satisfy them. We almost always have choices, and the better the choice, the more we will be in control of our lives.

Most of us have had the experience of trying to console a friend who is trying to deal with a sudden and unexpected marital breakup. She repeats over and over again, "How could he do this to me? How can I start all over again at my age? What right has he to destroy all we worked for all those years?" It is clear to everyone but the friend that she is choosing to remain hostage to a marriage that is over.

All of us have lived through times like this—suddenly the picture we have is so different from the picture we want, we feel as if we have lost control of our lives. We believe things are hopeless, and we don't know which way to turn. What never occurs to us in these desperate situations is that we are choosing the misery we are feeling, and better choices are available if we can learn how to make them.

In this book I explain that we are not controlled by external events, difficult as they may be. We are motivated completely by forces inside ourselves, and all of our behavior is our attempt to control our own lives. When, for example, we blame our misery on a child, spouse, or parent, we are acting as if they, not we, are in control of our lives. Our friend did not have to be miserable when her husband left—she chose to be miserable in a desperate, but ineffective, effort to regain control over a part of her life she believed was slipping away.

This book will teach you control theory to help you keep effective control of your life. You will learn to make more effective choices than the painful, ineffective ones that too many of us now make as we attempt to satisfy powerful and unrelenting needs within us. But to learn control theory, you will have to give up your lifelong, commonsense belief that almost all you do is a reaction or response to events around you.

This will not be easy. Lifelong beliefs, especially if they are held by almost everyone you know, die hard. I encourage you to be skeptical. Believe nothing in this book, no matter how persuasive my argument, unless you try it out in your life and discover it works for you.

CONTROL THEORY

1

Everything We Think, Do, and Feel Is Generated by What Happens Inside of Us

We are in your car and come to a red light. You stop, and I ask you why you did this. You point to the red light and say, "It turned red—I always stop at red lights." Later your telephone rings, and I ask you why you picked it up. "Because it rang," you say, and start to wonder what kind of a fool I am. But am I really as foolish as you think? Do you always stop for red lights and answer the telephone when it rings? Haven't you ever crashed a red light purposely for what you considered a good reason—perhaps an emergency? Don't you sometimes pay no attention to a ringing phone because you are doing something better at the time?

I don't claim that the red light and ring of the phone have nothing to do with stopping or answering, but they are not what *causes* us to stop or answer. We stop because we all carry around inside of us a powerful desire to do all we can to stay alive. We pick up the phone when it rings because most of us also have a strong desire to talk to anyone who is willing to talk to us. Just think about the possibility of crashing a busy red light or letting the phone ring when you are home alone with nothing to do, and it will become apparent that what moves you to act is inside, not outside, of yourself.

Nothing we do is caused by what happens outside of us. If we believe that what we do is caused by forces outside of us, we are acting like dead machines, not living people. Because we are alive, we can choose whether or not to answer the phone, depending on whether or not it fulfills a current goal. In fact, what I will explain in this book is that everything we do—good or bad, effective or ineffective, painful or pleasurable, crazy or sane, sick or well, drunk or sober—is to satisfy powerful forces within ourselves.

A telephone-answering device is a dead machine. It has no choice but to answer the phone. Its actions are controlled by the outside ring, and its sole purpose, put into it by its "all-powerful" designer, is to respond without question to that ring. It is as truly a slave as only a robot can be. But if we believe that, like machines, we are controlled by outside forces, whether as simple as a red light or as complex as a tyrannical husband, and give up the idea that we always have choices (limited as they may be), we embrace slavery.

If I believe that the motivation for all I do, good or bad, comes from within me, not from the outside world, then, when I am miserable, I cannot claim that my misery is caused by uncaring parents, a boorish spouse, an ungrateful child, or a miserable job. If I were a machine, this claim might be valid. I could be programmed to "feel good" only if those I "needed" treated me well. But I am not a machine, and although I strongly desire good treatment from everyone in my life, if I don't get what I want, *it is my choice* whether or not to be miserable. The fact that it does not seem as if I choose my misery does not make it any less a choice. Again, to refute our old friend common sense, you can no more *make* me miserable than you can *make* me answer the telephone.

By now you may be taking strong exception to my claim that we choose most of the misery we feel. I know that when you lose a good job, it feels as though you've been pushed off a cliff. Everything you have learned all your life tells you that you are not choosing your misery—it is caused by your being out of work. I am sure you are also thinking, It's bad enough that I've lost my job; how could choosing misery make it better? I promise, if you will give me time to prepare the groundwork, I will explain in detail why I make this claim and how you can use this knowledge to take more effective control of your life.

But for now, can you think of at least a few people you know who have made better choices than misery when they have been laid off from a good job? Somehow, without fear or resentment, they dealt with this situation as a challenge and chose not to be overwhelmed. To become more effective, you must learn what these people have learned: How you feel is not controlled by others or events. You are not the physical or psychological slave of your parents, husband, wife, child, boss, the economy, or anything else unless you *choose to be*. Later, as I explain much more about our choice to be miserable if people don't treat us the way we want to be treated, it will turn out that choosing misery may be, at least for a while, a good choice. What is important to learn now is that *it is always a choice and, after a while, almost always a poor choice.*

My cousin tells a joke about a young man visiting a large civic cactus garden in Arizona during the summer. Everyone admiring the cacti, including the young man, was lightly dressed because of the heat. Suddenly he jumped into a large patch of low cacti and rolled around on the spines. Horrified, the others quickly pulled him out, but not before he had become a bloody mess. When they asked why he had jumped in, he said, "It seemed like a good idea at the time."

Haven't we all done our share of cactus rolling? Stop and think of the last foolish thing you chose to do; didn't you do so because at the time it seemed like a good idea? While what we do always seems sensible to us when we do it, even a moment later it may seem like the stupidest thing we could have done. Therefore, good or bad, everything we do is our best choice at that moment. Even though I often say, "I knew it was foolish when I did it," the facts are, foolish or not, at the time it seemed better than anything else I could do.

If, as I claim, the world never causes us to do and feel what we do, I must acknowledge that billions of people, especially those who live their lives in poverty and misery, might bitterly resent this contention. For them, the telephone never rings, the light never turns green, and almost all they have are cacti in which to roll whether they like it or not. Nevertheless, what I will explain is that, regardless of our circumstances, all any of us do, think, and feel, effective or ineffective, is always our best attempt *at the time* to satisfy the forces within us. I recognize that there are countless numbers of people whose best efforts do not work; no matter what they are able to do, they are cold, hungry, or brutalized. But I also claim that it does them no good either to accept their misery or blame it on the world. To do so deprives them of all the opportunities they desperately need to take control of their lives. Those few of the huge numbers of deprived who do beat the odds and take effective control of their lives learn early not to spend much energy blaming the world for their predicament.

For many of us, who are not so desperately situated, taking effective control of our lives is much more possible. But even with all of our opportunities, we will never succeed if, for example, we blame our school failure on the teacher or our lack of work on the economy. And the "spare tires" around our waists are not the fault of Baskin-Robbins, but because we spend too much time eating mocha fudge ripple. When you learn to put control theory to work in your life, you will spend your energy attacking the problem—not blaming it. No matter how you get into the cacti, complaining is ineffective; you may as well climb out, patch yourself up, get going, and learn to stay away from those thorns in the future.

2

Our Basic Needs—
The Powerful Forces
That Drive Us

To be alive is to be driven. Rarely are any of us so relaxed that we feel nothing inside pushing for attention and satisfaction. Built into our genetic instructions, into the very core of our being, is a group of basic needs that we must satisfy continually. One need is immediate—the need to breathe to stay alive. Anytime we get short of air, everything else is unimportant. But immediate or not, all our needs are urgent in the sense that we quickly become aware of any that are not satisfied. Once aware, we have no choice but to attempt to satisfy that need. As soon as that one is satisfied, another need, or perhaps even several acting together or/in conflict, begins to push for satisfaction. There is no respite from the forces that drive us.

Through a careful examination of my life, I have come to believe that I am driven by five needs that together make up the forces that drive me. While lecturing, I have discussed these with thousands of people, and almost all agree that they are driven by the same needs. As I describe them, examine your own life and see if you are driven by these needs. I believe you will find that you are, because it is likely that all creatures of the same species are driven by similar forces.

THE NEED TO SURVIVE AND REPRODUCE

This need seems to be located in a group of small structures clustered at the top of the spinal cord in the most ancient part of our brain. Generally referred to as the "old brain," these structures are assigned the important task of keeping our necessary body machinery functioning and healthy. Breathing, digesting, sweating, and regulating blood pressure are examples of the many vital functions automatically controlled by one or more of these old brain structures. When there is a threat to the body, the old brain is capable of both detecting and coping with this threat, often without our having any awareness of this activity. For example, if a streptococcus invades our throats, the old brain automatically mobilizes our immune systems to cope with the invader; if we exercise, the old brain increases our heart rates to provide our bodies with more oxygen. These and many more old-brain survival activities go on without any awareness on our part that they are occurring.

Much of the time, however, the old brain cannot function effectively by itself. It needs active, conscious help from the other part of the brain, the huge and complicated cerebral cortex, or, as it is often called, the "new brain." When, for example, we are low on water, somewhere deep in the old brain this lack is detected as a threat to our survival. We are not aware that this has been detected because the old brain has neither consciousness nor the ability to initiate any conscious behavior. What it can and does do is send a help-me signal to the new brain, a signal that we have learned to recognize in this instance as thirst. Then, directed by our conscious new brain, we begin to search for water or something else that we have learned will satisfy our thirst. The same operates for food, warmth, air, and sex. When these are needed by our bodies, the old brain signals the new brain, and because we have learned to recognize these signals as hunger, cold, impending suffocation, or sexual desire, we begin the conscious search for what will satisfy these urges. Once any of these is satisfied, we pay it no further attention until, in the natural course of time for our species, it again needs satisfaction.

The cerebral cortex is called the "new brain" because it evolved much later than the old brain. Calling it by this simple name will make it easy for the reader to keep in mind that the brain itself is made up of two major divisions that are in constant communication with each other: the small, unconscious *old brain* and the huge, conscious *new brain*. The new brain is the seat of all our awareness, the source of all our voluntary behavior, and the origin of all we learn.

When we talk about our existence, ourselves, who we are, our minds, or our psychologies, we are talking about the conscious functioning of our new brain. In routine situations where there is no need to make a choice, the new brain is also capable of functioning unconsciously and automatically—e.g., when we walk on familiar ground, we do not have to be aware of where we place our feet—but anytime we make a choice, its functioning is learned and conscious. In these nonroutine situations, we may not be aware of why we are doing what we do, but we are always aware that we are doing it.

Without the new brain, the old brain can keep our bodies alive, but as human beings we do not really exist. If our new brains are destroyed, as in an accident, we can live in an old-brain-supported coma as long as people or machines perform simple new-brain functions such as feeding us and keeping us clean. Most of us have heard of someone who has lapsed into a coma and, with care, has continued to survive for years as an unconscious body.

In affluent countries where survival is rarely a problem, many people encounter difficulty satisfying the frequent, old-brain-generated adult need for reproduction that we become aware of as the urge for sexual release. This difficulty, however, does not concern the old brain, because it is not capable of concern. If it senses that we are well fed and healthy but have not recently engaged in reproductive behavior, it sends a barrage of reproductive signals that we (our new brain) have learned to recognize as sexual frustration. It is then up to the new brain, which is really ourselves, to find a way to satisfy these signals. While there is almost no way we can eat or drink without finding food or beverages, or warm ourselves without shelter, people driven relentlessly by sexual signals have searched for, discovered, and are still discovering a wide variety of sexual activities, many of them even nonreproductive, such as masturbation, that satisfy these signals.

The ultimate sources of these sexual signals are our genes, which carry within them the blueprints for our lives. *What the genes do is best understood if we think of them as providing us with a series of biologic instructions that we must carry out if we are to exist, survive, and prosper.* Many of these instructions have to do with our existence as the bodies we are; for example, the color of our eyes is the result of our cells obeying a blue or brown instruction from an eye-color gene or group of genes. It is also our genes that instruct our old brain to carry out all of its survival activities that, if success-ful, lead us to be healthy and reproductive. If these can be done automatically—for example, sweating or shivering—we have no choice but to carry them out exactly as they are given to us because they are functions of our old brain alone. When cold, we will shiver; when hot, we will sweat; and even if we decide to try to interfere with these basic old-brain functions, we will not be able to do so.

When an old-brain survival or reproductive instruction gets more complex and must be carried out by a new-brain conscious behavior, we have to learn what to do. And because we usually learn more than one way to satisfy most old-brain instructions—breathing is the exception—we learn to choose which way we think is best at the time. As mentioned, with the reproductive instructions that we have learned to satisfy through sexual activities, we have even learned ways, like masturbation, that thwart the purpose of the genetic instruction. But whether we satisfy the purpose of the instruction or not, and no matter how many ways we figure out to do it, what is impossible to do is to be *unaware* of any instruction, survival or reproductive, that is encoded in our genes.

People can starve themselves (as do anorexics and hunger strik-ers), or renounce sex (as do priests and nuns), but they are not so much disregarding a survival instruction as obeying a conflict-ing genetic instruction, centered in their new brain, that they judge is more important to them at this time than staying alive or reproducing.

Therefore, as important as our old brain is to our survival as individuals and as a species, it is by no means the dominant force in our everyday lives. As long as it functions reasonably well, as most old brains with the help of their new brains do, satisfying our sur-vival needs occupies only a minor part of our lives. Most of us are concerned with satisfying the much more difficult and often *conflict-ing needs* that arise not in our unconscious old brain but in our complex, conscious new brain. A politically motivated hunger striker is attempting to satisfy his new-brain need for power, but as meal after meal is put in front of him, he can't help but be tortured by conflict.

These much more complex and difficult-to-satisfy new-brain in-structions are best called "psychological needs" because, like love or power, they have to be satisfied more by people than by things. In fact, a good way to define the term *psychology* is to think of it as the various ways we relate to each other as we attempt to fulfill strong conscious needs that arise within our new brain. But even though new-brain needs are much less specific than old-brain needs (food is much more tangible than love), and even though the behaviors that we use to fulfill them are more psychological than physical (loving is more complex than eating), their source is as much in our genes as the need to breathe. *We are at our core biologic beings: that we satisfy some of our genetic instructions psychologically rather than physically makes neither the instructions less urgent nor the source less biologic.*

The following are the four psychological needs that I believe are encoded in our genes:

THE NEED TO BELONG—TO LOVE, SHARE, AND COOPERATE

Because the instructions to survive, like eat and drink, are so clear-cut and, when we sense them, so urgent, most of us tend to accept the commonsense idea that survival is the basic need, the strongest of the forces inside of us. But again, common sense is wrong, because if the need to survive were basic, there would be no suicide. It would be impossible to kill yourself or even risk your life for fun, as many skydivers do, if the need to survive were basic. Survival is strong, but in a person who attempts suicide or jumps from an airplane for fun, other instructions must be equally strong.

Several years ago I talked to a man who had barely survived a serious attempt to kill himself. When I asked him why he had tried, he replied that he was lonely and had been lonely for so long that being dead seemed a better choice than living in such pain. Research bears him out. Most people who commit or attempt suicide describe incredible loneliness as the reason.

As I look inside myself, I find that the need for friends, family, and love—best described as the need to belong—occupies as large a place in my mind as the need to survive. It may not be as immediate as thirst or hunger, but if, over the long pull, I did not have the close, loving family and friends that I almost take for granted, I think that the idea that life is hardly worth living would come occasionally to mind. Even if we have friends and family, many of us also enjoy a sense of belonging with pets, plants, and even an inanimate object like a "beloved" boat or computer.

THE NEED FOR POWER

We are all aware of how much of their fortunes some wealthy people spend trying to get elected to public office. Even though they have a great deal of power, they seem to be driven by the quest for more—and politics, for many, is the acme of power. This need to get others to obey us, and the esteem that accompanies it, drives all of us. Even the most humble compete with other self-effacers for humility. As we walk down the street, most of us attend to how we appear in comparison to other people. Are we as well dressed, well groomed, younger or older? Do we walk as well, as fast, as carefully, or as recklessly? Are we as rich, good-looking, tall, or trim? And this is just walking down the street. Imagine how competitive it would be to run for office against someone who wants to win as much as you do.

In the struggle for power, men, because of their greater physical strength, have until now grabbed and held the largest share. Women, however, have no less a power need, and in our culture are now asserting themselves publicly to satisfy what is written in their genes. We have the privilege of living through this historic struggle, and those who think women will give up do not understand that they have no choice except to continue: The struggle is written in their genes. What is different today from years ago is that the fight is now out in the open; beneath the surface it has always been there.

In this need for power, I believe we differ from all other living creatures. Most nonhuman creatures have only a minimal drive for power beyond what is needed for survival. Mammals and birds struggle for a strong mate or to protect a limited territory, but only the human competes for power for the sake of power. George Orwell said it best in his book *Animal Farm* with the cogent observation that "all animals are created equal and some are more equal than others." Only we have a need for getting to the "top" that keeps us competing long past the time when any rational use exists for this much power or recognition. King Midas is much more the rule than the exception as families feud to the point of bloodshed over money, property, or who tells whom what to do. We must be descended from people who struggled successfully not only for the strongest mate but for the biggest cave, the best place by the fire, and, as societies evolved, the leadership of the group.

As individuals, our drive for power is often in direct conflict with our need to belong. People marry for love and belonging; but once married, driven by the need for power, they struggle to take control of the relationship. As they assert themselves to bend their mates, however, they find it harder and harder to behave in loving ways. Insufficient love, I believe, is not what destroys close relationships; what tears them apart is the power struggle that seems inevitable. It crowds out love when husbands and wives fail to negotiate and find power compromises that are acceptable to both. Many a divorced person will state quite honestly, "I still love him [or her], but I can't live with him—it is too much of a struggle."

But power also brings people together. Tennis star Jimmy Connors commented that as he lost tennis matches, he also lost "friends." After slipping for a year or two, he once again rose to the top and quickly regained those same "friends." Having become a little wiser, he realized they hung around him more to share his power than because they cared for him.

Although people are attracted by power, when it is too unequal, it is hard to maintain friendships. How many of you still maintain an active friendship with someone who was once financially comfortable and is now poor? And even when we try, don't they make it hard for us because, no longer able to compete, they feel uncomfortable around us?

When we are faced with a direct conflict between the need for power and the need to belong, we try to resolve it by juggling. As soon as we are sure of a little power, we go out of our way to be friendly. When we are sure of our friends, we may take a chance and try for power even though it may take time away from friends and family. How many men reading this have worked long hours for the recognition and power that accompanies a lot of money, hours that were hard on your family because they missed you and wanted you more than your promise of all the good things that money would buy? How many women reading this have risked the love of an insecure husband to go back to school or work for recognition? You may have rationalized that you needed the money for financial security, but chances are it was as much power and recognition that drove you to make the move. The conflict between belonging and power is a great threat to any relationship; those of us who can negotiate a balance between these needs are fortunate.

THE NEED FOR FREEDOM

Can you conceive of staying alive if you were not free to move around? Could you survive if you were tied up? Some species move more than others, but all living creatures must move to stay alive. "Nudge it and see if it moves" is the usual way we test whether or not something is alive. But we want to be free far beyond the ability to move—even the worst dictatorship allows people to move. What we want is the freedom to choose how we are to live our lives, to express ourselves freely, associate with whom we choose, read and write what satisfies us, and worship or not worship as we believe. These and more are the freedoms that people have fought and died for throughout history because those in power always find their power threatened by people who have freedom. If you were restricted by those in power from enjoying them, you, too, might consider risking your life. Freedom is a powerful motivator when we become aware of its loss, but keep in mind that those who kill for power always claim they are killing for freedom. Most of the time they are killing for the "freedom" to tell other people how to live their lives.

Most of us in the free world have reasonable political freedoms. What we don't have in many cases is both freedom and love. Like power and belonging, these needs are in conflict in many people's minds, and the best many of us can do is to compromise—to try to find a livable middle course. A frequent complaint of many young people, especially women, is that it is so hard to find someone who will commit himself to marriage. Many young men say that they want the freedom to keep their options open, and they look at marriage as a loss of these "options," whatever they may be. Today, because many of us have the money to have more options, we look for someone who is not only close and loving but also sensitive enough to our need for freedom so that we can exercise some of these options. People like this are hard to find, because both men and women tend to believe that if we "give" too much freedom to the one we love, we may lose some love—and in some cases, we may. But we may also lose it if we try to control them, so, again, this common conflict between our basic needs is difficult to resolve.

Recently my wife was doing errands when she met a casual friend —let's call her Susan—whom she had not seen for several years. Susan poured out her misery because Dave, her husband of a quarter of a century, had abruptly left her, filed for divorce, and moved in with another woman. A large part of what he had done was to exercise his need for freedom. What she complained of was her sudden lack of belonging. Perhaps Dave will find even less freedom in his new relationship, but it was partly his need for freedom that drove him to this step. I have a friend who has never married and, except for his long-deceased mother, has had only superficial relationships in his life of over sixty years. He is as wealthy as Croesus and free as a bird, but suffers so from loneliness that his freedom is of little value to him. Although he recognizes his loneliness, he continues to claim he can't get involved, because the smallest involvement infringes on his cherished "freedom."

To satisfy all of our needs requires a constant give-and-take. If you are my boss and exercise power, you deprive me of some freedom. But in order to have some power and freedom of my own, I need the money you pay me. Without it, I can't support my family, with whom I feel a powerful sense of belonging. But as much as I love my children, they tie me down. If they are too demanding, or if we have no one who will give us some time away from them, we may grow to resent them. The problems of single parenthood are in many cases money, but underneath the lack of money is the loss of freedom that a little money could purchase. All our intricately intertwined needs are also separate, and rarely can we figure out how to live so that we fulfill each to the extent we would like. When we do, for that period of time, however short, we are very much in control of our lives.

THE NEED FOR FUN

While most of us do not feel as driven by fun as we are by power, freedom, or belonging, I believe it is as much a basic need as any other. We will make drastic alterations in the way we live, even risk our lives, as we attempt to play to satisfy this need. It might have been as much the need for fun that caused Dave to leave Susan as the need for freedom. Many long-term relationships grow empty because fun is neglected, taken for granted, or not felt as much needed by one of the partners as the other.

I believe that fun is a basic genetic instruction for all higher animals because it is the way they learn. Higher animals are born with very little knowledge of how to fulfill their needs. They must learn this, and the fact that learning is fun is a great incentive to assimilate what we need to satisfy all our needs. If a man and wife have a relationship in which they are learning together and also encouraging each other to learn separately, theirs will likely be a fun-filled, solid relationship.

Experimenters have shown that female apes and monkeys that are isolated, and thus deprived of the normal social play of childhood, fail to learn even the basic lessons of how to mother a child. Mothering may be innate in lower animals and birds, but in primates almost no behaviors are innate and play is how we learn much of what we need to know to live effectively. Most animals, even primates, stop playing as they grow to adulthood, because, having both simple needs and little conflict between these needs, by the time they are full grown they have learned almost all they need to know. Humans, driven by complex psychological needs that are always in some conflict, must learn all their lives and therefore continue to play and look for fun well into old age. In fact, losing interest in looking for fun may be a sign of mental deterioration in older people.

We are the only creatures who believe so implicitly in learning that we establish formal schools, but in doing so we have mostly failed to appreciate that learning without play is difficult. We laud our astronauts for joking in space because we recognize that a grim atmosphere is not conducive to the intense mental demands of their missions, but we have little tolerance for a child or teacher who jokes in the classroom. Think back to a teacher whose lessons you still vividly remember and you will almost aways recall that, whatever she taught, her class was fun. It is unfortunate that even educators who recognize the need for fun in the classroom are intimidated by those in power from suggesting that grim and boring classes may be a major failing of our educational system. If our genetic need for fun is tied to learning, as I think it is, then harder assignments and longer hours alone may do little to remedy the failings of our schools. When we are both learning and having fun, we often look forward to hard work and long hours; without fun, these become drudgery. Try to teach "better" procedures in a no-fun atmosphere to competent employees of any large organization and you will soon be lecturing to empty chairs.

Laughter is a unique human behavior, but why we laugh is not well understood. I believe the main reason we laugh is that, for the moment, we experience a powerful sense that our need for fun is fulfilled. Animals who do not have the mental capacity to get this experience cannot laugh. But what is funny and causes us to laugh is that we are made aware of a quick and powerful insight into a new truth and/or have been vividly shown the falsity of an old tradition. The punch line of a joke always contains a valuable lesson delivered in a new, quick, and usually irreverent manner. The reason adults do not laugh at children's jokes is that they do not usually teach us anything new, and children do not laugh at our jokes because they are not ready to learn what we find funny.

Comedians instruct us in the truth about ourselves, and it is because the lesson is so apt that we find it funny. For example, the late comic Joe E. Lewis is well remembered for "I've been rich and I've been poor and, believe me, rich is better." With it he so completely destroys the inane "virtues of poverty" argument that we are hard pressed not to laugh when confronted with the clear truth of this simple statement. The next time you laugh, think a moment and I am sure you will find that you have unexpectedly encountered a short burst of truth and wisdom.

While some people pursue fun on their own, most of us like to play with interesting people. But what makes them interesting is that we learn from them, and the way we learn is to talk to them, sharing ideas and experiences. For example, I play tennis for fun, but I look for partners who are interesting to spend time with because we share more than just a game of tennis. As much as I like fun, however, I don't think I would kill or die for it as I might for freedom or power (though I'd risk a lot for a good tennis match).

Fun is such an integral part of our lives that most of us could not conceive of life without it. Yet it can be as much in conflict with the other needs as they are with each other. It can be in conflict with survival (people parachute or mountain climb for fun), with belonging (men watch football all weekend while wives and children nag for their attention), and with power (some people become so obsessed with the struggle for power that they leave no time at all for fun). But when you have power, you also have more time for fun, so power can also be very supportive of this need.

There may be other needs, but these are the ones I find in my head, and most of the people I talk to find the same ones. Many of these same people also claim a need for belief in a higher power, and, certainly, many people have died and will continue to die for their religious beliefs. If you feel this need inside your head, you are in the majority, but you will also find that it, like the others, is often in conflict with another need. For example, I know several priests and nuns who have left organized religion because they could not satisfy their need for personal belonging, a family of their own, if they remained. Others find such a powerful sense of both belonging and power in their religion that they have no need for the close sexual and family relationships that most of us desire.

It is not important to the thesis of this book that I establish with any certainty what the basic needs are that drive us. To gain effective control of our lives, we have to satisfy what we believe is basic to us and learn to respect and not frustrate others in fulfilling what is basic to them. All you will ever know is what drives *you*, just as I will know only what drives *me*. We cannot look into other people's heads and see what drives them. We can listen to what they tell us and look at what they do, but we should not make the mistake of assuming that we *know* what drives them. This means that we can never be sure of satisfying anyone else no matter what we do. It is reasonably safe, however, to assume that what drives us is similar to what drives other people, so there is no harm in trying to satisfy another person. But if what we do does not work, we should be careful not to persist or we run the risk of losing that person for a friend or lover.

As I lecture on the ideas in this book, I hear frequently from people who claim that there is just one universal need: the need to know. They claim that this single need underlies everything: All of our behavior is initiated by this need to find out more and more about the world around us. I don't deny that knowing about the world, and ourselves as part of it, is important, but I don't believe this is a basic need and that we try *to know* just for the sake of knowing any more than I believe that people climb mountains just because they are there. They climb for power, fun, freedom, or companionship, but not to find out what's on top. People who are satisfied can live in blissful ignorance; my wife has no more interest in scuba diving than I have in baking. Ask your neighbor if he would like to join you in learning to read Chinese, and if he can't wait to start, I will believe in the need to know.

Others argue that religion, or the holy spirit inside us all, is the single need from which all others are derived. This may be, but there is no hard evidence that this is the case for many people. Iraqis and Iranians are fighting as I write this, killing and dying for the same Moslem faith. I don't dispute their beliefs, but it seems to me that despite their strong religious claims, they are fighting for power. It is inconceivable that any religion would advocate killing as a holy function, but there are plenty of religions that advocate and encourage their followers to struggle for power the same way many politicians do. On the other hand, religious leaders have always been in the forefront of those who fight for freedom as evidenced by what the pope is trying to do to aid the solidarity movement in Poland. To survive, people have temporarily put aside their religious beliefs as some in the Donner party did when they practiced cannibalism. The bulk of the evidence is that for many, religion may be a basic need, but it is unlikely that it is any more *the* basic need than the need to survive.

If there were one overriding need, life would be simple indeed. We would be like lower animals and plants that struggle only to survive. We would all get along much better because there would be no conflict within ourselves. Fish who eat smaller fish have no idea that they are depriving the small fish of their lives or freedom, nor do most of us (some vegetarians excluded) feel for the turkeys' rights on Thanksgiving Day. If the need to belong were overriding, families would get along much better than most do; and if the need for power were absolute, it is likely that we would already have had nuclear conflict. It might be a better world if the need for fun were supreme, but all fun and no work also tends to make Jack a dull boy.

What has led us to become the most intelligent of all living creatures is the constant conflict between the separate needs. Our continual struggle to satisfy these disparate forces—and especially to resolve the ever-present conflicts between them—has pushed us to become the most intelligent of all life. And, driven by our genes, we are unable to escape this conflict, so it is likely we will get even smarter. We will need all the sense we can garner to deal with our most powerful creation, nuclear energy, and still survive, belong, and be free.

The purpose of this book is to help increase our knowledge by attempting to teach the *control theory* through which we attempt to satisfy these needs. I believe that far too few of us have any clear idea how these unrelenting needs cause us to behave the way we do. If we continue to follow the dead-end belief that we have no internal instructions, that our genes are mostly concerned with the color of our eyes and hair, and that what we do is caused by forces outside ourselves, we never will.

3

The Pictures
in Our Heads

Suppose you had a grandson and your daughter left you in charge while he was taking a nap. She said she would be right back, because he would be ravenous when he awoke and she knew you had no idea what to feed an eleven-month-old child. She was right. As soon as she left, he awoke screaming his head off, obviously starved. You tried a bottle, but he rejected it—he had something more substantial in mind. But what? Being unused to a howling baby, and desperate, you tried a chocolate-chip cookie and it worked wonders. At first, he did not seem to know what it was, but he was a quick learner. He quickly polished off three cookies. She returned and almost polished you off for being so stupid as to give a baby chocolate. "Now," she said, "he will be yelling all day for those cookies." She was right. If he is like most of us, he will probably have chocolate on his mind for the rest of his life. I'm sure grandparents reading this will sympathize. After all, what are we for if not to introduce grandchildren to the finer things of life?

I tell this story to illustrate how we develop the pictures in our heads—the specific pictures that we believe will satisfy our built-in needs. At the time we are conceived, the requirement that we satisfy our basic needs is built into our genetic instructions, but when we are born, we have not the slightest idea of what these needs are or how to fulfill them. To satisfy them, even before birth, we begin to create what is best described as a picture album in our heads and begin to fill it with detailed pictures of what we want. Our whole lives will be spent enlarging these albums.

The baby in the above story had begun to understand that when he woke up, the urge he felt was hunger. He also knew, when he looked through his small picture album, that the picture of his bottle was not what he wanted to satisfy his hunger. I doubt that he had the picture of any specific food in his tiny album, and I am sure that he knew nothing about chocolate-chip cookies, but he had the hazy picture of something that was not a bottle.

He also knew how to cry. He learned that moments after he was born and had been crying ever since with great success to get his urges satisfied. Well aware that when he cried, people started moving to pacify him, he used this behavior to control others besides his grandfather. To those of us who have long had a picture of choco-late-chip cookies and a thousand other delicious foods in our albums, this all seems quite simple. But for a baby, it is far from simple to find out what will satisfy the urges he feels when, in the beginning, he hardly knows what these urges are.

It is like going to the store and telling the clerk that you want something—"Please bring it quickly." When he asks you what it is, you say, "Something that will satisfy me, you fool, and bring it right away!" He is a willing clerk and he brings you one item after another, but you keep yelling that he is a miserable incompetent and he should please hurry up and get what you want or you will take the store apart.

We've all been in that clerk's position with babies, animals, and even plants: If a favorite plant starts to die, we say, "If only I knew what it wants." But when we start out, none of us knows what we want; we only know we desperately want something—so we may scream, cry, pout, or thrash about randomly to try to get it. The way we learn what we want is: When what we do gets us something that satisfies a need, we store the picture of what satisfied us in a place in our heads. From now on I will refer to this place as a *personal picture album.* When that baby learned how satisfying chocolate-chip cookies were, he pasted the picture of those cookies in his personal picture album, where it's my guess he will keep it for the rest of his life.

He was crying to get the world to offer him something to satisfy his hunger. Although he did not know what would do it, he was able to master the simple logic that if he didn't have it, it must be outside himself. This means that to recognize whatever it was, he had to make contact with the world. The way all living creatures make this contact is through the senses associated with our eyes, ears, fingers, tongues, and noses. But it is also important to keep in mind that it is through these same senses that we make contact with our own minds and bodies, both of which are, to us, a very important part of the real world.

I like to think that all our senses combine into an extraordinary camera that can take visual pictures, auditory pictures, gustatory pictures, tactile pictures, and so forth. In simple terms, this *sensory camera* can take a picture of anything we can perceive through any of our senses. I like to use the word *pictures* rather than the technically correct term, *perceptions,* because pictures are easier to understand. Since more than 80 percent of the perceptions we store in our albums are visual, *pictures* is also a reasonably accurate term.

After biting into the cookie, the baby liked it very much. Immediately, he took a picture of that cookie with his sensory camera and stored it in his picture album as a picture of something to look for again when he got a similar urge. He might not yet have completely understood that the urge was hunger, but what he did know was that whatever it was, chocolate-chip cookies satisfied it.

This means that we store in our personal picture albums the pictures of anything in the world that we believe will satisfy one or more of our basic needs. For the rest of his life, when that baby gets hungry, he will start turning the food pages of his album. Many times, when he comes to the pictures of chocolate-chip cookies, he will say to himself, "That's what I want right now," and he'll try to find a chocolate-chip cookie in the real world. I have some friends who tell me that there are times, especially when they are on a diet, that they think they could kill for chocolate. With a little thought, it will become apparent that your personal picture album (the pictures in your head) is the specific motivation for all you attempt to do with your life.

Everything you know, however, is not stored in your picture album—it is not the same as your memory. For example, to satisfy our needs, we speak and read, and to do this we store all the words we use and recognize in our memory, but these words are not in our picture albums unless they are a part of a need-satisfying picture. It satisfies many people to say grace before meals, so that prayer is in their albums, but the specific words that make up that prayer are stored in their much larger memory. Therefore, the picture album or the world in my head is a small, selective part of my total memory. It is the "world" that I want right now—it could even be called my "ideal world," but it is more than ideal; it is the world I believe I must have or my needs will not be satisfied.

Our personal picture albums are never hazy or general; they always contain very *specific* pictures of what will satisfy our needs right now. Anything that satisfies me in any way, I store. If I see something that does not fulfill any part of any need, I will pay little or no attention to it. I may, of course, be aware that something is there, and I may even know what it is; for example, I still remember that I had a green Chevrolet in 1950. But that picture, while it may be in my memory, is no longer in my album as it does not presently satisfy any need.

While I am making up my mind whether a picture satisfies me, I may store it in my album temporarily, but if it does not pass the test of being something worth keeping, I will remove it. This is why old people, who are feeble and can no longer actively fulfill their never-ceasing needs, have little memory for the present. What is the sense of storing what is unsatisfying? For the past, however, when they were capable of dealing effectively with the world, their memory is excellent. As we grow older and less effective, we tend to paste fewer and fewer pictures in our albums. To maintain our self-esteem, we want to talk about the good old pictures, the ones we pasted in permanently when we were young and effective.

When a picture that has been in my album for years is no longer as satisfying as I would like it to be, I will often look for a new, more satisfying picture to replace it. It is like my old car: I replaced it with a better new one. This is what Dave did when he left his wife for another woman. He had Susan in his album for many years as a need-satisfying wife until for reasons known only to him, which he may never choose to share with anyone, he replaced her with the picture of someone else. It may be that the new woman better satisfied his need for love. If she was wealthy, she may have satisfied a long frustrated need for power; or, if she was more tolerant of his life-style, she may have satisfied his need for freedom. For whatever reason, maybe even for fun, he put her picture in and took Susan's out. And when we change important pictures, we change our lives.

It is likely that we have hundreds and even thousands of pictures that will satisfy each need. If we come from large, loving families, we may have a hundred relatives that we like to be with—*but we must have at least one picture for every need.* If we have no picture at all, the need that is unsatisfied will drive us first to look for a picture that may satisfy it, and then for a way to make satisfying contact with whatever it is in the real world that the picture represents. To have a need without quickly finding a picture to satisfy it is almost impossible. But keep in mind that *we commonly have pictures in our albums that cannot be satisfied in the real world—if wishes were horses, then beggars would ride.*

The man I talked to who attempted suicide said he had no one, and he despaired of ever finding someone. In his despair he attempted to kill himself; life without a picture to satisfy the need to belong is really life without hope. My guess is that he did have someone, but because he could not make contact with that person, he was so hopeless that he said he had no one. The problem is rarely that there are no pictures, but that we can't satisfy the pictures we have. Unless we are genetically flawed—as are psychopaths, who seem to have a strong need for power but no need to belong—we usually have at least one picture of someone to love in our albums at all times.

The power of the pictures is total. In our relentless efforts to satisfy them, we may go so far as to choose behaviors that endanger our lives. For centuries parents have become distraught when a teen-age daughter chooses to stop eating and begins to starve to death. It is still called by its ancient Latin label, anorexia nervosa —loss of appetite for no known physical reason. Some understanding of this crazy choice not to eat can be gleaned through the concept of the picture albums in our heads. A researcher who did an ingenious experiment with anorexics showed them pictures depicting their heads superimposed on a series of bodies ranging from what most of us would call "normal" all the way to skeletal. Then he asked the young women, "Which of the bodies do you like seeing your head attached to?" To the researcher's surprise, they said none of them—all were too fat. What they were saying was that they wanted to be thinner than whatever they saw in the mirror. To achieve this irrational degree of thinness, they had no choice but to starve themselves, and they did.

This example illustrates that the pictures in our albums do not have to be rational. Crazy or sane, all any picture has to do is fulfill the need that the person decides is most important at the time. Although this does not explain why an anorexic pastes in that life-endangering picture, it does lead any sensible physician treating her to tell her that he will not allow her to starve herself to death. If necessary she will be force-fed to keep her alive. Because they aim to be thinner, but not to die, this treatment makes some sense and, more important, keeps them alive while a good counselor attempts to help them change the pictures in their albums. Once they change the pictures, they are horrified that they are so thin and they start to eat. Later we will talk about how this is done.

Alcoholics are dominated by the picture of themselves satisfying any and all of their needs through alcohol. As long as this "wonderful, all-satisfying" picture is in their albums, they will drink not only when they are frustrated but also to prevent possible future frustration. Any therapy that does not change the picture of alcohol satisfying their needs to something less destructive will be ineffective. When they join Alcoholics Anonymous, as many do, they begin to replace the picture of alcohol with AA. If they attend AA regularly, they are able to stop drinking, because being involved with this satisfying organization keeps the picture of AA predominant. All alcoholics who are AA regulars believe that the picture of them drinking alcohol is never completely removed from their albums. It may be moved far to the back, but not out. They contend—and they should know—that if they fail to attend AA and do not keep the AA picture large and active in the front of their albums, they will slip back to drinking.

To some extent the pictures explain why homosexuals and others who do not satisfy their sexual urges in the usual heterosexual ways find it almost impossible to change their sexual behavior. This is because in their albums they have pictures of themselves satisfying their sexual urges with other than what most people consider usual sexual activities. For reasons that no one yet can explain, once we get any sexually-satisfying picture, usual or unusual, into our albums, this picture is almost impossible to remove. If we attempt, because of cultural pressure, to engage in any long-term sexual activity that is different from the pictures in our heads, we will be either unable or unwilling to perform. If we can't change the pictures ourselves, and there is, as yet, no counseling technique that can lead us to change most of them, then we must accept the pictures we have. Difficult as this may be, we must learn as best as we can to live with them within the rules of society.

If the sexual pictures are destructive to others—as in the case of men who have the picture that they want sex only with children—these men will have to learn to live sexually frustrated lives or risk going to prison. Even though the subject of unusual sex practices has been much researched, the main finding so far is that, almost impossible as it is to change any sexual picture, normal or abnormal, *they are not innate.* We know this because studies show that children of homosexuals are statistically no more likely to be homosexual than is the general population.

That the pictures can cause you to engage in nonreproductive homosexual practices that conflict with the basic need to reproduce illustrates not only how powerful they are but also how specifically they determine the course of your life. The pictures, therefore, represent the *specific* life you *want* to live. And if this involves real people who may not want to play the exact part in your life that you assign to them in your album, you may engage in a long, miserable struggle to get them to change. Susan is now engaged in this struggle because Dave refuses to be what she wants him to be. If he won't go back to what she wants—and it is likely he won't—her choice is to either continue her losing battle or replace his picture. Fortunately, the picture of whom we love is usually replaceable with someone else, and my guess is that eventually Susan will do this.

Large-brained humans are more capable of changing their pictures than lower creatures, but at any one time we want what we want and nothing else. I eat my eggs over hard, because that is the picture in my head of how eggs should be eaten. My wife shudders as she cooks them, because that is not the picture in her head. When she urges me to eat my eggs softer, she has no chance of succeeding unless she can persuade me to change my picture. It is likely that before he left, Dave had many arguments with Susan over the different pictures of marriage each had in his and her albums. Husbands, wives, and families that do not get along together always have vastly different pictures in their heads of how each wants to be satisfied by the other.

It is not easy to change our own pictures, but it is even more difficult to persuade others to change theirs. To change a picture, we have to replace it with another that, if not equally satisfying to the need in question, is at least reasonably satisfying. *This can be done only through negotiation and compromise; force will not work.*

Most people do not know that they are motivated by the pictures in their heads and have no idea how powerful and specific they are. In most relationships, even good ones, we constantly attempt to force others to change to what we want. Try to force your son to play little-league baseball, your daughter to cut her waist-long hair, your husband to play bridge, or your wife to jog five miles before breakfast and you risk a hornets' nest of resistance. Think how hard it is for you to throw away a favorite old sweater, now in tatters, a relatively insignificant picture, and you begin to see how quickly you resent anyone who pressures you to change a picture.

People who live together must learn that it is impossible for any two of us to have the same pictures in our heads. Expand this to a family and the odds against this sharing grow even greater. No two people can live exactly the same life, and though we are all driven by the same needs, even these usually vary in strength from person to person. I may need love much more than you do, and you may be more driven by power than I am. But both of us need some of both, and our success as a couple will depend on how well we can agree on some specific pictures that will satisfy these needs. If you and I live together and share half the pictures in our albums, we probably have more in common than most. Therefore, if we want to satisfy the need to belong, which drives us together, we must learn to share what we have in common, and accept, or at least tolerate, the pictures we don't share. If we want to take effective control of our lives, the knowledge that *no two of us can share the same pictures must become an integral part of the way we deal with all those around us.*

Tim, your teen-age son, refuses to work in school, listens to "weird" music all night long, and admits to smoking marijuana. You and he have very different pictures of what his life should be. It seems to you that it is impossible to talk to him about anything—just looking at him "makes" you upset. Variations on this theme run through all families. When the pictures get to be impossibly different in a marriage, a divorce is possible, but you can't divorce a child or a parent. It's even hard to separate completely from a brother or sister. Frustrating as they may be, they are not easy to replace.

In our attempts to patch up failing relationships, we usually try to force a change. We pressure Tim to work in school and stop smoking pot. We take away the car, cut his allowance, restrict his friends from the house, and impose a curfew. But this rarely works. Whether you like it or not, Tim will live by his pictures, not yours, as long as they satisfy him. Tim may even rub it in by saying, "Look, I don't hassle you, why don't you leave me alone?" And you always rise to the bait with a lecture that you are not hassling him, only trying to point out how he is ruining his life. As you do, things between the two of you continue to deteriorate. Still, you nag because you can't accept Tim's attitude toward school or his use of drugs no matter how hard you try. The way he chooses to live his life is incompatible with your album.

To get along with Tim and perhaps eventually persuade him to change some of his pictures, you need to start the process by trying to find some pictures that you and Tim still share. One shared picture will get the process started. The only way any relationship can be patched up when the pictures are very different is to try to find one or more new pictures that can be shared or to try again to share some old ones that once satisfied you both. You must look for something that you and Tim can do together, something you both want to do, and then do it. Let's suppose that at one time you enjoyed fishing with Tim, but for a long time you have been getting along so badly that you haven't even considered asking him to go fishing. You now realize that you must find a satisfying way to get together, so you offer to take him fishing, saying, "Just fishing, no lectures." He accepts, you do it, and get along well for a weekend. It's a little like old times. If you are patient, don't lecture, and do a few more things together that work, you have a chance to patch up any once-strong relationship. If what Tim is choosing to do with his life is not need-fulfilling in the long run, as it usually is not, he may begin to pay attention to what you have been saying. Remember, you have already said it many times, you don't have to say it anymore.

With many children, parents, brothers, or sisters this may be all we can do. We may have to settle for what we can share and accept that many of the pictures in our albums will never be the same, *but the better we get along, the more pictures we will begin to share again.*

If, in frustration, you kick Tim out of the house, all you are likely to accomplish is losing him. But your concern is that if you do nothing, he may destroy himself before your eyes. This is a tough dilemma with no easy solutions, but if you keep in mind that you must find some pictures to share, you will realize that you can't accomplish this if you kick him out. A compromise might be to try a middle course—let him stay, but set rules for no loud music and no pot smoking in the house as minimal conditions. If he breaks these rules, tell him he has to leave for twelve hours and come back and try again. Continue to talk to him pleasantly (no lectures) and try to share at least one pleasurable activity with him each week, but offer no money or other tangible support unless he goes to school or work. Then wait and wait.

Persuading someone to change pictures always takes a long time. Don't look for anyone to prescribe the exact path to follow between toughness and laxness. It does not exist. But if you stay close to Tim through keeping good contact at home and with an occasional fishing trip, the path widens. He has more choices than the limited ones of destroying himself at home or leaving with little ability to take care of himself on his own.

If we want to stay with others, we must spend our time enjoying what we do share, always trying to find a new picture to share, and accepting or at least tolerating what is not shared. If you find that you just can't accept a different picture in your wife's album, perhaps you can work out an agreement that today we'll do it my way and tomorrow we'll do it yours. Many people work out vacations that way. If, right now, you are in the midst of a deteriorating relationship, you should take the initiative to try to work out some compatible pictures with your partner. Don't wait for him to do this; he doesn't know how. Even if only one of you understands the importance of the pictures in your heads, you have a better chance of getting along together.

The new pictures we put in our heads often conflict with old ones. Dave may have a picture of himself as a very loyal person and feel miserably disloyal as he tries to find a better life with his new wife. But if he were to return to Susan, as he may, there might still be insufficient love, fun, or freedom to satisfy other pictures that are important to him. Later in this book I will explain conflict in great detail, but for now it is important that you understand that there is nothing in control theory that says the pictures in our heads have to be compatible. In fact, incompatibility and even conflict are common in all of our albums. Dave's picture of himself as loyal will not disappear just because he has met a new and, to him, exciting woman. It may put a damper on this new relationship for years. To continue to see himself as loyal, he might act in a financially responsible way to Susan, so that to this extent she might benefit by that picture.

Since the only way we can take pictures out of our albums is to replace them with others that will fulfill the same basic need reasonably well, people will endure a great deal, sometimes choose a lifetime of misery, because they can't replace pictures. Many women endure brutal beatings and humiliations in marriage, but stay with these husbands because they are still the only "possible" picture of a loving person. After suffering abuse, these women may complain that their lives are living hells, but still they stay, because they do not believe they can replace their husbands in their albums. If these women could understand the picture-album concept, they would find that it is a possible answer to the question they continually ask themselves, "Why do I stay?" They might seek more actively for a better picture to begin to take more effective control of their lives.

But what if we are deprived of the way we have fulfilled a need for years? Suppose a beloved spouse dies—what happens to that picture? For a while, nothing. It remains the same as always; in fact, sometime it gets a little better as we tend to glorify the dead. In the real world we have lost a loved one, but in the album she is still very much alive. This is why we choose to suffer so much when we lose someone. As I will explain later, when there is nothing we can do, we almost always choose to suffer. But grieving is also sensible. Those close to us gather around, and we are reassured that many still care. In time, we accept that we cannot bring the loved one back to life. Supported by friends and relatives, we begin the slow, painful process of removing her from our albums, realizing that to keep her there would cause us to grieve forever.

Although it is never possible to deny the pictures in our albums, at times we still try to push them out of mind, because to admit that we can do nothing to achieve them is a painful admission. We all have pictures in our albums of how our marriages could be better or our jobs more rewarding, but we try to deny these pictures, because to admit their existence opens up wounds that we would rather keep closed. We try to tell ourselves everything is fine, but we are still unsatisfied.

A lonely woman once came to me for counseling and said that the previous day she had gone to an emergency room because she could hardly breathe. She was still short of breath. The doctors had not been able to find much wrong except that she smoked too much. Gasping as she spoke, she vehemently denied that her shortness of breath might be psychological. But as we talked about what she wanted, which was a good relationship, and she felt that with my help she might learn to find one, her breathing eased. She found it hard to admit that she needed help; her shortness of breath became her way to ask for it.

Your picture album—in which you find love, worth, success, fun, and freedom—is the world you would like to live in, where somehow or other all your desires, even conflicting ones, are satisfied. None of us has a picture in his album of himself doing badly. We may at times choose to do what those around us say is self-destructive, but we don't do these things to destroy ourselves. The pictures we are trying to satisfy make sense to us. Tim did not think he was destroying his life; his father did.

Sometimes we may choose to "fail" (in the mind of someone else —a father, for example) because it seems to us that this "failure" will get us more of what we want than if we "succeeded." To Tim, success in school might set the stage for a career, like law, that he does not want. Or, less specifically, to succeed would be to put himself in a position for his father to make greater and greater demands that take Tim farther and farther from the pictures in his head. None of us wants to fail, but we must keep in mind that no two of us have the same picture of success. It is the picture of success in *your* head, nobody else's, that causes you to do what you do.

4

What Makes Us Behave

The best way to begin the explanation of why we behave is to take a look at how a thermostat controls the air temperature in a room. Most of us don't realize that a thermostat is not activated by the cold or hot air—what activates it is the difference between its set temperature and the air temperature in the room. It no more turns on because of what happens outside of it than Susan's upset was caused by Dave's leaving. Just as we are, the thermostat is internally motivated and attempts to control the temperature of the room to the temperature it "wants." Susan, therefore, was not upset because Dave left; she chose to be upset as her best effort to deal with the difference between the picture of Dave in her head, living with her as her husband, and the picture of Dave in the real world, gone with another woman. Why she chooses upset to deal with this difficult situation, I will explain in later chapters; first I must explain the cause of all our behaviors—anything that we do, think, or feel.

The thermostat also has an internal world—simple, I'll admit, but still a very specific picture that will not be satisfied until the air around it is at its set temperature. It also has a sensory apparatus, a sensory camera, which can detect whether the temperature in the room is below or above its setting. Then, like us, it can act to reduce that difference. But, *unlike us,* if it can't get the temperature it "wants" through the furnace or air cooler, it is stuck. There is nothing more that it, a dead machine, can do. Living creatures are never stuck. If we can't get what we want with what we know, we will create new behaviors that may be more effective. But old or new, all our behavior is our constant attempt to reduce the difference between what we want (the pictures in our heads) and what we have (the way we see situations in the world).

These newly created behaviors may not work. They may be no better or even worse in practice than what we have. But there is always the possibility that they will be better, and when we are desperate to get what we want, we will always consider them and often try them. Everything wonderfully innovative, from the wheel to the computer, has been achieved by people struggling to create something in the real world that was represented by a picture in their heads. But, as I will explain in detail later, everything miserably innovative, from heart disease to psychosis, has also been created by people involved in this same struggle.

If Dave's wife won't take Dave out of her album, she will try to get him back by doing all she knows and all she can learn. She will also consider seriously any new idea that may come to her. In a sense, she was probably doing something new by "spilling her guts" to casual aquaintances like my wife. If these attempts fail, as they often do, she cannot quit. Pushed by the picture she wants, she will expand her efforts, and in doing so almost always choose increasingly painful and senseless ways to behave. Whenever there is a difference between what we want and what we have, *we must behave* —which means acting, thinking, feeling, or involving our body, all of which are components of the total behaviors we generate as we struggle endlessly to get what we want.

Take a moment and look back into your own life to a time when you were very frustrated, a time when the picture in your head was far better than the real situation. Didn't you stubbornly hold on to this picture, even though the longer you did, the further you got from what you wanted? Didn't you *do* fewer effective things, *think* more irrational thoughts, and *feel* a variety of painful feelings that you may never have felt before? Didn't you approach acquaintances and pour out your tale of woe, driven in this frustrating situation to try a variety of actions, thoughts, and feelings that were to some degree new to you? Did you perhaps think some genuinely *crazy* thoughts, or feel more depressed than ever before? Maybe you "got" sick or began to act irresponsibly. Perhaps you began to use drugs or alcohol in larger quantities than ever before.

You frequently act, think, and feel this way if you suffer a severe personal rejection or lose a good job. It could be that you were desperate to get into a prestigious educational program, such as medical school, but no one would accept you. Many of us persist in a losing business venture long after we should have quit, to cut our losses. Why do you hold on to the picture in your head long after all possibilities of achieving that picture in the real world seem exhausted? It is probably for one of two reasons: (1) You do not believe that a better picture or at least a reasonably different picture would satisfy you as well as the unattainable one or (2) you do not seem to be able to give up the hope that somehow you can come up with a behavior that will get you what you want.

As you read this book, aren't you are still holding on to at least one picture you can't get and, if so, becoming more and more miserable and inneffective as you continue the losing struggle? This is because we are constructed in such a way that whenever there is a difference between the picture we want and the picture we now see, a *signal,* generated by this difference, starts us behaving, and we will continue to behave as long as that signal persists. We actually feel this signal as an urge to behave. Try to look at a painting hanging crooked on a wall and ignore the immediate urge to straighten it out. For most of us, who have a picture in our heads that all paintings should hang straight, this urge is overwhelming. It is almost impossible to ignore the crooked picture.

Just as your furnace whirs into action because an electric signal has been generated in the thermostat by the difference between the temperature it wants and the temperature in the room, Susan is sending a large signal to all the parts of her brain that generate behaviors. All her obsessive complaining, sympathy seeking, anger, misery, and scheming for revenge are initiated by the strong continuing signal generated by the difference in her pictures. If my wife had known Susan better, she might have tried to persuade her to remove Dave from her album. Susan, driven hard by the signal to keep doing something, would very likely have paid little heed to that advice. Remember, Susan does not know anything about needs, pictures, or signals, only that she has a strong urge to continue trying to get Dave back.

For purposes of this nontechnical book, I would like to group all the parts of the brain where behaviors are generated and call them our *behavioral system.* It is this system that is turned on, and stays on as long as there is a signal to behave. It is this system that is pouring out all miserable behaviors Susan is presently using in her desperate attempt to get Dave back.

By the time you are old enough to read this book, you have a huge behavioral system in which everything that you have learned to do, think, and feel is stored and organized in a way that it is ready for use whenever the system is signaled. Any signal generated by the difference in the pictures will immediately cause us to look into our behavioral systems and select from this large stock of organized behaviors one or more that we judge is the best available behavior to reduce this difference. What Susan selected when she met my wife was one of her well-used give-me-some-advice-I'm-desperate behaviors in the hope that perhaps my wife would be able to help her. But keep in mind, our behavior is always related to what we want. If she had hated her marriage but stuck to it because of a sense of loyalty, and then, to her relief, Dave pulled out, she would have chosen a far different behavior when she met my wife. She might not have mentioned her marriage, but spoken instead about her plans for a new life without the drag of a husband she no longer loved.

When we are born, our behavioral systems are almost empty except for most of the essential physiological activities like swallowing, blinking, urinating, and sucking. Compared to lower animals, who have quite a few well-organized behaviors like walking or swimming built in at birth, we have almost none. But in contrast to lower animals, who learn very few complex behaviors after birth, we continue all our lives to learn an almost infinite number of complicated behaviors, which we organize into an easily tapped stockpile from which we select those that we believe will best satisfy our needs. Think about how much a two-year-old already knows how to do and you begin to appreciate how large this system will become in time.

But even at birth, we are far from helpless. Along with most mammals and birds who depend on parents to survive, we are born with one powerful and well-organized behavior: *the ability to express anger strongly.* If we couldn't, our chances of survival would be slim. Even small babies know that to survive they must do all they can to control the world around them. There is no doubt that a normal newborn has the capacity to act as mad as a hornet when she realizes that her present surroundings are far different from the tranquil, all-fulfilling world of her mother's womb—probably the first picture in her tiny album.

The baby has no idea that she will die if she can't do something to make her world more comfortable, but sensing strongly the difference between the pictures, she immediately signals her behavioral system for a behavior that will get the real world to be more like the comfortable world of her head. The only behavior in her tiny system that will actively affect the world is her strong ability to express anger. But an angry baby is doing much more than simply feeling; she is involved in a total behavior in which she not only feels angry but is thrashing about angrily and, as much as she can, my guess is, thinking angry thoughts. Since this is a total behavior, instead of calling it anger, I would like to call it *angering,* a term that not only better describes the feeling but implies that doing and thinking always accompany the feeling. I realize that the more accurate verb form, *angering,* is unfamiliar, and in the beginning will seem cumbersome. I promise, however, to explain in the next few chapters why learning to express behaviors not as nouns, but as the verbs they actually are, will help us to take more effective control of our lives.

Angering is the only behavior we are born with that has any direct effect on the world around us. Swallowing, grasping, blinking, coughing, sneezing, urinating, or defecating are needed for survival, but without angering to get someone in the world to take care of us, these behaviors have little value; it will do no good to swallow if no one feeds us. As we mature, we will learn an almost infinite number of ways to do, think, and feel that will strongly affect the world; but in the beginning, all we can do is anger, and, for us who survived, this was enough. Today, in most of the world, babies who do not anger will probably still survive, but I'm sure in some of the desperately poor, overpopulated parts of the third world, the ability to anger strongly is often the difference between infants who survive and those who don't. From the standpoint of evolution, infants who survived and left us the genetic instruction to anger did so because they were able to generate a lot of angering.

We become acutely aware at birth that we are being driven by a variety of urges, but we don't have the faintest idea what they are. It will be several years before we can begin to sort out what the urges inside us mean, and even longer before we have a specific idea of what our general needs are. But to survive, we must immediately figure out how to fulfill powerful urges that are a mystery to us. Not only do we not know what these urges are, but we don't even know that they must be fulfilled in the world. In fact, we don't even know what the world is or who we really are. All we know is that we are uncomfortable, and we have an urge to be as comfortable as we were in the hazy picture in our tiny albums of what life was like inside our mothers.

So we anger in the hope of becoming more comfortable; and whoever senses our anger, usually our mothers, do all they can to please us because they are driven by powerful pictures in their heads to take good care of us. As we are being taken care of, we use our sensory cameras to observe that it seems to be done in just one way or another, and soon we observe that it is a person who is doing all these wonderful things for us. Because this person is so satisfying, we take her picture and paste it in our albums, where it will likely remain for the rest of our lives.

We continue to take careful notes of what she does and how this satisfies the various urges of which we are becoming more aware each day. Sometimes we want attention to satisfy our need for belonging, other times food to satisfy our need for survival. We might even just scream to see how quickly she will come, and when she rushes to us, we feel satisfied that we have a lot of power. We are more and more sensing who and what is out there and learning new behaviors that we can use to *control* whatever it is to our satisfaction. Our sensory cameras become more sensitive as they mature, and the pictures they take, which we paste in our albums, become more and more specific. As they do, we begin to organize our primitive angering into a small but powerful repertoire of angering behaviors to satisfy what we now realize are a variety of different and rapidly clearing pictures.

Though mothering a child is highly satisfying, even a devoted mother will find it difficult to subordinate her needs completely to those of a demanding child. An angering child is a tyrant, and a mother's need for freedom will begin to assert itself. A good mother also recognizes that if she becomes a slave to her baby, he won't learn to take care of himself. So not long after birth, she stops letting the baby totally control her with angering. She starts giving him the message that he has to begin to consider doing some things for himself. After he is fed, loved, cleaned, and obviously tired, his mother puts him down and does not run to him when, to assert his power, he screams for her attention. Now that angering does not work, the baby is forced to begin to consider something else to fulfill the urges he feels.

If their mothers do not become their slaves, most babies learn that they cannot control them as completely as they would like. If you throw a tantrum and no one responds, further angering is useless. And if you decide to do something for yourself, angering is more harmful than helpful in getting started. Try to accomplish anything worthwhile when you are angering and you will see what I mean. Therefore, when they scream and nothing happens, most babies learn quickly to look for something new. Remember, we are all creative, and one of the first new behaviors that most babies create is to smile. Once they have created it, they may use it to get what they want, and it may work better than angering in many situations.

Smiling, and later chortling for joy, is a powerful controlling behavior. Mother finds it almost impossible to resist a smiling and soon laughing baby. In fact, this behavior is so effective that it will even control strangers—something angering rarely did. Smiling is a marvelous creation, and we store it in our behavioral systems to use for the rest of our lives. Once the baby has learned that there are other behaviors besides angering, through imitating and creating he begins the rapid process of adding to his behavioral system a well-organized group of powerful acting, thinking, and feeling behaviors. Almost all of these are more effective and more pleasurable than angering.

As we grow and go to school, read books, and watch television, we learn many new behaviors, but most of what we store in our behavioral systems, effective and ineffective, we learn from the people we care for or respect. Driven by our need to belong, we have put these people in our albums and they become our most effectual teachers. It is the behaviors we have, and our ability to learn more and create more, that we must use to gain as much control over the world as we can. But there are great differences in how well people do this, and this difference is directly related to the adequacy of our behavioral systems. But, adequate or not, the way we are constructed, our behaviors are all we have to satisfy our needs.

5

We Are a Control System

We use a great deal of control-theory terminology in our lives without realizing it when we talk about "being in control" or "losing control." When we successfully diet, we tell others with great pleasure that we are in control of our weight; we say we are in control of our fitness when we prepare for our first marathon. We feel good when our children, students, golf game, employees, or even our congressmen are "under control." Our most painful times are when we lose control: if our children are in trouble, or the company for which we have worked thirty years goes bankrupt, or our doctor tells us we have a crippling disease.

Most of us recognize that our greatest problems arise when we try to control ourselves or other people. Controlling *things,* like the crabgrass in our lawns, is much easier. How, for example, do I control my daughter who wants to marry someone she hardly knows, or my son who refuses to work? If I make up my mind to save some money, I find that I can't control myself because I love to buy clothes. Or if I want to be thin, how do I control myself when all the food looks so good? Even if I buy a car that turns out to be a lemon, it is not the faulty car I find so frustrating but the dealer that I turn to for help. Everywhere we turn, the problem of gaining or losing control over ourselves or others surfaces. This is because all living organisms, as well as many dead machines, like thermostats, function as *control systems.*

A control system acts upon the world and itself as part of the world to attempt to get the picture that it wants. When I am thirsty and satisfy my thirst by drinking some water, my behavior is that of a simple, well-functioning control system: I am in control of what I do, and what I do satisfies a thirst-quenching picture in my head. By contrast, if you could always get me to drink by handing me a glass of water, you, not I, would be in control of my life. In theory, you could make me drink myself to death if you were cruel enough to keep giving me water. This machinelike example sounds silly, but it is representative of the most common theory of why we behave the way we do. It is called "stimulus-response theory," and anything that functions by this theory would be called a stimulus-response (S-R) system.

As I explained in the first chapter, any theory that contends that our behavior is a response to outside events or stimuli is wrong. I have also explained that all of our behavior is generated by needs inside ourselves; for example, we are not an S-R system that stops because a light turns red, *but a control system that stops because it satisfies our need to stay alive.* To take effective control of our lives, we have to learn how we function as control systems and make that learning an integral part of the way we live. Most of us have a long way to go, because the mechanical S-R system is not only the system that almost all "scientific" psychology embraces, but, even more important, the commonsense system that almost all of us embrace.

For example, parents believe that they can and should control their children to get them to do what the parents think is best, and they will often resort to force to "stimulate them to make the correct response." Some employers believe that all their workers really want is money, so that with wages employees can be made to do almost anything, satisfying or not. Husbands attempt to control wives, and wives, husbands, because they believe they can. Teachers attempt to control students; doctors, patients; politicians, constituents; and lobbyists, politicians—all because they believe that this is not only possible but desirable. And because we often do something that satisfies someone else, and they do "respond" in the way we wanted, we are fooled again and again into believing that we *caused* them to do what we wanted.

Children frequently do obey parents who exert tyrannical control, some workers will do almost anything for more money, and spouses often go along with their husbands or wives even when frustrated.

Many teachers find that their classes are obedient even when the subject is boring; some patients follow their doctors as if they were holy; elected politicians often lead people to their own destruction. But, keep in mind, those who follow, who seem as if they are being controlled, do so only as long as following satisfies them. When it no longer does, they not only stop following, they begin to struggle to gain or regain control of the situation. More often than not, this struggle is expressed in a variety of miserable behaviors, such as choosing to depress, or getting involved in a self-destructive illness such as heart disease.

In the following chapters I will explain in great detail why we do this. First, we must learn how we function as control systems. Only then will we accept that directly or indirectly we often choose pain and disability as our best attempts to control ourselves or others around us, and often both. We may even believe that people are accepting control when they are not. For example, a wife may act subservient to her husband and appear to welcome his authority over her. As she does, she will be unaware that she is choosing to suffer excruciating migraine headaches as her way of rebelling against or even counteracting his control. But whether we are aware of it or not, and no matter how hard we try to convince ourselves that their control may be good for us, if people's attempts to control us, or even our attempts to control ourselves, frustrate a basic need, we will in some way choose to rebel. This rebellion is rarely direct. It is almost always in painful, indirect ways, like choosing to depress, or migraine, or even in more self-destructive ways like developing illness. Our hospitals are filled with people who have lost effective control of their lives. Together with many of the physicians who treat them, they are unaware that their rebellion against the control of others, or their ineffective attempts to control themselves, are being expressed in illnesses like peptic ulcers, colitis, asthma, rheumatoid arthritis, or heart disease.

Regardless of how we struggle to control or to escape from control, whether with conscious angering or less-conscious sickness, if we can learn that this is what we are doing, we have the beginning of what we need to know to take more effective control of our lives. With this knowledge we will be able to start making more effective choices than these painful and self-destructive behaviors. Norman Cousins, a renowned journalist, was instrumental in causing his recovery from a crippling form of spinal arthritis by separating himself from traditional medical care and taking control of his own life even while critically ill. How he did this, especially how he fulfilled his need for fun, is beautifully described in his best-selling book *Anatomy of an Illness.* *

As much as we like to believe we can control other people, we cannot unless what we do persuades them that it satisfies some picture in their heads. We can usually persuade more effectively with the carrot than the stick—that is, praise seems more effective than punishment, because most of us have in our albums a need-fulfilling picture of being praised. But if we suspect that the praise is just to get us to do something we don't want to do, praise may be even less persuasive than punishment. Many of us resent being tricked even more than we resent being hurt.

Not only is it almost impossible to control people to get them to do willingly what does not satisfy them, it is extremely difficult to get animals to accept our control if it does not satisfy them. I make this point to show that if we can't control an animal, there is little chance that we can ever sucessfully control a person. This is well illustrated by a man who trains piglets to perform in amusement parks. Using food as a desirable "stimulus," he gets them to climb up a ladder and then slide down a slide. At the bottom of the slide, they trip a lever that releases a small amount of food into a dish. To get more food, because they never get enough to satisfy the hunger of a growing piglet, they have to climb the ladder and slide down again, again, and again.

According to S-R theory, a healthy, hungry piglet, never getting enough food, should climb and slide until he grows too feeble to climb the ladder. In practice, however, he will do it for only a few weeks and then quit. He is through climbing, and no amount of food will "stimulate" him to climb again. This means a new piglet is needed on stage every few weeks—but, to quote one of the more philosophical of the retired piglets just before he was turned into bacon, "That's show biz."

There is no way to explain this seemingly antisurvival behavior through the carrot-and-stick theory. Only through understanding

---

*Norman Cousins, *Anatomy of an Illness* (New York: W. W. Norton, 1979).

control theory, or how the piglet functions as a control system, can this refusal to slide be explained. People who have worked with animals have long observed that when an animal, using the limited intelligence it has, decides that it has lost control, it gives up. Rats who are restrained in the trainer's hand until they stop struggling and are then put into a barrel of water will drown in a few minutes, while rats put into the water without prior restraint will swim for hours before they give up. The pig, seeing an endless life of feeding indignities (I like to think animals have dignity), also senses such a loss of control that he gives up and starves. No external "stimuli" will work if the animal decides that to deal with it, he can no longer control his life.

How long would you slide down a slide in the same circumstances? Maybe longer than a piglet, but few of us would continue for very long if we were convinced that it was the only way we could eat for the rest of our lives. Because we have a sense of the future, we will submit to indignities as long as we have hope, but there is a point at which we, too, will rebel even at the risk of our lives. History is filled with martyrs who died for one or more pictures in their albums—and in the right circumstance, many of us are capable of becoming martyrs. There is a point beyond which none of will submit to authority, but long before we reach that point, most of us will choose to suffer long-term pain and disability as our way of attempting to gain or to regain control over our lives.

If you can begin to think of yourself as a control system, you will have less trouble learning that your motivation is always to control not only for present needs but, after those are satisfied, future ones. For example, suppose, having just finished a big, satisfying dinner, you go to the refrigerator to put away some leftovers and you notice that you are out of eggs. You don't want an egg right then, perhaps not even in the morning, but you still feel a little loss of control. Not because you are out of eggs, but because you have a picture in your album of a well-stocked refrigerator, and "no eggs" represents a slight loss of control over the food supply.

During a recent gasoline shortage, many of us stopped at gas stations and "topped off" every chance we had. Of course, we wanted to have enough to get where we wanted to go, but the shortage represented far more than just not having enough gasoline; in our heads, a full tank represented control, and topping off was our effort to regain control. Why is Monopoly such an intriguing game? Despite the chance involved, it represents an opportunity to gain control for a short time. Most of us who have less control than we would like are attracted to getting more even in play. It is fundamental to a control system that it always wants to have a sense of control, and any way that you can gain this, even in play, is pleasurable.

Almost all parents reading this book have pictures in their heads of their children as successful and happy. In an attempt to achieve this, we constantly tell them what to do. Our motivation is not necessarily selfish; we are convinced that what we want is best for our children. But when we attempt to exercise some control, we almost always run into problems. *This is because as much as a control system likes to be in control, no control system wants to be controlled.*

This explains why people who have been in control most of their lives resent taking charity. Hungry enough to accept a handout, they still resent the giver. This is because when they take charity, they lose some control. When what we try to do seems, even to them, more for our benefit than theirs, if they sense that we are trying to control them, they may reject the benefit rather than accept the control.

You can observe your resentment of control in your life every day. You tend to anger quickly when anyone makes even the smallest move to control you. Just a simple question such as "Why are you late?" can cause you to bristle if you regard it as a challenge to your sense of control. You have to be very careful when you play a competitive game with a child. You risk having an enraged child on your hands if he senses that you "let" him win. To him, this represents the ultimate loss of control, and for a long time he may refuse to play this or any other game with you.

How many of you either work for yourselves and earn less than you did when you worked for someone else or know someone else in this position? It is likely that you were well aware that you struck out on your own to gain more control over your life. You may now work longer hours for less money, but during these hours you are more in control, and to you this is what freedom and power are all about. Control is not a need; it is the way we must function to fulfill our needs. But since we are all built in the same way, we are all engaged in a never-ending struggle with each other. We are so aware of this struggle that we tend to regard anyone who can live in happy harmony with all around him as a superhuman saint or a subhuman fool. What makes this struggle possible for those of us who are neither saints nor fools is our need to belong; because we need each other, we are all willing to accept some control—but not too much.

Our lives, therefore, are a continual struggle to gain control in a way that we satisfy our needs and not deprive those around us, especially those close to us, of satisfying theirs. Easy as this is to say, and logical as it sounds, very few of us realize how little attention we pay to this claim in practice. Just as nations prepare for war and go to war to control others who they believe are trying to control them, much of our pain, misery, and insanity, as well as many of the chronic illnesses we suffer, are our personal battles to gain control of people around us.

In the end, whether we engage in national wars or personal wars, human beings have only one avenue, negotiation and compromise, through which to work out a way to live in harmony. Susan and Dave show little more faith in negotiating or compromising than a newborn baby as they choose the self-destructive behaviors that brought their marriage to an end. My hope is that if the Susans and Daves of this world can learn the control-theory common sense that our only effective tools for getting along with each other are negotiation and compromise, maybe as a nation we can learn the same lesson before it is too late. Since there will be no one left to talk peace after the next war, it makes good sense to break with tradition and hold the peace conference first.

6

We Always Have Control Over What We Do

My closest friend runs a highly competitive business in which he frequently encounters unexpected problems, such as bad weather, supplier strikes, and rapidly changing government regulations. Sometimes they bunch together and he feels as if he is losing control of the whole operation. At these times, rather than sit at his desk and mope, he goes to the supermarket. He tells me that no matter how tough things get, as he fills his cart with items like fresh raspberries, blueberries, succulent mushrooms, vintage wine, and expensive ice cream, he feels better with each item he tosses into the basket. By the time he gets home, his mind is so filled with pictures of ice cream topped with raspberries or blueberries that the troubles at the office seem to melt away.

I tell this story as a way to begin my explanation of what we can and cannot control as we behave to satisfy our needs. What I will explain in this chapter is that, regardless of how we *feel,* we always have some control over what we *do.* When my friend loses control, he goes food shopping. If nowhere else, in the market he is in command.

To satisfy any picture, however, we must, as control systems, be capable of sensing what is going on both around us and inside of us and then be able to act on that information. To find out what is going on around us, we use our five well-known external senses: vision, hearing, touch, taste, and smell. We learn what is going on inside of us through a group of less well-known internal sensors that feed us pertinent information about the state of our bodies. These sensors tell us when we are hungry, tired, thirsty, sexually aroused, sick, tense, or depressed, to cite just a few of the many internal sensations that inform us about what is going on inside of us. Our internal sensors also keep us in touch with our internal world so that we are continually aware of what need-satisfying pictures are presently available in our albums.

While our internal sensors are usually individual (thirst is sensed as thirst and nothing else), our external senses can be thought of as components of a total system that provides us with a composite sensory picture of the world around us. In most situations we pay more attention to some of these sensory components than to others. For example, when I go to a movie, I attend mostly to what I sense through my eyes and ears and little to what I sense from my nose, mouth, or skin. But even though I pay little attention to smell, taste, and touch, information continues to come in through these senses. If the aroma of hot buttered popcorn is all around me and I have an eat-popcorn picture in my album, I may decide to go to the lobby and get some for myself. We cannot turn off any of our senses—all components function all the time—but, depending on what we want, we can and do pay more attention to some than to others on most occasions.

When we sense that what we have is not what we want, we generate behaviors that act on the world and, of course, on ourselves as part of the world. As we examine our behavior, it may seem, at first glance, to be made up of four different behaviors, but these seemingly different activities, like our five senses, are actually *four separate components of what is always a total behavior.*

The four easily recognizable *components* that together make up our *total behavior* are as follows:

1. *Doing* (or active behaviors): such as walking or talking, which means voluntarily moving all or some part of our bodies in some way that we want to move it. (Some involuntary behaviors necessarily accompany most routine activities; for example, I don't voluntarily position my tongue when I talk.)

2. *Thinking:* voluntarily generating thoughts or involuntarily generating thoughts as in dreams.

3. *Feeling:* such as anger and joy, which means we have the ability to generate a wide variety of feelings, both pleasurable and painful, just as we initiate thoughts and actions. Some of these may be known only to us, as when we hide pain or joy, but most of what we feel is readily apparent to those around us, especially to those who know us well. Difficult as it may be to accept, our feelings are just as much a part of our total behavior as what we do and what we think.

4. *Physiology:* such as sweating or clenching our fists, which means the ability to generate the voluntary and involuntary body mechanisms involved in all we do, think, and feel.

There is a complex physiology that provides the bodily where-withal for doing, thinking, and feeling. For example, the intense pleasure that accompanies satisfying sexual activity is the result of a natural morphinelike chemical that is injected into our brain through the action of special cells that become active before and during orgasm. Not only our actions but also our thoughts can have a dramatic effect on the physiology of our bodies. While watching a horror movie, we usually become aware of our heart racing at a rate far above normal. As much as we tell ourselves it is only a movie and "ask" our hearts to stop racing, the fearful thoughts that now occupy our minds send a speed-up message to the part of our old brain that regulates heartbeat.

While there is little practical value in learning more about how we sense the world than what I mention here, there is tremendous value in learning as much as we can about how we behave—especially how we can control our behavior so that we are more effective in satisfying our needs. To do this, let's take a close look at how I might deal with a very frustrating situation—failure to pass an important examination. When I went into the test, the dominant picture in my head was of passing, but now all my senses are busy informing me of the bad news that I flunked. Because I still want to pass, I will begin to generate some mostly sensible (at least to me) behaviors that I believe will help me to regain control of this unsatisfactory situation.

In this case, what makes immediate sense to me to *do* is to go home, sit in my chair, drink a few beers, and avoid my classmates, most of whom I believe passed the examination. What I may *think* is sensible is to condemn myself for not studying hard enough, wish that I had passed, wonder what to do now, and hope it was all a mistake—a whole series of thoughts that are my immediate best attempts to both deal with and rationalize what happened. I will also generate a variety of *feelings* that also make good sense to me right now. Probably I'll be depressed, irritated, somewhat resentful, despondent, anxious, tense, and fearful—a whole series of emotions that seem to me appropriate to this failure. I also may be "suffering" from a headache or diarrhea, which, added to what I am doing, thinking, and feeling, comprises my *total behavior* in this situation.

When we encounter unfortunate situations like this, most of us are much more aware of one of the components of our behavior than we are of the others. Because of this, we tend to think of that component as a separate behavior rather than be aware that it is just one part of a total behavior. For example, if someone asked me how I was doing after I failed the examination, I would be unlikely to mention all the components I've just listed. What I probably would talk about is the feeling component: "I'm upset," I would say. "I'm miserably depressed about the whole situation." I would do what we all tend to do when we talk about anything complex, which is to describe it by its most obvious or recognizable component.

When I fail, the most recognizable component to me, and to anyone who knows me, is the depression. While I may also be sitting home thinking discouraging thoughts, I am more aware of the depressed feeling than of what I am doing or thinking. This is why, when you asked how I was doing, I told you I was depressed. But this feeling component, while it is the largest and most obvious component to me and those who know me, is still just one of the four components that make up my total behavior. The more we are able to recognize that it is just *one of the four components that make up our total behavior,* the more we will be in control of our lives. Therefore, as you learn control theory, you will stop using the inaccurate noun forms, like *depression,* that describe only the feeling component of your four-component behavior and begin to use verbs to describe the total behavior. When you do, accurate verbs like *depressing, anxietying,* and *headaching* will become as much a part of your speech as the inaccurate nouns *depression, headache,* and *anxiety* are right now.

As soon as we begin to think of our actions as total behaviors, it will become apparent that when I fail a test, the "depression" I feel doesn't happen to me; it is the feeling component of the total behavior of depressing that I am choosing in this unhappy situation. This means that I not only choose to sit in the chair and choose to think miserable thoughts, both obvious choices, I also choose the "depression" I feel and the headache or diarrhea that I "suffer." It is impossible to choose a total behavior and not choose all its components.

If, however, we want to change a total behavior, the way we can do it is to choose to change its doing and thinking components. To show how this works, let me carry the test example a step further. Suppose, after I told you I was depressed, you tried to cheer me up by saying, "Come on, stop moping. You can take the test again in a couple of months. The world hasn't come to an end. Do a little work and you can still pass the course. There's no sense in sitting around and just acting miserable." All this would be perfectly reasonable for you to say, but regardless of your good intentions, *if I continue to choose to sit there,* it is almost impossible for me to cheer up. Unless I choose to change what I do, think, or both—and almost always I can—I will not change what I feel, because the total behavior of depressing makes good sense to me right now.

It makes sense because, as I will explain in the next chapter, whenever I am severely disappointed, there are four powerful, rational reasons for me to deal with this situation by choosing a total behavior that has as its major component a miserable feeling. Based on these reasons, depressing is not only a sensible choice, it actually seems to me, as it does to all of us in similar situations, to be the best possible choice at this particular time. Therefore, no matter how hard you try to cheer me up, and as much as I "claim" I would like to, I will not, because misery, as a large part of my total behavior, makes the most sense to me right now.

Not only are we almost totally unaware of why we choose misery, we are also unaware of why it does not feel like a choice. I will explain the three reasons why it does not feel like a choice in chapter 8. But what you now know is that when you are frustrated and "miserable," it seems to you that you have no choices: You feel locked into the misery you are experiencing. You would certainly have every right to argue, "If my misery is a choice, then why, after I depress a while, can't I make a happier choice? Besides, if I can't change how I feel, what good does it do to know it's a choice?"

The answer is that, as important as the feeling component is, we are fortunate that it is only one of the four components that make up the total behavior, depressing. *When I fail the test, I have no ability to change how I feel, separate from what I do or think, but I have almost complete ability to change what I do, and some ability to change what I think, regardless of how I am choosing to feel.* I have arbitrary control over both these components, especially over what I do. Suppose as I sit huddled in my chair thinking miserable failing thoughts, concentrating mostly on how miserable I feel, you asked me, "What are you thinking about?" I might reply, "Well, I'm thinking, What's the sense of going on? I'm a failure. I may as well quit college altogether."

But it is also likely that if you tried, and struck upon a subject that interested me, you could engage me in a nonacademic conversation. Perhaps you might try football or music, and, quickly, I could choose to think some different thoughts. I might continue to depress as the feeling component, but I can separate my thoughts from my feelings and divert my mind to the new subject. I can also choose to turn on the television and watch a game or an opera. As soon as I do, however, I can't fail to notice that as hard as it is to change a sensible feeling, even as I continue to depress, I have some control over what I choose to think and almost total control over what I choose to do. Not only can I turn on the game or the opera, I can get up and go to the refrigerator to get an apple. After the game is over, I can go for a walk, go to a movie or the library, play tennis, or even start to study for another examination. Just as my friend chooses to go marketing when he is upset, there is a whole gamut of things I can do, *regardless of how I feel,* if any of these doing behaviors makes sense to me.

Right now, while reading this chapter, please try this simple experiment. Try to feel angry. Go to work at it and try to generate rage. You will probably find it impossible. Because there is no sense feeling angry right now, you can't arbitrarily choose to anger. Even an actor has to have a reason (character motivation) before he can generate a feeling. Try as we will, it is almost impossible, *arbitrarily,* to choose a feeling that makes no sense.

Now try to think green; blot out all else and think green. This may be possible, but it takes a great deal of concentration. If you relax even for a moment, green will slip from your mind because it makes no sense. Now raise your right hand—pick it up and raise it above your head. Immediately, you see that this doing behavior is easy to accomplish because, as we have evolved, the *doing* component of our behavior has come almost completely under our voluntary control whether what we do makes sense or not. Therefore, as you sit trying to change your feeling to "anger," you can't do it. You may be able to change your thoughts to "green" for a short while, but then it will slip away. But deciding to raise your right hand in the air is something you can do indefinitely regardless of whether it is satisfying or ridiculous.

At this stage of our evolution, we have almost total control over the doing component, some over the thinking component, almost none over the feeling component, and even less over the physiological component of our total behavior. For example, it's very hard not to be scared at a horror movie; and once scared, it is impossible to stop our hearts from racing. But any time we want, we can get up and leave. When we do, we will quickly stop being frightened and our heart rates will soon return to normal. Once outside, we can begin to think about what to do next and, if it is feasible, do it.

Therefore, if I fail an important test and "sensibly" choose to depress, there is no way I can arbitrarily stop depressing and cheer up just because I don't like being miserable. I have, however, the arbitrary ability to change what I choose to do. I do not have to sit huddled in my chair depressing; I can, regardless of how I feel, call a friend and arrange a game of tennis. When we begin to play, I may still complain of how bad I feel, say I'm sorry I got him out on such a "bad" day, and, between games, tell him over and over how bad I feel and that, educationally, I'm doomed. I may not play my best, but I still can play.

As I play, however, invariably I will notice that I begin to think different thoughts, feel different feelings, and experience a different physiology. My headaching or stomachaching clears up, my depressing seems to go away, and I start to think more about winning the match than failing the test.

All of us have had experiences like this, and from them there is a very important lesson to be learned: *Because we always have control over the doing component of our behavior, if we markedly change that component, we cannot avoid changing the thinking, feeling, and physiological components as well.* The more we get involved in an active doing behavior that is markedly different from what we were doing when choosing a misery, like depressing or headaching, the more we will also change what we think, feel, and experience from our bodies. And if what we do gives us greater control, it will be accompanied by better feelings, more pleasant thoughts, and greater physical comfort.

If it were not this way, once we chose a miserable behavior like depressing, we would be stuck not only with our painful feelings but also with our discouraging thoughts and our rigid "confinement" to our chairs. The only way out of this potential bind is to learn that we always have control over the doing component, and unless we are physically restrained, we can, for example, choose to do something more effective than sit in our chairs and depress. We can go to the library, buckle down, study hard, and petition the department for a reexamination. And as we do, we cannot help noticing that we are thinking more effective thoughts, feeling more pleasurable feelings, and our physiology has returned to its prefailure state.

With this in mind, let me now go ahead and explain why people who are severely frustrated do not usually choose effective doing behaviors; why most of us find it *sensible* to choose a wide variety of miserable feeling behaviors—for example, depressing, migraining, or anxietying—as total behaviors.

7
Why It Makes Sense to Choose Misery

Even if you understand what has been explained so far, you probably find it difficult to believe that you not only choose most of the misery you suffer, but that choosing misery almost always makes good sense at the time. An incident that happened some years ago will illustrate what I mean. I was driving slowly just a few blocks from our house with my three children. We live in a quiet residential neighborhood and the street was deserted except for a boy about ten years old riding his bike rapidly toward us on the other side of the street. Suddenly, for no apparent reason, he fell. It was a nasty fall, and I stopped the car to see if he needed assistance. He was stunned for a moment and then quickly hopped back on his bike and pedaled away fast in the direction from which he came.

As soon as he got on his bike, I said to my three kids, "Look, he won't cry!" And he didn't. I was trying to teach them a little psychology, and when, as I predicted, he didn't cry, I asked them why. My children seemed surprised at the question, but then all three of them, almost as a chorus, said, "He won't cry here, he'll wait until he gets home." They then explained what I had also concluded: He could choose whether and when to cry, and it made no sense crying to an empty street. (He never looked in our direction at all.) If he was going to cry, he needed someone to cry for and he was headed home to perform for his mother. We all predicted that he would start crying when he turned into his driveway and would be going full blast by the time he got inside the house.

Compare this quite conscious choice to feel bad at the appropriate time and place with an experience a friend of mine had recently and see if they really aren't the same. He had been trying to get a date with Janice for months, and finally she agreed to forget her career for a night and go out with him. But at the last minute, she called to tell him she was sick. Instantly, he felt miserable, but there was nothing about the way he felt in this disappointing and frustrating situation that would lead him to have even the remotest idea that he was choosing the pain he was experiencing. If anything in his life had ever seemed to be happening to him, *and not chosen by him,* it was what he felt that disappointing night. It didn't seem to help much that her hoarse voice and hacking cough backed up her claim to be sick, and his mother's delight in taking the theater tickets off his hands seemed only to rub salt into his wounds. By the time Janice was well, her career took her out of town for six months and he has been "depressed" for weeks thinking about how much different it would have been if only she had not gotten sick.

If, despite all he believes to the contrary, I could teach him that, just like the boy on the bike, only longer and stronger, he was also choosing the time and place of his misery, he would begin to understand that other, more effective choices might be possible.

Keeping these examples in mind, let's take a further look at how Susan has chosen to behave since Dave left. Following common sense, which is all she knows, she blames Dave for her present situation and would bitterly resent any implication that she is choosing the misery she feels. We know that what is driving her present behavior is the difference between what she wants and what she has, and as long as she wants Dave back, she must continue to attempt to get him back.

As time goes on, she will reach deeper and deeper into her behavioral system, trying desperately to find a behavior that will help her to regain control, but, remember, what she finds will always be a total behavior made up of what she is doing, thinking, and feeling to get what she wants. (In this case her physiology is not pertinent so I'll skip that component in my explanation.) What she has found so far are depressing, complaining, angering, crying, plotting, and guilting, all total behaviors in which the feeling component is both predominant and painful. Remember that all our behaviors are made up of doing, thinking, and feeling, so that any behavior that is predominantly feeling (pleasurable or painful) is best described *as a feeling behavior.*

Instead of the miserable *feeling behaviors* that she is choosing, she could have chosen a more effective *doing behavior.* For example, she could take a trip to some place that she has always wanted to see; or she might decide to write a book about her separation after a long marriage, which would be mostly a *thinking* behavior. What she has chosen are a group of *painful feeling behaviors* that, through long experience, she, like most of us, chooses because they exert powerful control over our own lives and the lives of most of those we encounter. However, she has learned neither that she chooses them nor the sensible reasons for making these painful choices. And powerful as they are, they still may not work, and in this case they do not. Susan has been depressing for months, but Dave is still gone.

Understanding control theory, I know that Susan is choosing her present misery, and if she were to ask me for help, after listening to her story with compassion, I would ask her the same simple question I would ask my disappointed-in-love friend: "Is your complaining to me, and I suppose to a lot of other people, about Dave's leaving, helping you?" She probably would stop complaining long enough to ask me what I meant.

I would repeat the question, again with a lot of compassion, but without backing off. If she really wants help, I want her to realize how important this mildly confrontive question is. I want her to think a little about her total behavior—all she is doing, thinking, and feeling. Her paining and complaining may deter others from asking her this vital question, but I am not deterred. I know she is choosing her misery, and I also know that she can't abruptly cheer up, but if I can get her to focus more on the *doing* aspect of her behavior, it is likely she can make a better, much less painful choice. As I explained in the last chapter, we have almost no ability to change what we feel or think, but we have almost total control over what we do, whether it satisfies us or not.

Even while depressing, Susan could choose a wide variety of active behaviors. She could, for example, force herself to go to work, fix up her house, travel, pursue a career, get involved in a physical-fitness program, tell her friends she is looking for a new social life, and even start to entertain to get one started. In the final chapters of this book, I will pursue this important process; I introduce it here to point out how vital it is that we know that we choose total behaviors in which painful feelings predominate. To take effective control of our lives, we must try to replace painful feeling behaviors with the only behaviors we can choose in any situation: doing behaviors like those above. If what we do is even a little effective, we will feel better because the feeling component of successful doing behaviors is always pleasurable.

Right now, look back into your own life to the last time you depressed and complained about how badly the world treated you. Ask yourself how your complaining helped you. This is not a rhetorical question—this is a real question with a relentlessly logical answer. Our biology, or the way we are constructed to function, may not always be effective, but it is always logical. When we choose to depress because Janice broke the date or Dave left, there is reason for our choice: We believe that depressing in these instances, or any other of a variety of painful feeling behaviors in other situations, is our best choice to regain control over the frustrating situation in which we find ourselves. *Hard as it may be to accept, we are all more than willing to pay the price of severe pain and misery as a part of the total behaviors we choose as we attempt to regain control.*

Specifically, I believe that there are four distinct reasons why we choose the suffering that is so much a part of most of our lives. As I explain these reasons, review in your mind a recent time when you were "depressed" and ask yourself if my explanation of these, as the reasons for your choice to depress, makes sense to you. The more aware you are of *why* you make these choices, the more able you will be to accept that they are, indeed, choices. While this is, for many of you, a strange new responsible way to view your behavior, once you accept that misery is a choice, you will look for better choices to replace it.

THE FIRST REASON: TO KEEP ANGERING UNDER CONTROL

By the end of the first year of life, a baby has learned a whole repertoire of angering behaviors to control his mother or anyone else who helps take care of him. As babies grow older and evaluate how well their angering is working for them, they discover that there are many serious flaws in using angering to attempt to get what they want. It just doesn't work as well as it did when they were infants. People who once ran to their angry screams now pay little or no attention. Even a serious, all-out, head-banging tantrum is more apt to cause parents to laugh than to sympathize—very discouraging indeed.

The magic of anger starts to disappear when a child gets to be about two years old, and he begins to question the effectiveness of this behavior. He cannot, however, give it up until he can replace it with another behavior that works as well or better. He may try smiling because he has learned how effective it is, but if he is seriously frustrated, it's hard to smile. Looking for a stronger behavior, the baby begins to tap his creative behavioral system and soon learns to depress, a powerful behavior that he will use to replace angering for the rest of his life.

Let's say that a two-year-old wants to be taken for a walk, but everyone is too busy to take him. They tell him to go play and that maybe they will take him later. He already has discovered that angering will not work and now he tentatively takes the newly created depressing out of his behavioral system and tries it. Unlike most adults who depress and have no idea that this is a choice, at age two he is perfectly aware he is making a choice when he depresses, a choice that he hopes will get him the control he believes he has temporarily lost.

He becomes listless, stares at the floor, is unresponsive, pays no attention to his toys or the television, and generally does a pretty good job of depressing for a beginner. He lacks Susan's sophistication, but she has had fifty years of practice. He, too, will become an expert in due time, but his amateurish first attempt works remarkably well. He gets attention and is "cheered up" with the walk that he wanted. But most important, when he is taken for the walk he enjoys, he regains control and soon stops depressing. He has learned that he has created a very powerful new behavior, and he stores it in a behavioral system ready for instant use. He will spend a lot of time and effort the rest of his life improving it in all kinds of sophisticated ways.

It has, however, a serious drawback: It is very painful. Even when it works, it is much more painful than angering. But it is so powerful and controlling of those around him, he decides the pain is worth it and begins to use it frequently when he is frustrated. He also discovers that he must actually use the behavior and feel the pain. If he only pretends to depress and does not pay the price of the pain, people see through him and it does not work.

When Dave left, Susan angered powerfully, and maybe even tan-trummed, but she learned that if she continued to anger, she would make things worse. Few of us are willing to spend much time with an angering person, and she didn't want to lose those still near and dear to her. She also was aware that if she did not get her anger under control, she was in danger of doing something destructive to herself or someone else, so it was important to stop angering. If we get too destructive, our survival itself is threatened.

Recognizing the destructive and alienating force of angering, Susan chose to replace it with depressing as a safer and more effective way to attempt to take control. She had to pay the price of the suffering, an integral part of depressing, but she was more than willing to pay this high price to try to get the control this powerful behavior may give her. Depressing also gives her time. Angering is such an urgent, active behavior that it usually involves us in precipitate action that can, and usually does, make any situation worse. When we depress, we move much more slowly; we have time to think things over and figure out what else we might do, think, and feel that may work.

Few sober adults anger for more than a short time, because we recognize that if we replace angering with depressing, we gain more control. But unfortunately, since we all depress so often, most of us tend to pay less and less attention to a long-term "depresser." It is a much more powerful behavior in the beginning than later on. If we wish it to continue to be powerful, we must increase its intensity, and the threat of suicide is the common way many chronic depressers do this.

By the time we are adults, we have created or learned from others (usually a combination of both) a wide variety of painful, feeling behaviors, all of which we store in our behavioral systems for future use. But if we wish to take effective control of our lives, it is important to learn that these behaviors, controlling as they are in the beginning, rarely work for more than a short time. We need to learn more effective, less painful behaviors to replace them, but this is hard to do until we understand that these are chosen. With this understanding we can choose better ones; without it we tend to lock ourselves into long-term misery because we wrongly believe it is happening to us.

Not everyone gives up on angering when frustrated. There is no shortage of violence around us. I recently saw a documentary on television depicting the increase in wife and child beating by unemployed fathers, men who had pictures in their albums of being hard workers. Unable to find employment, they are out of control, and have no effective behaviors to deal with the long-term unemployment associated with the recent severe recession. Most of the men interviewed recognized that they were choosing violence to deal with their frustration at being out of work—a recognition that is the first step toward choosing to depress. If their unemployment continues for years, most of them will replace angering, which is making their lives worse, with depressing. There is some indication this is already happening as the program mentioned that almost two million people had given up even looking for work, an unmistakable sign of severe depressing.

THE SECOND REASON: TO GET OTHERS TO HELP US

The second reason we choose to depress when we are frustrated is to attract help. Susan was asking for assistance by trying to enlist sympathy for her misery. Depressing is probably the most powerful help-getting behavior we have in our behavioral systems. It is even hard to ignore an obviously depressing stranger, and still more difficult to walk by a depressing child. We immediately sympathize, since we all know what it feels like to depress.

Susan's depressing was not only her attempt to enlist general sympathy and help, it was her ongoing attempt to get Dave's sympathy: If he would realize how upset she was, maybe he would come home. This is why Dave deals with her only through his lawyer. He knows how vulnerable he is to the power of strong depressing. The ultimate of depressing is to threaten or attempt suicide. Committing suicide is very powerful self-control, but worthless to gain control of others, so it is the *threat* of suicide that most people use to gain control.

It would be logical to ask, "If we want help, why don't we just ask for it? Why depress?" One reason is that we are afraid of being refused, especially if we have asked before and been refused. Since we still want what we want, we have to find another, more powerful way to ask, and depressing is what we try. Most of us, when making a request that we fear may be denied, tend to blend a little depressing into our asking, as if to say, "If you turn me down, you are going to make me upset." This indicates how we are going to be if you refuse to help and adds a little more power to what we ask.

An even more important reason we don't like to ask is that asking is an admission of weakness. It is frustrating to our need for power, and to many of us it is tantamount to begging. Depressing, painful as it is, is the most powerful way that human beings have found to ask for help without begging. Many of us have become so skilled at the "art" of depressing that we are able to depress just enough to get help without asking—to choose to depress more would be to suffer needlessly.

Depressing, therefore, allows us to plead for help and at the same time maintain our self-esteem by denying that we need it. Have you ever depressed strongly and, when people offered help, said, "Don't bother about me, I'll just upset you. Leave me alone, I'll work it out somehow on my own"? Aren't "leave me alone" and "don't upset yourself on my account" the hallmarks of an expert depresser who very much wants help, but also doesn't want to lose the power that she will lose if she asks for it? We have to pay the price, but, considering how many of us depress, the price is evidently worth it. What is important to understand is that since we are not aware that we choose to depress, we have no idea that we are also *choosing* to pay the heavy price in pain that always accompanies this choice. After we learn it is a choice, we are much less willing to pay the price and we tend to look actively for effective doing behaviors that do not hurt.

THE THIRD REASON: TO EXCUSE OUR UNWILLINGNESS TO DO SOMETHING MORE EFFECTIVE

It is common to use pain and misery as an excuse for either ineffectiveness or fear or a combination of the two. We often recognize that there are better things to do when we are frustrated than to sit around depressing. Feeling the way we do, however, it is hard to get started. It often involves a lot of work, and in our heads we don't have pictures of ourselves working hard the way we feel right now. Our present pictures are of others helping us and solving our problems. The best way that we can justify these nonworking pictures to ourselves and others is to claim that we aren't lazy, that we really want to get going and we'll start just as soon as we feel better.

Many times, however, we use our depressing to avoid coming face-to-face with a fearful situation. For example, my friend Tom loses a very good job and I spend a lot of time at his house trying to cheer him up. I realize he is choosing to depress, and I know enough control theory to know that he will do this for a while to keep his anger under control and seek help. But after I sympathize for a week or two, I can't help telling him to start getting out his résumés and begin to look for work. He agrees that I'm right, he would like to start looking, but he's just too upset to get going.

Tom isn't lazy, and may not even want much help. He is frightened that the kind of job he has in his album is not available, and fearful that if he looks and is rejected, he will be even more frustrated than he is now. So he "protects" himself by using his present "upset" as an excuse to prevent what he fears may be a series of rejections that will make his life even harder to control than it is now. If he knew he was doing this, he would not suddenly shape up, but it would be more difficult for him to continue to use this self-induced excuse for long. And the sooner he looks for work, no matter how hard times are, the better his chances of finding it.

THE FOURTH REASON: TO GAIN POWERFUL CONTROL

By now I hope I have begun to drive home the important point that we are willing to pay the price of these painful behaviors because they do provide control. How many of you have an old aunt —let's call her Aunt Carol—who for years has been a "professional" depresser? Her expert ability allows her to control the whole family; she is like a virtuoso in her ability always to steer the conversation around to the theme of her life, her unrelenting misery. No matter what people do for her, it is never enough. Yet, in the same breath, she expertly asks why anyone even bothers with her—why don't people just leave her alone to die quietly and enjoy their lives without her putting a damper on everything?

She has depressed so long that most of the family are fed up and pay less and less attention to her, but she is so dependent for control on this behavior that she redoubles her efforts because, regardless of others, she can always control her daughter, Phyllis. Carol's ability to get Phyllis to choose to guilt if she does not attend to her mother is phenomenal, and continues because Phyllis has no idea that her mother is choosing her misery. However, don't forget that when Phyllis guilts, she controls her anger, which might otherwise rage out of control.

If Phyllis can learn a little control theory, she will change the way she deals with her mother. She will stop listening to the endless telephone conversations and stop running over when Carol tells her on the phone that she is so beside herself that she cannot even talk. Phyllis will very slowly, but with calm and firmness, tell Carol that she will no longer listen to her complaints for more than a few minutes. If they can't talk about something pleasant, she will hang up. She will not run over in "emergencies" but set up regular times for them to visit and do things together. If Carol depresses on these visits, Phyllis will cut them short and do less, not more, with her. Knowing that her mother is choosing to depress and, with help, can learn to make better choices, Phyllis will free herself from the pain of guilting.

Later, when I explain how to put control theory to work in your life, I discuss what to do in much greater detail, but by now I am sure that many of you are already beginning to realize that we should never let anyone control us with these miserable, ineffective behaviors. It does neither them nor us any good.

These are the four reasons that we employ the common, painful, feeling behaviors that make up most of our misery, all of them chosen, although we are almost never aware that we choose them. Angering, however, is the exception; we often recognize that we choose to anger. If we believe it is justified, it can even feel good, and then we usually recognize it is a choice. Most of the time, however, we blame our anger on someone else, saying, "You made me angry," and on these occasions it is usually painful, and we have little awareness that we are choosing it.

Miserable as depressing is, I would be remiss if I did not point out that it is useful if we do not use it for too long. For example, when someone close to you dies, a few months of depressing that we call "mourning" is extremely helpful as you attempt to regain control over your life. Mourning helps keep inappropriate anger in check and helps you to gain support from your family and friends. Far from resenting your attempts to control them, those close to you welcome a chance to show they care. Only if the mourning extends too long—six months seems to be as long as most responsible people choose this behavior—does mourning become ineffective and self-destructive.

In any severely frustrating situation, a short period of passive, inactive depressing—several hours to several weeks—helps us to avoid hasty, angry behaviors that might make any out-of-control situation considerably worse. Depressing may be painful, but it is safe. If more people depressed when they lost control, there would be much less violence in our society. Regardless of the situation, however, there are many times when the best behavior is to do as little as possible, and depressing is often that behavior.

Later, in chapter 12, when we look at psychosomatic illness, I will explain that these self-destructive diseases often occur in people who do not use painful feeling behaviors to attempt to control their lives. Miserable as they are, these behaviors often give us enough control to prevent our bodies from getting involved in the disease process. Even suicide is less likely in a person who is strongly depressing than in someone who has tried depressing and found it does not give him the control he is looking for. If you have a friend or family member whose life *continues* to be seriously out of control, *who has been depressing for months and then stops for no apparent reason,* you should be cautioned that he now may be considering suicide. In this instance, when he stops depressing, it is because things are getting worse, not better.

As we go through life encountering a variety of frustrations, we diversify and learn additional feeling behaviors to supplement the angering with which we are born and the depressing that we soon learn. Each of us becomes adept in the use of a small group of these powerfully controlling behaviors, usually specializing in a few, and sometimes in only one if it works well.

These additional behaviors—such as anxietying, guilting, and headaching—are very different from each other, and why anyone chooses one rather than the other depends on what that person may have created or learned and his or her evaluation of how effective any one behavior is. Most people find that one works better for them than others. Carol is a world-class depresser, and Phyllis an expert guilter. But when Carol gets too controlling with her depressing, Phyllis has also learned to migraine as a way of escaping Carol's control. Regardless of what the behaviors are, however, they are all chosen for those same four reasons.

To gain more understanding of how people use these painful behaviors, let us take a look at a few people you may recognize. Randy was a highly intelligent college student who, as an undergraduate, made almost straight A's. He continued his success through the first year of the graduate school of business, but in his final year he became suddenly incapacitated with fearing and anxietying. He chose to anxious so strongly that he could not sit through an entire class. If he forced himself to stay, he increased his anxietying to the point where he felt total panic, as if he were doomed to die immediately unless he left the room. His stomach became queasy, hands sweated, heart pounded, ears buzzed, and his mouth became so dry that he could not speak coherently. Although he was easily able to do "A" work on all assignments, he could not pass the course unless he took the final exam in class, so he was stymied. In his album he had the picture of becoming a highly successful business executive. In the real world he was suddenly an unsuccessful graduate student. The last thing he thought was that he was choosing what he was doing.

Randy saw himself as excessively shy and unattractive, and believed that no matter how well he did in school, no one would hire him. If he succeeded in school, he would have to face the real world and possibly find out that he could never be the successful business executive of his album. But he enjoyed his academic success too much to drop out of school, so he took control by fearing to go to class and anxietying if he went. Through these behaviors he gained painful control over his anger at not being attractive and gregarious. He was also able to ask for help with the school problems his behavior was causing. When he learned through counseling to take more effective control, he finished school with honors. Maintaining this control and continuing to work very hard, in a few years he became vice-president of a very successful company.

Mary controls her husband through her overwhelming fear of leaving the house. Psychologists call this incapacity a "phobia." There are tens of thousands of people like her and many more with a variety of other phobias, ranging from fear of flying to fear of germs. She will leave the house only in the company of George, her husband, or Janet, her daughter. She has convinced herself, her family, her minister, and her physician that she has no responsibility for her disability. She is suffering from agoraphobia (fear of the marketplace), a "disease" of the nervous system. How she "caught" this "disease" is unclear, but there is a clue in her recollection that her mother suffered from a similar condition.

On the rare occasions when Mary must leave the house (perhaps it is being fumigated), she suffers from the same anxietying symptoms that Randy did, so she stays home and keeps her husband a virtual prisoner except when he is at work. Even when he calls her, as he frequently does to reassure her, she sometimes lets the phone ring awhile before she answers—a powerfully controlling ploy. She tells him she was afraid to pick it up as someone might overhear and learn that she is home alone. Every once in a while he "has" to leave work to come home because she doesn't answer the phone when he calls.

In her internal world, Mary has the picture of a wonderful marriage with a strong, devoted husband. In the real world, she has not had a good marriage. She sees her husband as a weak man who is successful in business only because she pushed him to work hard. With success, he is now resistant to her pushing, so more and more she is satisfying her need for power by controlling him through her choice to phobic. She keeps him at her beck and call all day with calls to his office for things he has to do for her because she is afraid to leave the house. Mary also wants to control her daughter, but Janet has escaped to college and comes home as little as possible.

Mary's fear of leaving the house controlled her anger, satisfied her need for power, and got her a great deal of attention as a "sick" person. It is interesting that after years of being her "prisoner,"

George left her without warning and made a new life for himself. Her control was too much. Her daughter had the strength not to get drawn in to replace her father, so Mary, no longer able to control anyone with her phobicking, and short of money, pulled herself together. She got a job, made friends, and has a better life than she has had in years.

We will usually give up behaviors that don't work if we are capable of better ones. Mary was. People who don't understand control theory look at this as a miracle cure, but Mary has an inkling that no miracles were involved.

Richard never liked his job as an insurance adjuster, but it paid adequately and he felt trapped into it by financial responsibility. One day he lifted a heavy bottle for the office water cooler and says he heard his back snap as it gave out. He did suffer a mild back injury that probably healed in a few weeks, but he was immediately incapacitated and remains that way four years later. He has "survived" two back surgeries and over $150,000 worth of medical care. His back "hurts" worse than ever, he spends almost all his time in bed, and it is doubtful that he will ever return to work.

To test whether his pain was physical or mental, a doctor gave him some Amytal, an anesthetic drug that produces a mild hypnoticlike trance but does not kill pain. Under its influence, Richard was able to follow the suggestion that he get up from bed, bend, hop, and lift with no pain—activities he would not be able to perform if his backache had a physical cause. He needs full consciousness to concentrate on this painful choice and the drug breaks his concentration to the point where he can no longer backache. When he was shown movies of himself doing all the exercises under the effect of the Amytal in a vain effort to prove to him that he is not disabled, he continued to be in control by saying, "That is what I have been telling you for years. I'd be fine if you would give me some real medicine. Can't I have more of that wonderful drug?" Of course, he can't live in a trance, so while the experiment was good "medicine" to protect him from further surgery, it did nothing to help him take more effective control of his life. No medicines that chemically affect the brain can be, in themselves, rehabilitative.

It is easy to see how backaching gets the anger at being on a hated job under good, if painful, control. Many people who see doctors in their offices and many of our hospital patients are like Richard, "professional patients," who learn to use paining as their way of dealing with life situations that, to them, are intolerable. Some people call this chosen pain "imaginary," but it is not; this pain, like all pain, is real. If Richard's pain could be measured, it would be more intense than if he had something physically wrong with his back. When we are injured, we have as much pain as our bodies (our old brain) "believe" is necessary to cause us to immobilize the injured part; but when we backache, we choose as much pain as we need to take control of our lives. This usually requires much more pain than the limited and localized pain necessary to immobilize an injured body part.

It is very important that the reader not conclude that I am claiming that *all aches and pains*—whether in the head, joints, back, neck, abdomen, or anywhere else—are chosen by the person who suffers from them. If there is a good medical reason—for example, an injury or some congenital defect—then medical care plus rest is always the best treatment. The diagnosis of paining should be considered only when there is no definite cause, and when rest or good medical treatment is ineffective. Perhaps the best way to tell if you are paining is to ask yourself how long this has been going on. Even a fairly serious injury for which you are receiving rest or corrective exercises will heal in three months.

Richard was probably healed in about six weeks; after that time he was paining for the reasons cited earlier. Almost any chronic ache in the back, neck, or joints starts as an injury but continues as paining in many cases after the injury heals. Of course, an injured body part, even after it heals, may be weakened or adversely affected by scar tissue and prone to reinjury. In the case of a back injury, the person has to be careful about heavy lifting and violent twisting exercise like playing basketball or disco-dancing.

I realize that it is very hard to accept that your pain may not be physical, especially if this is not confirmed by your physician. You must be aware that most physicians are too cautious to suggest a psychological cause to patients in severe pain even when they can find no physical cause. They don't believe that because they couldn't find it, it does not exist. But with all the exhaustive tests and X-ray capacity now available, it is extremely uncommon for the physical cause of a severe pain to elude a competent physician. If your doctor tells you she can find no cause, and the pain has persisted for more than three months, you may have to draw your own conclusion. For you, facing that you may be paining is big step in the direction of taking effective control of your life.

Suppose you do conclude that you are paining and set about regaining control of your life and later it turns out that the pain had a physical cause that was treatable. You have still done yourself no harm and probably a lot of good because the more you are in control of your life, the more effective any treatment will be. I do not suggest that you draw this conclusion without seeking good medical care and/or resting any injury for several months. If, however, *the doctor can find no physical cause, and the pain does not steadily decrease with rest but, like Richard's, gets worse, and tends to subside when you are happy and recur when you are frustrated, you should suspect you are choosing to pain and treat yourself by attempting to regain control of your out-of-control life.*

Terri washes her hands fifty times a day compulsively and calls her obsession with cleanliness "crazy." She has been married to Mr. Steady-But-Dull almost twenty years and has little excitement or sexual satisfaction in her marriage. She is attractive and men are attentive to her. She claims that the only thing wrong with her life is her compulsion, and although she makes fun of Mr. Dull, she does not relate her handwashing to him. In her album, however, is a picture of a far different marriage from the one she has.

Some time before she became, to use her words, "crazy clean," she got an offer from Fred, an attractive married man they see socially. In a gentle, joking way, she turned him down, but not off, and she continues to enjoy the genteel attention she gets from this mild flirtation. Mr. Dull laughed when she told him about Fred, and said maybe she shouldn't be so virtuous. This surprised her, but rather than pursue what, if anything, he meant, she simply didn't mention it anymore. But she upped her soap-and-water time significantly and is now busy day and night with cleanliness and personal hygiene.

Terri is safe. As long as she carries on so compulsively, she has no time to stray. How long she will be able to keep her life under "clean" control, I don't know, but if she doesn't do something to get more fun and excitement, she will literally scrub herself away. She shares her craziness with millions of other women who find themselves "locked" into a lifetime of no fun, no excitement, and little sex. Some wash, as she does; many more depress, phobic, headache, backache, stomachache, and anxious. They also eat to excess, drink, and use addicting drugs, legal and illegal. Many husbands do the same. Anytime we lock ourselves into an unhappy relationship, we will struggle in painful and self-destructive ways to get out or improve the relationship. Many of these ways we choose—as Terri is choosing to wash, and Susan choosing to depress—but there are many more *we do not choose.*

Some of those are irrational mental behaviors like psychoses, others are irrational physiologic behaviors best called "psychosomatic disease," but either can become part of a self-destructive effort to regain control over our lives. When over a long period of time we are unable to satisfy our needs, we are like a starving man who will eat anything. I once read about a man marooned at sea who eventually ate toothpaste and leather shoe soles to alleviate his hunger. In the same way, while none of us wants to be crazy or sick, these can become a part of a desperate effort to regain control of our lives. I will explain how we make these forced, irrational choices in later chapters when I discuss creativity and reorganization. I mention them here to make it clear that I do not claim that we choose all of our misery. We do, however, choose the painful feeling behaviors discussed in this chapter, and I think I am safe in saying that we choose most of the misery that all of us suffer.

8

Why We Are Unaware That We Choose Much of Our Misery

As long as you feel good, it is easy to accept my explanation that you choose your misery. When you are getting along well, this radical claim becomes a challenging intellectual insight that makes good sense. But to put this claim into practice, to move from intellectualizing to living, is not at all easy. For example, the next time you headache, you will find it almost impossible to say to yourself, "I'm choosing to headache because my marriage is in trouble and I must control my anger or I'll do something drastic. I also want help with my marriage, but I am too proud to ask for it. The truth is, I would rather look for help for my headache than face the fact that I have to make some major changes in my life."

This is a mouthful of self-awareness that takes a long time to integrate into your life, but people who practice control theory learn to do it. They have not, however, learned it easily or quickly, because, like all of us, they have had a lifetime of practice acting and feeling as if their misery has happened to them. No one has to tell you that when you headache or depress, it does not feel like you are choosing your misery. What you have to learn is that you want it to feel this way because you do not want to take the responsibility that becomes yours as soon as you accept that misery is a choice.

The last thing I want to be aware of when I am depressing is that I am choosing this (or any other) painful feeling behavior. If I become aware that I am choosing to depress, for example, when my elbow is sore and I can't play tennis, it will be very hard to ask for the sympathy I want. To get sympathy, it is important that neither I nor those around me know I am choosing what I am complaining about. If, through learning control theory, I can become aware that I am choosing to depress, I will also become aware that better choices are available. When I put this knowledge to work in my life, I will stop wasting time and energy with depressing (and other miserable choices). I will learn that I can live well with less sympathy, and go about my business while my elbow is healing.

What blocks most of us from taking effective control of our lives is our resistance to changing a lifetime of feeling as if our misery happens to us. Learning the four logical reasons for choosing to suffer, explained in the last chapter, will help, but not enough to overcome the experience of a lifetime. This is in large part because there are three equally logical and extremely powerful reasons that block us from becoming aware that these are choices.

1. SOME SHORT-LIVED BUT INTENSE FEELINGS ARE NOT CHOSEN—THEY HAPPEN TO US

At a recent control-theory seminar, after I had finished explaining that we choose most of our feelings, a woman approached me and said that although she generally agreed with my explanation, she did not believe it applied to the immediate pain or pleasure she felt when she was suddenly frustrated or quickly satisfied. She was right. While we choose all of our long-term feelings, painful as well as pleasurable, as the feeling component of a total behavior, we do not choose the immediate short-lived feelings that she questioned. Some immediate, intense, but very short-lived feelings do happen to us. Because of this we tend to jump to the seemingly logical but *wrong conclusion* that all of our feelings happen to us, when in fact these immediate feelings are only a very brief part of all we feel.

What we feel, therefore, is divided into two distinct parts, which always occur in sequence.

First: We *experience* an immediate, usually intense, short-term feeling, which occurs at the moment of frustration or satisfaction. This brief burst of pain or pleasure is best described as a *pure feeling*.

Second: Either to deal with the frustration or prolong the satisfaction, we almost always choose a long-term feeling behavior such as depressing or loving. These behaviors may last for years and even increase in intensity with time, but our short-term pure feelings begin to attenuate as soon as they occur. They are completely superseded in a short time by whatever behavior we *choose* to deal with the frustration. It was these short-term intense feelings that we do not choose that the woman at the seminar correctly asked me to include in my explanation of pain and pleasure.

In the early stages of evolution, when the fundamental need was survival, there had to be some way that we could quickly become aware that we were or were not in danger—or, in the terms of this book, were or were not in control of our lives. The way we evolved to gain this information was through feelings: If we felt pain, we moved into action; if we felt pleasure, we stood pat. For example, when caught in a severe lightning storm, even before we evaluated the danger, we first felt pain and then chose to run for shelter. But as soon as we chose to run, the pure pain we felt at the first flash of lightning began to diminish, and by the time we were moving, it was gone. It had been superseded by the behavior of running. If, as we ran, we feared the storm, the feeling behavior of fearing added to the doing behavior of running would have superseded the pure pain we felt when the lightning first flashed. If our running and fearing brought us to a safe dry cave, we would immediately experience the *pure pleasure* of regaining control. This would also quickly attenuate as we sat in the dry cave, and would be replaced by whatever we chose to do next—perhaps to explore the cave. We might later enjoy the pleasant feeling behavior of sharing the experience and discovery with our friends and family. In either case, the immediate pure pain or pleasure is short-lived and quickly superseded by whatever we choose to do, think, and feel in the situation. Therefore, *we choose what to do, think, and feel, but we do not choose the pure feelings that precede any of these behaviors: Those are built into our control systems to tell us immediately whether we are or are not in control.*

It was from these simple, initial feelings, which are tied to our survival, that all of our complex feelings eventually evolved and became a vital component of many behaviors. But even though our feelings have become complex, the purpose of all feelings, short- or long-term, remains the same: We feel good when we are in control and bad when we are not.

A good way to understand pure feelings is to go back to my friend Tom who had just lost a good job. When he opened his pay envelope and saw the dismissal slip, there was a sudden, large difference between what he wanted (work) and what he had (unemployment). At that moment he felt a sharp pang of disappointment—a pain with which we are all too familiar. This pain alerted him to the fact that he had lost control of an important part of his life and that he had better start to do something about it. The frustration may be anything from an endless list: losing a job, having your house burglarized, breaking a priceless Ming vase, or being told that you need immediate surgery. But regardless of what it is, I believe the pure pain we feel is almost the same. It may vary in strength, but for any one of us, it is essentially the same pain. Mine is a sharp, stabbing, constricting pain in my chest. I have never had a heart attack, but this stabbing, twisting pain feels just like what people describe as the pain of angina. It doesn't seem to make much difference what my disappointment is, this is mostly the pure pain I feel.

Different people have described their immediate pain: a sudden headache, a feeling of impending doom, stomach pain accompanied by nausea or shaking and shivering. Whatever it is, however, all describe it as an acutely painful feeling that does not last very long —usually from a few moments to several minutes. Much longer is rare because it is almost immediately supplanted by whatever feelings are associated with the behavior we choose to deal with the frustration.

I have already described that to deal with his sudden loss of work, Tom chose to depress, perhaps the most common of the long-term feeling behaviors we choose when we lose control. But because he did not choose the pure, immediate pain of the disappointment, it was very easy and very natural for him to conclude that he also did not choose the long-term pain of depressing that quickly superseded the pure pain. As the pure pain attenuates and is replaced by the feeling behavior, for a short time they blend together, making it very difficult for us to tell when the pure pain ends and the chronic pain completely takes over. *Because it is so difficult to tell when this occurs, we tend to think that the long-term pain of the feeling behavior happens to us just as the pure pain did.*

There is a simple test you can try that will clearly point out the difference between these two pains, and also show you that the immediate short, pure pain is not chosen, but the long-term pain is. All you have to do is notice what you feel when you quickly handle an acute frustration with an effective doing behavior that solves the problem. The acute pain is quickly over, and there is no chronic chosen pain because the effective behavior you chose does not have a painful feeling component; it does not hurt.

For example, if Tom had immediately called a friend at another company who had recently talked to him about taking a good job that was open, even as he dialed the phone his acute pure pain would have subsided. If the friend, then and there, had offered him the job, Tom would never have depressed. In fact, as he took control, he would have felt an immediate acute "pang" of overwhelming pleasure that again he will not have chosen—this, too, will have happened to him.

If, on the other hand, Tom's friend at the other company had been encouraging but noncommittal, Tom would have begun to depress almost immediately, but the acute pain of the disappointment would have completely dissipated. What he would have felt was the nagging pain of depressing. In a situation similar to this, if you have learned the amount of control theory that I have explained so far, you will have no difficulty knowing the difference between the immediate acute and the later chronic feelings.

If, as in the first instance, Tom had immediately gotten a good new job, the pictures, once far apart, would immediately and pleasurably have coincided, producing a moment of pure, intense pleasure. The farther apart the pictures were, and the more quickly they come together, the more ecstatic this feeling. But this ecstasy is also short-lived. At times it may last a little longer than the pain of disappointment, but never very long. Like the pure pain of sudden frustration, this pure joy is also felt for about the same amount of time by anyone, regardless of what we have accomplished or what has fortuitously happened to us. Then, because we need to belong, in most cases we choose the behavior of sharing our good fortune with those we care for, and if it is extreme, perhaps even with strangers. Lottery winners on television who hug and kiss everyone in sight are a good example of this—joyful sharing is a wonderful behavior. If Tom had gone out and celebrated his new job, the joy of that behavior would have been chosen and would have been quite different from the short burst of pure pleasure that occurred when his friend gave him work.

To simulate the intense pleasure of suddenly gaining control, people have looked for, found, used, bought, sold, and fought for drugs for thousands of years. Recreational drugs imitate the pure pleasure that we feel when we suddenly take control, and may even give us a variety and intensity of pleasure that we do not normally experience even when we achieve sudden and very effective control of our lives. Scientists are now finding that some chemicals can cause the immediate, pure pain of frustration, but people have known for years that there are drugs that bring the user ecstasy. With drugs like heroin and cocaine, the ecstatic feelings can be prolonged much longer than any natural experience of pure pleasure, and as drug users become addicted to these drugs, their lives career increasingly out of control.

2. MOST OF THESE PAINFUL CHOICES HAVE BECOME AUTOMATIC

Take a moment to do this: Stop reading, get up, walk across the room, and then return to your chair. Now, sit down and tell "me" exactly where you placed your feet on this short walk.

You don't know. Your purpose was to walk across the room and back, and what your feet did to assist you was automatic. If you started paying attention to where you placed each foot every time you took a step, you would probably stumble. But you do place them, and quite precisely.

If we examine any behavior, what we attend to most while we are behaving is our purpose or goal. Much of what we do to reach that goal, especially if it is a goal we have often reached, has long since become automatic. The first time you walked, you paid a lot of attention to your feet and where you put them. Even now, if you should suffer an injury or stroke and can't walk for a while, as you relearn to walk you will pay a lot of attention to what was recently automatic. Even complex behaviors can become automatic; while thinking of something important, we can drive a familiar route and arrive at our destination with no real awareness of how we actually got there.

If, for reasons cited in the last chapter, you have been depressing for years, you will have no more awareness that you are choosing it than you had of where you put your feet when you walked across the room. It becomes automatic with use—the fact that it is more complex than walking does not make us more aware that it is a choice. Tom began to depress moments after he saw his dismissal slip, without the slightest realization that he was choosing to use this powerful but painful feeling behavior in an effort to regain some of the control he had just lost.

But if you look at a frustrated two-year-old (or even the ten-year-old who fell from his bike), you may see him quite consciously figuring out whether to sulk or anger. He may try first one and then the other, but he is well aware of what he is doing. By the time we are adults, sulking has matured into depressing, and we have selected a few powerful feeling behaviors that, when we are frustrated, we use quickly and automatically with little or no awareness that we choose them.

Feeling behaviors can be pleasurable as well as painful, and most of us are more than willing to accept the responsibility for what we do that satisfies our needs. You don't make me hug and kiss you; I want to because it feels good. While distinctly painful behaviors such as headaching are limited to less than twenty (and most of us use only four or five that we have discovered "work well" for us), the variety of pleasurable behaviors we choose is almost infinite. A control system, however, cannot work one way for pleasure and another way for pain. They are all feeling behaviors and, therefore, chosen. What is different between choosing to pain or to pleasure is awareness: We are much less willing to take responsibility for painful choices, so we are much more willing to block these choices from awareness.

3. WE DO NOT WANT TO LOSE SELF-ESTEEM

Our need for power and self-esteem is so strong that if I were to become aware that I was choosing, for example, to depress or to headache, this knowledge would cause me to lose some control. So, to maintain as much control as I can in a frustrating situation, I repress from awareness that I am choosing misery. Besides, if those around me are controlled, as many are, by their belief that my misery is happening to me, my "apparent vulnerability" is my strength rather than my weakness. If I admit or they learn that I am choosing pain or misery, I would lose this control. Remember, getting help without begging is one of the reasons I choose to suffer.

To maintain self-esteem, my best course is to repress from awareness that I choose much of the misery I feel. By the time I am an adult, I am so good at this that even if I discover a new, highly controlling feeling behavior—such as a phobicking that ties me to the house—I am quite able to repress that I have chosen it. I am happy to agree with my doctor that I am suffering from a nervous disease that happened to me.

The next time you depress or use any of these feeling behaviors long past the time that they may be effective, leaf through your album, find the picture you want, and say to yourself, "Is choosing to depress my best choice to get this picture right now?" If you have any reasonably effective, alternative behaviors, you will quickly stop depressing and choose one of them. I doubt that after you read this chapter you will ever be as "comfortable" depressing as you have been previously. It is almost impossible for anyone, even the most ineffective among us, to continue to choose misery after becoming aware that it is a choice.

9

The Values in
Our Cameras

"Beauty is in the eye of the beholder," and so, of course,
are ugliness, genius, greatness, and meanness. All our values, good
and bad, come from within ourselves. In the real world, where
everything exists, there are no values, labels, or designations of any
kind. In order to communicate sensibly, as language developed we
began to agree on what to call the many objects we encountered.
Over many years, in a variety of languages, a tree became a tree, up
became up, and sweet, sweet, until all we knew about had one or
more descriptive designations.

As long as we were describing a particular configuration like a
man or a river, we could usually agree. But later—to warn others
about someone who might harm them, or to tell someone about a
crystal-clear river—we began to add values to our descriptions. We
talked about a "bad" man or a "good" river, but when we did, we
often disagreed vehemently, and this disagreement over values is still
very much with us. It is almost impossible to avoid discussing values,
because by now we have evolved to the point where our sensory
cameras add either a good or bad value to almost every significant
thing we see. Unless we consciously intervene, this happens quickly,
automatically, and without any awareness on our part that we are
doing it. Values seem to be as much a part of what we see as color,
shape, or size; but, unlike these more descriptive labels, they are
much more personal. For example, although few of us argue about

a person's skin color, we do argue about the value of the person whose skin is that color.

With "good" intent, I once told a friend not to encourage his son to act so "stupidly," and it took five years to reestablish the friendship. I did this quickly and without thinking, because when I said it, the boy was doing something so patently "foolish," in my view, that I could not imagine his father could think otherwise. In control-theory terms, I have a picture in my head of how kids should behave, and when I saw my friend's son behaving so differently from that picture, I called his behavior "stupid" before I could stop myself. The reason I could not stop myself was that it did not seem to me that first I saw him and then I added the adjective *stupid*. What I saw through my sensory camera was one picture—stupid boy.

How many people did you pin a value to yesterday with no awareness on your part that you were doing it? As you drove to work, didn't you hear some "fool" on the radio claiming you could lose weight and still eat all you wanted? And no matter how many times you have given instructions, didn't your "lazy" secretary fail to open and sort your mail? Did your "deaf" boss refuse for the fifth time to listen to your "great" plan to reorganize your department? Upon arriving home after a grueling day, didn't you see that your "good-for-nothing" son had failed to mow the lawn and set out the trash? And did your high-school-senior daughter, who obviously "doesn't know right from wrong," hit you with her "harebrained" plan to hitchhike through Europe all summer with a boy she hardly knows? Didn't it seem to you, as you encountered these people behaving so differently from the pictures in your album, that *deaf, lazy, good-for-nothing,* and *harebrained* were as much attached to those people as their arms and legs?

But those values have not always been attached to your son, daughter, boss, and secretary. For years your son was a "good" kid struggling to "find" himself, and until the sudden advent of the hitchhike scheme, your daughter was your "darling" who could do no wrong. Even your secretary had been a "hard worker" until recently, when personal problems began to occupy so much of her time that she could not keep her mind on her work. And for years, until he became harassed by a "power-mad" vice-president, your "understanding" boss took time to listen to all your suggestions.

If you want to take effective control of your life, you must become aware that your sensory camera is no ordinary camera faithfully recording the world as it is. It is an extraordinary camera that, as much as it can, pictures the world as you would like it to be. The way you want to "see" the world is as close as possible to the pictures in your head. Therefore, to fulfill your need for love, for a few years you saw your unemployed son "struggling to find himself." To have seen him otherwise would have been frustrating. Thousands of European artists painted Christ not as the dark Mideasterner that he was but as the fair-skinned Nordic of the picture in their heads.

When what we see has little to do with what we want, our cameras record reality quite faithfully. For example, when I am working inside, I see a gray, windy day as just that; the weather is unimportant. But on my day off, when I want to play tennis, the same day is a perfect day for a game. This is why our friends tell us frequently to face reality. It is easier for them to see today as it is because as it is does not frustrate them. My wife, who does not play tennis, often says with great accuracy, "How can you consider playing on such a rotten day?" But I want to play so badly that my sensory camera steps in and does its best to improve the weather.

Even the most obedient sensory cameras, however, have limits as to how much they can distort the world. Much as we want to live the pictures in our heads, we must live in the real world where a son's two years' sitting home no longer fulfills our needs. As it does not, we slowly begin to see him more as he is and less as we *hope* him to be. Finally, in an effort to regain control because hoping is a very ineffective behavior, we begin to pin the label "good-for-nothing" or "vegetating" on him, just as yesterday we called our secretary "lazy," the boss "deaf," and daughter "harebrained."

Our frustration drives us to make this change in values when kindness, patience, and tolerance seem not to get us what we want. Pushed by our ever-present need for power, we begin to think, "If he won't change, I will change him." But before we act, we want to define as sharply as possible the *difference* between what is right (the pictures in our heads) and what is wrong (how he is acting).

Labels like "lazy," "deaf," or "good-for-nothing" quickly make this difference clear and help us to justify whatever we choose to do to get him to "see the light." We may righteously kick this "good-for-nothing" son out. We also consider cutting off our "harebrained" daughter's allowance, lecturing our "lazy" secretary, and even sabotaging our "deaf" boss—all in the guise of getting them to change. If we have any doubts about the wisdom of what we are doing, our own labels reduce these doubts. To gain support for what we have done, or plan to do, we talk to friends and family about these problems, always using the labels to help convince them we are right. After all, who would argue that we ought to extend our patience beyond two years with a son who sits and "vegetates"?

It is very likely that values became part of the way we saw the world early in our evolution. Those who could "see" dangers had a clear survival advantage over those who stopped to figure out what was going on. For example, when our ancestors came face-to-face with a saber-toothed tiger, they had to be able to look at him, "see" he was dangerous, and act immediately. We are not descended from people who stopped and thought things over in this situation. Today we teach our children to "see" a gun or a stranger as dangerous, not to wait and make this determination for themselves. Most guns and strangers are not dangerous, but enough of them are so that we believe it is a good idea that they be seen this way.

When we assign values to those we love, these values can cause a great deal of frustration. There's no problem with good values like loving, hardworking, or generous, but when you fall into the trap of seeing your son as "good-for-nothing," the gap between the two of you widens every time you look at him or think of him. If your son "reforms," as many "good-for-nothings" do, it may take a long time to reconcile because of the way you saw him for so long. You would have been better off if you had never pinned this label on him.

Once a value is in our cameras, we tend to use it. To avoid frustration, we should make a continuing effort to remain aware that *we put it there and we can take it out.* If, as a small child, you put the label "strangers are dangerous" into your camera, you may be uneasy with people unless you've known them for years. Long after any rational danger from them has passed, you may still be ill at ease because the value remains in your camera.

Just as we can gain a great deal of control by learning that we choose to depress and that better choices are available, we must learn that far too often we choose to add bad labels to what we see. One of the most difficult lessons to master as we struggle to take effective control is *to learn not to label something "bad" just because it is different from what we want.* It is much easier to satisfy our needs in a different world than a bad one. The fewer bad values we attach to what we see, the more effective we will be.

For example, take an imaginary walk with me around my neighborhood. Immediately I see my next-door neighbor's lawn "cluttered," not with children's toys but with a "pile of junk." It is not easy to get along with a neighbor who has a "junkyard" for a front lawn. Then I see a "disreputable bum" "cruising" "my" neighborhood in an old, "beat-up" truck. He becomes a "burglar" looking for a house to rob and my heart starts an unhealthy pounding.

It is as if we have two stockpiles of labels—one good, the other bad—stored in the back of our cameras. As soon as we see anything that significantly differs from what we want, without any awareness we attach a label from the "bad" stockpile and see it as bad. If what we see coincides with what we want, a good label is instantly added to the picture in the same way.

Good values present few problems, but bad labels cause us a great deal of difficulty—because as we add them, we increase the difference between what we see and what we want; and the larger this difference, the more we must act to reduce it. Too many bad labels will lead us to exhaust ourselves in unproductive arguing, fighting, rejecting, backbiting, gossiping, moralizing, preaching, and conspiring. For example, calling a son "good-for-nothing" or a daughter "harebrained," because these bad labels are too readily available from a large stock, may give us a temporary sense of superiority. But they also lead us to argue, fight, or depress, hardly effective ways to get them to be the children we want them to be. We all know this, but we seem unable to stop, because we fail to realize that the source of our ineffective behavior is as much *our* labels as *their* behavior.

Tolerance, a virtue more professed than practiced, means making an effort to accept that others, even those we love, have different pictures in their heads. Probably the reason so many of us are intolerant is that once we choose to pin a bad value on anyone, our own action increases the difference beyond what we ourselves can accept. To be tolerant, we must learn how quickly we add bad values, and we must make an effort to recognize that this need not be automatic. We can say to ourselves, "What good will it do to call my son 'good-for-nothing'? How will this help me to persuade him that he has to do more than sit around? If he needs my help, how will he get it if I call him bad names, fight with him, or depress?" Whenever we see someone as bad, we must stop and ask ourselves,

"Will this label help me get what I want?" If the answer is no, we should try to remove the label. The less we label, the more we will be in control of lives.

At the back of our sensory cameras, behind the stockpiles of values, all of us have value systems that become the final filters through which passes almost all we perceive. For example, people who have fashion as a personal value system look at the world through a fashion filter. Anything in style is seen as good; what is not, bad. Fashion predominates all they do. If they play tennis, the style of their apparel may be more important than how well they hit the ball.

Many people have a money filter in their camera and view all they see in terms of what it costs. If they are economical, cheap is good, expensive is bad. If they are status-conscious, or anxious to impress with wealth, expensive is good, cheap is bad. A rose has more beauty if it is a rare, expensive variety. A sunset is more glorious if it is viewed from the veranda at Caneel Bay. The people with whom they associate are clever or attractive in proportion to their wealth: They filter their lives through their bank accounts. Fashion and money are good examples of the many personal value systems that color our lives.

When most of us think of value systems, what first comes to mind are universal systems such as religion, politics, patriotism, and civil liberties. Born-again Christians filter all they see through the teachings of the Bible: What supports the written word of God is good. Chicago Democrats may see all the "machine" does as good, anything opposed as not good. American Civil Liberties Union members see the world as good or bad depending on whether personal freedom is advanced or retarded; and many American Legionnaires see American as good, foreign as bad.

Many organizations also have a code of values: Companies like IBM encourage their employees to see the world through company eyes. Charlie Wilson's famous remark, "What is good for the country is good for General Motors, and vice versa," is a classic example of how the values of a company can dominate the lives of its executives. Lodges like the Masons, unions like the United Auto Workers, professions like law and medicine, and cults like the Hare Krishna are just a few of the organizations that provide value systems through which many of those who belong filter what they see.

In our sensory cameras, we may have a whole series of filters, each representing a different value system. For the most part, these do not conflict. For example, fashion usually supports politics; it is the rare politician in these media-conscious times who does not dress with conservative sincerity and have hair that is fashionably styled and blown dry. Occasionally, however, filters may conflict. For example, patriots who also believe strongly in civil liberties may at times have difficulty with "my country, right or wrong." Conflict in value systems is infrequent, however, because the purpose of value systems is to help us reduce conflict as we attempt to fulfill our often conflicting needs.

If, instead of using value systems, we attempt to make a separate evaluation of each component of an important situation, we can't help but run into a great deal of conflict. For example, a good friend is now drinking far too much and is probably already an alcoholic. Looking at each component separately, I see alcoholism as bad, but my friend is good. These values are opposed and I am in conflict as to whether to keep seeing him or not. If, however, I have a system that values all friends as good no matter what they do, I have no conflict. Following this system, I stick to him through bout after bout of drinking, with little discomfort, because my friendship filter removes my concern over his drinking. Conversely, if my value system holds that all alcoholics are no good, friend or not, I can tell him that until he stops drinking, he and I are through. Of course, as much as these value systems may help me, they do little for my friend—he needs my help, not my acceptance or rejection.

Therefore, while a value system may "work" for me to prevent conflict, it is often detrimental to people I need and may eventually frustrate my ability to get along with them. If my company, whose value system I fully endorse, orders me to relocate, I may be deaf to the legitimate complaints of my children, who don't want to move. Even those who torture and murder for religious or political beliefs—common crimes throughout history—filter away any conflict they feel by pointing to a higher-power value system to justify what they do. These people use duty, patriotism, and religion for power and ride roughshod, for as long as they can, over those who disagree with them.

But value systems also help us to get along with others. Members of organized churches feel the *power* of God behind them and gain *kinship* with those who believe as they do. Vegetarians gain the power of good health and the camaraderie of others who shun meat. No matter how personal and obscure the system, we will almost always gain a feeling of power and a sense of belonging. But the more we adhere to any system, the more this belonging will be limited to others who believe as we do. We even see our children as "bad" if they don't follow "our" way. Therefore, any rigid system we embrace may, by excluding others, frustrate our need to belong.

To reduce this frustration, those who believe in a system always proselyte for their beliefs. They feel a loss of control when they see people, especially those who seem to be in good control of their lives, following a different system. But even this they seem able to accept —these people at least have a sense of values. What bothers them most are people who seem "free" of any system and still get along well.

Therefore, the most serious and often fatal flaw in any value system is that they are always destructive of our need to be free. Whatever freedom any system allows is only available within it. I have several close associates who were, for years, members of an established religious order. They finally left, not because they stopped believing but because they could not abide the restriction on personal freedom demanded by the system. Because we need to be free, the more a value system dominates our lives, the less likely this system will work for a lifetime. Satisfying our often conflicting needs requires creativity, which is always variable and unpredictable— only a noncreative machine can follow a system forever.

Although it takes more effort, you will be more in control of your life if you evaluate each situation at the time you encounter it rather than rely too much on any value system. If our children join the Reverend Moon's church, most of us adhere to value systems that lead us quickly to consider rejecting those children. But if we can refrain from viewing their move through such a system, we will be less inclined to do what will separate us even more from our children. We must keep in mind that children join restrictive organizations searching for a set of values that will give them more control over their lives. If we reject them, causing a further loss of control, they will cling more tightly to what they have joined.

If you are not constrained to follow an anti-Moon value system, you will find it easier to keep in touch because you may be able to see only the *move* as bad, not the child. You must, however, be cautious not to criticize the Reverend Moon, because your son now has Moon's beliefs as the major filter in his camera. If he tries to get you to join, let him talk and don't argue. He is as much trying to convince himself as you, and if you argue, he will work harder and may succeed. When we label anyone "bad," we will have more trouble dealing with him than if we could have settled for a lesser label. We tend to anger much more at a bad child than at a slow or careless child, because the difference between the picture of the child you want and a bad child is greater than between a slow or careless child. The greater the difference between the pictures, the greater the pressure to behave, and under pressure we are less likely to find an effective behavior.

The fewer value systems we have in our cameras, the less we will label what we see and the less pressured we will be to act. With less pressure, we will have the time to figure out flexible and creative behaviors that may be more effective in any situation. We must recognize that we embrace value systems not only because they seem to work at the time but because they promise to work forever to satisfy our needs. Few, if any, systems consistently deliver on this promise. When, at times, they fail, as they almost always will, it is important to realize that much of our current problem may be in how our value systems have distorted what we see. Seen without these systems, the world is much easier to control.

10

Creativity and Reorganization

Every once in a while a story appears in my local newspaper about a "successful" middle-aged man who has abandoned his career and, after three years of scrimping, saving, and backbreaking work, has almost finished building a huge sailboat in his backyard and has a plan to sail to the South Seas. As he shows the newspaper reporter through his beautiful creation, he seems ecstatically happy. His story is that having been unsatisfied and mildly depressed for years, he suddenly got the sailing bug. He admits he has never been to sea; in fact, never past the breakers of the beach at Venice, California, so when asked where this creative idea came from, he smiles and says he really doesn't know. It just appeared one day, refused to go away, and here he is, almost ready to sail.

As I read this "human-interest" story, I am happy for him, as well as a little envious. I secretly wish I could do something similar to break the routine of my life before I get too old. I quickly dismiss the thought for "practical" reasons, but even as I put the thought out of mind, I wish I were as creative as some people seem to be. Then I, too, could make a big move in a new direction. It is my observation that most of us tend to have a low opinion of our creativity. We think of it as a special gift that a few lucky people possess but we'll never have. This is unfortunate because we are all much more creative than most of us realize.

Unlike machines, all living organisms are not only highly creative but always in the process of creating new behaviors. As I described in an earlier chapter, we never run out of things to do, think, or feel. Whether we are in control of our lives or not, new behaviors are constantly being made available us through a remarkable creative process that I would like to call *reorganization.* To understand how we *reorganize,* it is necessary first to understand that all the behaviors we have—that is, *all we know how to do, think, and feel*—that are presently available from our behavioral systems could best be described as *organized behaviors.* We use them day after day to maintain control of our lives. Even miserable feeling behaviors, such as depressing, are part of this well-organized repertoire from which we always try to select the best possible behavior to satisfy a current picture. Some of these behaviors we created, many we learned from others around us, but either way they are no longer new.

The behavioral system is a two-part system. One part contains our familiar organized behaviors; the other part, which is the source of our creativity, contains the building blocks of all behaviors in a constant state of reorganization. By themselves these building blocks could not be recognized as discrete actions, thoughts, or feelings; but as they reorganize, they may become recognizable and usable. Reorganization is an intangible process very hard to describe, but I visualize it as a kind of churning pot of disorganized behavioral material, a maelstrom of jumbled feelings, thoughts, and potential actions that are in a constant state of reorganization.

As active as this process is, we may have little or no awareness that it is going on. The one time when we almost always become aware of reorganization is when we dream. Our dreams seem to be creative attempts to deal with the frustrations of the previous day and, "crazy" as they may be, they seem to help us control our lives by resting our minds. If we take sleeping pills, we tend to paralyze our ability to dream normally and we do not get the restful sleep we need to maintain our health.

From this bubbling, ongoing creative reorganization comes a random stream of mostly minimal but occasionally well-organized new behaviors that are available to us to try if (1) we pay attention to them and (2) we decide that those to which we pay attention may help us gain or regain control over our lives. It was from this creative system that the boat builder got the kernel of the new idea that led him to a life totally foreign to the well-organized existence he had led for years.

But if new behaviors are always available, why, for example, do we continue to depress or headache for as long as most of us do? The answer is deceptively simple: We continue to choose misery because what our reorganization systems create and offer to us may be no more effective than what we have. All our creative systems can do is create—in simple terms, come up with new behaviors. There is no guarantee that what it creates has value to us or anyone else. During a week of strong depressing, we may create many new behaviors but continue to depress because not one of them is, in our judgment, as effective as our present misery.

The new behaviors offered to us may be unacceptably violent (to strangle the man who fired us from our job) or unacceptably crazy (to go to bed and stay there forever), neither of which in our opinion is better than our present well-organized choice to depress. We may seem to create faster when we are out of control, but more likely it only seems as if we are creating faster, because when we are out of control, we are much more on the lookout for something new than when we are in good control. But, fast or slow, our reorganization systems may never come up with anything better than what we have.

Only living organisms can create new behaviors. The most complex computer imaginable can create nothing, merely produce countless variations on the organized functions stored in its memory. It may take a long time, but after it has exhausted its capacity to vary what it has, it will run dry. A computer is like a gifted editor who can do wonders with what others write but does not write new material on her own. Our brain—or, more precisely, the behavioral system of our brain—is like the writer: It is always in the process of creating new behaviors, but much of what it creates may have little or no value. In a sense the creative part of the behavioral system is the writer, and the organized part the editor. No matter how creative his intentions, if the man with the dream of sailing to the South Seas did not have organized carpentry skills, he could not have built the boat.

Because we are constantly reorganizing, our chances of finding one or more creative behaviors that will help us to achieve control of any frustrating situation is greatly increased. Anytime a behavior we create helps us to achieve increased control, that behavior is stored in the behavioral system as an organized behavior ready to use in any situation where it may work. Many of the newly created behaviors that we accept and put to work in our lives are minimal and become tiny new creative variations of old, well-organized behaviors. For example, a slightly more efficient way to do your job is a small but welcome bit of creativity. At times, however, especially when our lives are dominated by painful choices, we accept much larger and more significant new ways to behave.

Mary, mentioned in chapter 7, may "lock" herself into her house by her well-organized choice to phobick because she has not yet found a more effective way to control her present life. If her fear of leaving the house does not give her enough satisfaction, as it usually will not, she will continue to examine the reorganized alternatives she is constantly creating. These, however, may be gibberish, a series of crazy thoughts and feelings that have no bearing on the frustrations of her life. As she continues to immobilize herself at home, the idea of suicide may begin to flicker through her mind, perhaps starting with the minimal idea "Face it, there is way to rid yourself of your pain."

The way the creative system works, new ideas do not usually appear in their final form. An idea may start as a tiny thought, a different feeling, or some combination of both. If we entertain it, it tends to grow in an irregular, nonpredictable fashion, until we slowly become aware that we might put it into action. In Mary's case, if the pain of her choice to phobick becomes extreme, and staying home becomes lonelier as her family and friends avoid her, the idea of expanding the creative suicide notion into action becomes more attractive.

Finally, she may attempt the creative act of suicide to try to regain control over the people she can no longer control with her phobicking. If her suicide attempt is serious, she may succeed in regaining this control for a while and make repeated attempts. Keep in mind that what we create and try by reorganizing does not have to be new under the sun—only new to us. Suicide, a well-known behavior, is always new to the person who attempts it. The wheel has been invented many times, but to the small child who reinvents it when he rolls a heavy toy box across the floor on some marbles, this is an exciting discovery.

Driven by our ever-present needs, we require a large supply of behaviors to deal with ourselves and the world around us. Most of us have learned enough ways to do this so that we usually believe we can handle the big issues in our lives: We see ourselves as well organized. But even the most effective among us often find themselves frustrated by countless small irritations, such as flat tires, rainy days, and missed phone calls, frustrations we encounter far more frequently than major setbacks like losing a good job or breaking a leg. It is these small, unrelenting frustrations of daily living that cause us to make constant demands upon our behavioral systems for new behaviors to help us to remain well organized and effective.

These demands are often answered; new ideas do pop out of our ongoing reorganization into our mind and are continually put to use in our daily lives. These new behaviors are usually simple, and individually almost inconsequential; but added together over a period of time as they shape and reshape the way we deal with the world, *they become our personality.* It is this constant reorganization that creates a stream of new ways to do, think, and feel that makes each of us a unique human being. Our individuality tends to take on a pattern, but even this pattern continues to change as we constantly add creativity in small, and occasionally large, doses to the way we behave.

If you focus on it, you can easily become aware of how creative you are—for example, when you bake a cake. For you, baking is a well-organized behavior that you have used many times to produce good cakes and cookies. It is one of thousands of similar, well-organized behaviors well known to you because you use them frequently, but they change as you continue to upgrade them with creative additions. Say you are assembling the ingredients and find you have no sugar. As you attempt to cope with this hardly earth-shaking problem, your *reorganization* gives you the hint that there may be a substitute for sugar. Looking around, you see a can of apple-juice concentrate. You say, "Why not?" and try it. This reorganization is minor—it pales beside the insights of da Vinci—but it is new to you, and you gain a satisfying sense of control when the cake tastes good.

For years people have surfed and sailed, both enjoyable ways to play on the water. Then several years ago, someone, probably while sailing or surfing, got the creative idea of combining the two sports. This new twist has become so popular that sailing surfboards are now seen on recreational waters all over the world. I doubt that the inventor sat down and figured it out; I suspect the idea just came.

What took a lot of figuring was how to design a board and a sail that would function together, and this, I am sure, involved a lot of creativity. Think of a regular thing you do, and then look back, and I am sure you will see many creative improvements that you have added over the years. When I write, for example, what I now do on a word processor is as different from what I did when I started as day from night. But long before I began to use the machine, I had figured out many ways to organize my writing that made it more efficient with each book. It is impossible to keep doing anything the same way; we always reorganize and improve in a myriad of small, creative ways—and while we do, we probably reject as worthless an equal number of "improvements."

Occasionally we read a story in the newspaper about someone who survived a plane crash in an isolated and barren location with no food. None of the survivor's organized eating behaviors worked, but he reorganized and ate something that he had never thought was edible, like insects, and stayed alive. In this extreme example, it was create or die, and books have been written about people in extreme situations who even ate human flesh to survive.

Creative as your reorganization system is, however, it may not come up with a successful behavior by the time you need it. All it can do is generate new behaviors, and, desperate as you may be, what it offers may have no relationship to what you need. It might offer you ideas such as standing on your head and meditating as a way to fill your stomach, or playing the kazoo as a way to make a living. But if you are severely frustrated, as your frustration grows, you become more and more susceptible to wild and even dangerous offers because you have nowhere else to turn to get anything better. Effective or ineffective, when you run out of all you know, reorganization in the hope of finding something new is all you have.

Most of us will never find ourselves in situations where we must create or die, and we deal reasonably well with most of our frequent frustrations through established, well-organized behaviors readily available in our behavioral systems. It is not often that we are even aware of any pressing need for the creativity, good, bad, or neutral, that our random reorganization systems continually provide. It would seem logical that when there is no demand for creativity, the reorganization system would shut down, but it never does. This is probably because, from an ancient survival standpoint, the ability to create is by far the most important function of our behavioral systems. No species that shut down its creative system could compete successfully against those who never stopped creating.

Therefore, without any frustration or particular need for anything new at the time, as our creative systems idle along, they constantly "stick their noses into our business," gently popping creative ideas into awareness. Most of these we reject with little or no consideration; but frequently, with little awareness of what we are doing, we accept small creative improvements in any organized behavior. Since I have become aware of its existence, I can't say that I am measurably more creative, but I am more aware of what it offers and more open to its "suggestions" than before I knew about it. I believe that if we know of its existence, we will tend to "listen" more to its usually quiet suggestions and give more of them the careful consideration they may deserve.

Brothers and sisters, even twins, as they grow and reorganize uniquely, may become so different that they hardly seem to come from the same family. One reason that some rise from humble beginnings and others never do is probably successful reorganization. Sometimes this is just good luck, but more often it's the willingness to take a chance and tap the creativity that is inside all of us. As we begin to become sexual, and begin the search for satisfying sexual behaviors, we do considerable reorganizing. Most of us add some creative aspects to our basic heterosexuality, but a significant number of people reorganize and find that homosexuality and other less usual sexual practices satisfy them. As I discussed in chapter 3, once we get a distinct picture of a sexually satisfying activity, we tend to keep that picture in our albums even though it may not be socially acceptable. Why we do this so rigidly is yet unclear.

When we are very young, we reorganize continually because it is the only way we can learn the countless behaviors we need to fulfill our needs. Moments after birth, we start adding creative additions to our total behaviors that, young as we are, seem sensible to us. These are the beginnings of our personalities, and even one-day-old infants have recognizable personalities to the trained eye and differ from each other markedly. Infants are similar for only a few moments after birth, and then they start the lifelong process of changing into what they will become.

Creativity is *the creation of something new that has never before existed in the life of its creator.* There will always be those rare occasions when something new and highly beneficial to everyone is created, as when the first human—perhaps a woman—who had the anatomy for speech fortuitously reorganized and spoke. Speech gave her and those she spoke to, who then learned to speak, such an evolutionary advantage that we are all descended from her and them. There is no human who does not have some remnant of her genes, but to speak as early as we do, each one of us still reorganizes much as the first person did. For each of us, it is not only imitation but also a creative act that almost all of us achieve if we have the mental and physical capacity to do so. If you waste your time foolishly trying to teach a little baby to speak, you will have no success and may even interfere with the normal process of reorganization that he is using to learn this complex behavior.

Creativity very often will provide the individual with more control over his or her life. But if it does not, it is not the fault of the creative process. If there is a fault, it is with how we, aware of it or not, decide to use this process. In and of itself, the reorganization system does not know right from wrong, good from bad, artistic from crass, scientific from silly. It doen't even know dumb from smart. All it knows is to create and to keep creating. If we use what it creates to take more effective control of our lives, this is fortuitous, but it is not and never will be the purpose of reorganization. Its only purpose is to create. If it had any other purpose, it would not work.

If a behavior that your reorganization system creates leads you to choose a self-destructive act such as suicide, there is no sense blaming this on the system, because, having no purpose except to create, it cares nothing about keeping us alive. If it were designed to have this or any other purpose, it would be unable to offer us any behavior that might be dangerous. But dangerous, unorthodox behaviors have been at the forefront of much that has proved valuable. Therefore, we cannot be truly creative if our creativity is in any way biased. As soon as any creative system has bias, it must lose creativity in the area of the bias. Reorganization, therefore, is always random and unpredictable. If it were not, it could not be truly creative. Columbus never would have sailed if his reorganization system had been biased toward believing the earth was flat. And if someone comes to you and convinces you to invest a thousand dollars in a process to make electricity from moonbeams, it could turn out to be the best investment you ever made.

When it occurs, however, creativity is only as valuable as any of us first decides it is, and progress depends on how much we can convince others that our decision is correct. This tends to be a slow process; people do not easily or quickly give up their old, well-organized behaviors for new ones. It took the Catholic church over 400 years to make up its collective mind that Galileo was creative, not heretical, so don't be impatient and stop listening to your creativity if what you discover is not immediately proclaimed as progress.

11

Craziness, Creativity, and Responsibility

Many years ago, a mother of a young man told me her son had broken down while attending college, and she made an appointment for him to see me. She said he was both willing and able to come to see me on his own, and she was right. When he came, he shook my hand, sat down, and, to me, looked fine. I asked him to tell me a little about himself and he said nothing. I tried again, and suddenly realized that, in his own creative way, he had decided to say nothing. When I asked if he would talk to me because that was the way I worked, he indicated by shaking his head that he would not. He would answer yes or no by a shake of his head. That was all. His behavior was mildly, but definitely, crazy. He had reorganized and accepted the creative idea that if he gave up speaking he would, in some way that made sense to him, regain control over his life. After he put this newly created idea into practice, it became an organized, need-fulfilling behavior that he chose to use with everyone.

Not speaking had a powerful controlling effect on his parents and the family doctor, and I am sure he expected to both frustrate and intimidate me with this symptom. I did not know control theory then, but I recognized that his refusal to talk was crazy, and that if he could control me with this symptom, I could not help him. I told him that it did not make any difference to me whether he talked now or later; I would wait. I added that as long as he refused to talk, I would talk to him. I told him that I didn't usually have such a captive listener, and I was encouraged that he smiled. Then, more seriously, I explained that it would probably be deadly boring to listen to me for an entire hour, but if all he would do was nod yes or shake no, I would have to do my best with this limited exchange.

At this, he evidenced some facial distress, so I offered him a deal: If he would talk to me in the office, I would make no demands upon him to talk anywhere else. In control-theory terms, all he would lose was control over me for an hour; all the others whom he controlled by his muteness, he could continue to control. He agreed, started to talk, told me his story, and in a few months we worked out a better way than his crazy silence for him to take control of his life. He is now a television producer with a family and with no more creativity than is normal for his profession.

When he first came to see me, he thought he would not be responsible for anything he did as long as he was "crazy." He was prepared to control me with his craziness just as he had controlled quite a few people before he met me. Had he succeeded, as do many people who reorganize with crazy behaviors, he might have taken a great deal longer to get his life organized than the six months I worked with him. There is hardly a more effective controlling behavior than craziness, because almost no one, including some mental-health and legal professionals, understands that although the initial idea is a creative reorganization, the decision to put the idea into practice is not. Any reorganization that is put into use becomes an organized behavior. If it does not work to help the user gain control, it may be given up; but as long as it is used, crazy as it may be to anyone else, it is organized for the user.

In frustrating situations, when you begin to run out of organized behaviors to satisfy your needs, you will necessarily begin to pay more attention to what is offered by your creative system. The more you lose control, the more you will consider trying an idea like not talking, and if it works (in this case, not talking removed this young man from what was for him a very frustrating situation), you will start to use it. All of us are potentially capable of creating new behaviors, and if we start to use them, some of these may be judged crazy by those around us. But if my life is out of control and "craziness" gets it more in control, then for me craziness becomes an organized behavior. This young man knew he had chosen a crazy behavior, but it worked so well that he went along with it for a while.

Crazy creativity is anything you do that most of us who are "sane" judge is very different from what we would do in a similar situation. The whole gamut of what is called "mental illness," including hallucinations and delusions, are creative behaviors. If I know what a voice is, I am perfectly capable of creating a new voice in my mind that I actually hear. All of us do this when we dream, but because we all do it, and few of us act on our dreams, we don't call it "crazy." While there are no restrictions on what we create, we are more likely to put tangible creations, like voices and ideas, to work in our lives than gibberish. Other people tend to pay more attention to what they recognize, and they don't recognize gibberish, so we get more control over those around us by saying we hear voices. If you are desperate, even a behavior you recognize as crazy is acceptable to you *if it gives you some control.*

To take effective control of our lives, we must learn that although we are not responsible for what we create, crazy or sane, we are responsible for what we choose to do with anything we create. If I had dealt with this young man as mentally ill, the victim of some brain derangement, either physical or chemical, that had happened to him and for which he had no responsibility, he might still be in "treatment"—still controlling me and others with his mutism. My responsibility was not to let him control me and at the same time to teach him more effective ways to take control of his life. Abnormal as what we create may be, our creativity itself is a normal, ongoing process, and when we put it into practice, *it is not illness.* If we call it "mental illness" and excuse the creator from any responsibility for what he does, we do him and our society a disservice.

There was a public outcry of frustration when John Hinckley, Jr., was found "not guilty" because of mental illness for his 1981 shooting of President Reagan and others. According to accepted psychiatric thinking as interpreted by the federal courts, the shooting was a product of a mental illness over which he had no control. This seemed wrong to the general public—and from a control-theory standpoint, the public is right and the courts wrong.

Hinckley was a young man with many frustrations. Lonely and powerless, he struggled unsuccessfully for years to fulfill his needs. Like all of us, he reorganized constantly; but unlike most of us, he acted upon his innate creativity more than we do, because he had so few organized behaviors that worked for him. But he still had control over that part of his creativity which he chose to put into practice, and in his case it is obvious that what he chose to do was to control someone else. Crazy as it was, he decided that he would have more control over his life if he shot the President than if he had behaved in a different way, and he is responsible for that decision. *He is not responsible for getting the idea—we all get crazy ideas—but he is responsible for putting it into practice.*

When we see any crazy, creative act that affects someone else, we have to assume, whether or not the other person is known to the perpetrator of the act, control was still the purpose. Only when a behavior is totally without observable external purpose—that is, purely creative and without observable effect on anyone or anything except the perpetrator—can that behavior be judged as nonresponsible. A man who sits at home staring at the wall, totally unwilling to eat or talk, is not responsible at this time, because he is still immersed in the act of reorganizing. This behavior is passive. If there is activity, then there is purpose to the behavior and it is no longer pure reorganization. If a man gets in his car or takes out his gun and runs amok spreading death and destruction to total strangers, these are organized behaviors that cannot be performed in a state of total reorganization, and it would be wise to handle them as criminal acts. To carry out these acts requires a much greater awareness of external purpose than is exhibited by the the man who is in a chair totally involved in his own creativity.

If, after committing a crime, the criminal reverts to total reorganization, he should not be tried until he is enough in control of his life to stand trial. If he never gains that control—a situation that almost never happens—then he should be treated in a hospital as long as he lives. Any creative act that is not a crime should be treated as a psychological problem if the person wants to be treated. If he does not want treatment, the case should be resolved according to whatever law applies, but my belief is that no one who does not infringe on the rights of others should be forced to take drugs or receive treatment for putting his or her creativity into practice. This does not mean that we should not try to convince them they need treatment; this is done all the time and is an integral part of any good mental-health program.

If a young woman, who is by our standards slender enough to be attractive, reorganizes and puts the crazy thought into action that she would satisfy her needs better by being much thinner than she is, we call her "anorexic." We often go further and say that she is suffering from a disease, anorexia nervosa, and therefore is not responsible for her choice not to eat. Her creativity may lead her to the well-organized behavior of starving herself, and although this is patently crazy, if she dies, who is responsible? It makes little sense to say that her disease was responsible, and we could not treat it.

What is sensible is to understand that she has embarked on a crazy course, keeping in mind that she is responsible for choosing this course. She is starving herself not because she wants to die but because she has decided that becoming thinner and still thinner is the best way she has to take control of her life. As she continues to lose weight, she makes the discovery that her refusal to eat gets her unbelievable power over her mother, father, many of the doctors that treat her, and others. Corrupted by this absolute power, she continues to refuse to eat. When she talks about how attractive she is now, what she is really talking about is how much power she has to control everyone around her.

Our job is to try to help her satisfy her needs in a less crazy way and to keep her alive while we try to give her the help she needs to find a better behavior than starvation. But she is just as responsible for choosing to starve as Einstein was for giving us insight into the secrets of the universe. Creativity is creativity. It is no less creative because it is crazy or self-destructive, and we are no less responsible because, lacking something better, we act upon what we create.

The vast majority of those who act upon their creativity are not criminal; they are like this young woman. Too often, however, if their creativity is far from what we accept as normal, we lock them up in a mental hospital and give them powerful drugs that paralyze not only their creativity but their whole behavioral systems. Even organized behaviors like walking and talking are made difficult by these drugs; feelings are almost totally eliminated, and thinking is greatly impaired. Since they can regain control only through organized behaviors, in my opinion paralyzing the whole system to knock out crazy creativity is excessive treatment. What they need is not drugs (or at most just a few drugs and only for a short time) but effective counseling to help them become better organized. They need to be locked up in a mental hospital only if they are a danger to themselves or others.

We can and should learn to recognize that when we lose control, we may begin to become aware of our ongoing reorganization, and we should not be afraid of this normal process. A young woman once told me that when the frustrations of her taxing job occasionally piled up beyond her control, she noticed what she described as her "personality slipping away." She thought she was losing her mind because she was becoming aware of a series of thoughts and feelings that seemed to her totally inappropriate to the situation she was struggling with at the time. Rapid random thoughts flooded her mind almost as if she were in a bad dream, and she began to choose to panic in an effort to deal with what was going on in her head that seemed so strange and frightening. She had an overwhelming urge to leave work, run home, crawl into bed, and try to deny the existence of her jumbled mind. She asked me if she was going crazy.

I told her that she was not going crazy in the sense that she was on the road to permanent insanity. However, during these episodes that lasted several minutes but seemed longer, she was crazy in the sense that she had no control over what she thought and felt. They occurred mostly in the middle of tense business meetings in which she had a lot of responsibility and absorbed a great deal of what she believed was unfair criticism. I explained to her that what she was describing was the initial awareness of her creative system that occurs when her organized behaviors are temporarily failing her. What was causing her to choose to panic was her realization that she was beginning to consider acting on some of this creativity, actions that would have been disastrous to her career. But I also pointed out the likelihood that she also got some very helpful creative ideas at these times, ideas that were part of the same random process. She laughed and agreed and was very receptive to my control-theory explanation of what was going on.

She has now incorporated a good working knowledge of control theory into her life, so when she occasionally reorganizes, she realizes what is going on and has some simple, well-organized behaviors ready to use when this occurs. She excuses herself for a moment, leaves the room, has a cup of coffee, or goes to the rest room, and during this brief respite she tells herself she has become aware of her ongoing reorganization because she is in a temporarily out-of-control situation. But she also tells herself that she knows she has the ability to reject the creativity if it is not useful, and to keep an open mind if it is. She is no longer worried about going crazy, because she realizes that what she is experiencing that seems crazy is her normal creativity. She also knows that while it may be happening to her, she need not choose to act upon it.

We can neither turn off our creativity nor avoid becoming aware of it when our lives are out of control. We can, however, learn that we do not have to accept what our creative systems offer if we can find an organized behavior to use for a while that will help us regain control. The young businesswoman decided to leave the meetings for a minute; you might take a walk, call a friend, bake a cake, or count to ten. Even a few minutes of a familiar, well-organized behavior will usually make us less aware of our ongoing reorganization. The more we know control theory, the more we are likely to smile, rather than panic, during the infrequent occasions when we become aware that a lot of crazy creativity has entered into our thinking and feeling. With this knowledge, we will be able to look past the craziness for ideas that are not crazy. We know they may be there, and if we wait, and keep our minds open to them if they pop into awareness, our creativity can become more available to us than if we know nothing about what is happening.

12

Psychosomatic Illness as a Creative Process

Few of us ever think of disease as a creative process. Yet just as insanity is an example of mental creativity, it is likely that most chronic illnesses are examples of physiological creativity. It is my contention that any chronic illness for which there is no known physical cause and no specific medical treatment may be our bodies' creative, but inadvertent, involvement in the struggle to satisfy our needs. In this group are some of our most common and disabling diseases, such as coronary artery disease, rheumatoid arthritis, eczema, ileitis, colitis, and peptic ulcers. Unlike usually treatable diseases of known physical cause, such as tuberculosis and diabetes, or preventable diseases such as polio, these are most likely the unwanted accompaniments of chronically out-of-control life situations. Often related to unhappy marriages or unsatisfying work, they are most aptly called "psychosomatic."

Since there is no specific medical treatment for them, the best advice to give anyone suffering from a psychosomatic illness is that she should try to regain effective control over whatever in her life is out of control, perhaps an unwanted person in the house, such as an aged and irascible parent. Unfortunately, as even your doctor may recognize, this approach is not supported by our present medical delivery system, which tends, in its "scientific" and mechanistic approach, to treat the physical side of all diseases much more rigorously than the mental side. This impersonal medical approach makes it harder, not easier, for sick people to regain the control over their lives that I believe they need if they are to recover from these serious illnesses.

While I recognize that what I will explain in this chapter is controversial, I will make every effort to support what I claim with a clear control-theory exposition of how these diseases come into being. To avoid any possible misunderstanding, let me begin by explaining what is and what is not a disease.

For a disease to be present, there must either be some observable structural change from normal to abnormal that can be seen either with the naked eye or under a microscope, or some life-endangering chemical or electrical malfunction, such as an abnormal electrical impulse to the heart. Therefore, even though we may seek medical care for painful feeling behaviors like headaching or backaching, these are not diseases, because there is no structural change in any tissue or organ, or any dangerous chemical or electrical malfunction.

There may be temporary changes in structures, as in migraining, when there is a marked narrowing of some of the major blood vessels that supply the brain before and during the headache. The painful symptoms are thought to be related to these changes, but when the headache is over, the vessels return to normal; and when the migrainer gains more effective control of his or her life, the headaches and the vascular changes disappear forever. Large changes in tension in the muscles of the back often are associated with a backache, but they, too, return to normal when the backache is over. I also want to make clear that a headache can be caused by an infection like meningitis, and a backache can be the result of a muscle spasm or slipped disk, so when I talk of migraining or backaching, I am referring to headaches and backaches for which rigorous medical examination has revealed no tissue damage.

Therefore, any disease, psychosomatic or not, always involves some observable structural abnormality in the part of the body involved in the disease or dangerous conduction malfunction. In heart disease there is narrowing of the coronary arteries, the vessels that supply the heart muscles with blood. In rheumatoid arthritis there is swelling and inflammation of the involved joints. In eczema there is reddening, oozing, bleeding, and loss of skin integrity; and in colitis, thickening, loss of elasticity, ulcerations, and loss of mobility in all or part of the large bowel. Disease may also involve temporary changes in nondiseased parts of the body. For example, along with heart disease there may be swelling of the legs as fluid accumulates. If the patient is treated properly, the fluid reabsorbs and the legs return to normal. The heart, however, never returns to its prediseased state.

The known causes of noncreative diseases may be an external agent like a streptococcus or an internal malfunction like diabetes; but external or internal, what we see as the illness is how our bodies attempt to cope with these tangible causes. Creative diseases, such as rheumatoid arthritis, have no tangible cause; their origin is in a normal body function that, for no apparent physical reason, begins to function abnormally. In a creative disease like rheumatoid arthritis, our immune systems—whose normal function is to protect us from toxic external agents like streptococci or internal pathogens like cancer cells by attacking and neutralizing them before they can do serious harm—attack and may destroy a perfectly normal wrist joint as if it were foreign to our bodies.

It is these creative or psychosomatic diseases that fill our hospitals today. Most of the once-feared noncreative diseases like cholera, the plague, and smallpox, which at one time killed people by the millions, have long been brought under control by sanitation, pest control, and vaccination. In the past fifty years, medical science has also done a superb job treating stubborn bacterial diseases, like gonorrhea, with antibiotics, and fearful viral diseases, like polio, through immunization. Even the latest feared disease, AIDS (acquired immune deficiency syndrome), is thought to be caused by a virus and may in time be brought under control by immunization.

Medical science has progressed enough so that if you contract a noncreative external disease that is not caused by a virus, you can be almost assured that it will be diagnosed correctly and treated successfully by your doctor. If it is a virus, there is a good chance that a successful immunization program is available or will be worked out in the near future if there are enough cases to warrant this effort. Genital herpes, a viral disease that is now spreading fear through our middle and upper classes, may be brought under control through an antiviral agent in the not-too-distant future. What medicine has yet to develop is a systematic method of dealing effectively with what I call the "creative" or psychosomatic diseases, because most medical education does not recognize that their cause may be our bodies' involvement in our attempt to regain effective control over some situation in our lives that is chronically out of control.

Alan, forty-four, has had a high-salary job for the past ten years. He works directly under J.B., the owner of the company, who seems to delight in making Alan's job a living hell. He criticizes Alan for everything and gives him no credit for his obvious contribution to the company. Occasionally he even goes through the aggravating ceremony of firing him and then "magnanimously" calling him back and raising his pay. A day never passes when J.B. fails to remind Alan of his "generosity." He is under J.B.'s thumb, but can't see his way clear to quit as he has a family and a life-style that needs the support of J.B.'s "generous" salary.

There is a huge difference between the work picture in Alan's album—to be treated with respect and given some credit—and the way J.B. treats him. He is continually aware of urges to do something to reduce that difference, but, short of quitting, he has not been able to figure out what. None of his organized behaviors works, and he is actively aware of some fairly crazy ideas as his creative juices seem to him to boil as he looks for a way to gain control.

Much as he would like to throw in the sponge and depress, to keep his job he must keep a stiff upper lip to deal effectively with employees and customers all day long. Maintaining a cheerful facade is difficult, but he does it—as do many of us who, like him, are stuck in bad jobs, or bad marriages, or with children we cannot abide. But what Alan can't stop—nor does he want to, because of the pleasure they give him—are the creative thoughts that run through his mind day and night, mostly about a variety of satisfying ways to kill J.B. The comforting fantasy that recurs over and over is the idea of slowly throttling him with his bare hands as J.B. gasps for mercy.

One day after a particularly trying late-afternoon meeting, during which he was "fired" once again, Alan went home to find that his teen-age son had put a deep scrape all along one side of Alan's classic Porsche while backing it out of the garage. The boy was heartbroken —he had wanted to surprise Alan by polishing the car—and as Alan looked at the scrape in the sculptured lines, he was beside himself. That night he was awakened by a severe pain in his chest, was rushed to the hospital, and was diagnosed as suffering from a massive heart attack. He lingered between life and death in intensive care for two weeks, but finally recovered enough to undergo bypass surgery to restore the impaired circulation to his heart.

He was sure his heart attack was caused by the "stress" of his job

—the Porsche episode was the coup de grace—but, needing the income, he returned to work, where he began to have chest pains almost immediately. His doctor advised him to consider retiring on the small disability that J.B. provided, but it would not have been enough to begin to support his expensive life-style. Although he does not know control theory, he knows that his life is seriously out of control and he does not know what to do to get it under control. In a later chapter, we will deal with how he might use knowledge of control theory to do this, but now let us take a look at how his chronic frustration may have led his coronary arteries to occlude, the most common of the creative diseases.

I mentioned earlier that all our physiology—the machinery of our bodies—is kept functioning and healthy under the well-organized direction of a small group of ancient brain structures generally referred to as the "old brain." When you turn a page of this book, it is your old brain that provides your muscles with the power to move. Your heart rate and blood pressure are regulated by your old brain; in a scary or sexy movie, if you feel your heart "speed up," it is the old brain that actually causes this to happen. Your food is digested under its direction, and your sexual capacity is greatly determined by hormones regulated by it. If you are lost in the desert, your old brain will send your new brain increasing messages that you recognize as thirst, urgent thirst, and finally such painful, urgent thirst that it seems you have no choice but to search for water. It is, however, only when your survival is threatened, or you have had no sexual release for a long time, that the old brain attempts, through painful messages, to direct the way you function.

The old brain has nothing directly to do with any conscious behavior; it "cares" nothing about whether we satisfy needs like power or freedom, needs that Alan's new brain cared desperately about because they had been unsatisfied for so long. To satisfy these needs, the old brain takes direction from the large, newer, conscious part of the brain, the cerebral cortex or "new brain." If, as often happens, the new brain asks it to function beyond any of its well-organized or usual ways of functioning, it will begin to reorganize and may try some new and "better" way to function. In Alan's case, although he had no awareness that it was occurring, his new brain had long been making huge demands not only on his mind but also on his body, demands that led his old brain to the creative functioning that became his coronary artery disease. To understand how the new brain does this, let us take a detailed look at how it functions.

My new brain is the source of my consciousness: It contains my picture album, through which I must satisfy all of my needs; my sensory camera with all its filters; and directs all of my conscious behaviors. *In essence, my new brain is me.* But on its own, my new brain can do nothing directly. All it can do is give orders that have to be carried out by my old brain or I cannot function. By itself, it is a general without an army: It can give orders, but unless the old brain carries them out, nothing happens.

No one has to teach me to breathe, blink my eyes, digest my food, or maintain my blood pressure or heart rate. And although I will learn precisely how to move my muscles, as when I learn to walk or focus my eyes, no one has to teach me to move my muscles; I am born with this knowledge encoded in my old brain. What my new brain does, as it struggles to fulfill my needs, is learn to give more and more specific and precise orders to do, think, and feel, which my old brain carries out with increasing accuracy until I grow quite old. Under the complete direction of my new brain, my old brain "learns" to provide the bodily wherewithal to carry out what my new brain asks of it. If I decide to cry, my old brain provides the tears and the sobbing. If I decide to think, it makes sure that the new brain has the blood and nutrients for it to perform this function. And if I feel ecstatic, it is because my old brain secretes some morphine-like chemicals that actually produce the ecstasy.

Most of the time, the old brain follows directions so quickly and efficiently that we pay no attention to what it is doing. But occasionally the new brain gives it an instruction that taxes its capacity to perform, as when you decide to run a marathon. The old brain has no trouble with running; it is running twenty-six miles that gives it a "problem." This is because it has its own built-in instructions to keep the body healthy and the new brain is now asking it to pay no attention to these innate instructions. The old brain can't "refuse" to run the marathon, but it can send back to the new brain a series of "slow down" or "stop" messages that are felt as pain and fatigue. The new brain, however, can disregard these messages, and the old brain can finally be so taxed that it fails to function normally and, still trying to keep running, you may get sick, lose consciousness, or even drop dead.

Few of us run marathons, but most of us suffer an occasional disappointment when our old brain stubbornly refuses to follow instructions. For example, I decide to engage in sexual behavior to satisfy a new-brain need like love or power. This decision is strictly new-brain—that is, I have sex frequently enough so there is no old-brain demand for sexual release. But to make love successfully depends on my old brain's "willingness" to get my sex organs ready. If I attempt to make love when I am physically exhausted, my old brain may "decide for health reasons" not to get my sex organs ready and I will not be able to make love. It is rare, however, that my old brain does not do as it is directed; these two examples are far more the exception than the rule.

If the old brain had the "sense" to refuse to follow instructions on more than these rare occasions, there would be much less psychosomatic disease. Its almost slavish attempts to carry out what it "believes" the new brain is commanding it to do is most likely what caused Alan's heart attack, and what causes all other psychosomatic diseases. Several years ago a man died after collapsing from exhaustion during the Honolulu marathon. If you were the coroner in charge of investigating this death, and you knew a little control theory, you might begin by looking into the parts played by each of his brains. The evidence against his new brain is highly incriminating. It was this part of his brain, perhaps in a desperate effort to gain a sense of power through competitive running, that drove him to this fatal effort. As he ran, as all long-distance racers will testify, he received a barrage of electrical and chemical fatigue signals from his overtaxed old brain, all trying to tell his new brain to stop asking the old brain to push his body to this extreme.

All of us are conscious of these old-brain signals as fatigue, and their purpose is to persuade us to slow down and take a rest. When they come hard and heavy, as in a marathon, it is impossible to disregard them. So, if his new brain had been more sensible, it would have given the order to stop or at least to slow down. But he didn't have that sense because in the past he had counted on his old brain, despite its complaints, to carry him through and it had not let him down. Still, you certainly would not be amiss if you blamed his new brain for his death, no matter how many successful marathons it had "persuaded" the old brain to run in the past.

There is, however, considerable evidence that his old brain was at fault also. It was given the assignment of running the marathon, it had "run" marathons before, and it should have "figured out" how to do it again. After all, the new brain can't pay attention to the "whinings" of a "lazy" old brain, and it had every right to expect performance when it gave an order that had been carried out well in the past. To drop dead was rank insubordination, because when the old brain failed and died, the new brain had to die with it. This, of course, is one of the dangers the new brain should keep in mind when it gives such extreme orders. The old brain is such a good soldier that it might be signing its own death warrant.

When the old brain was pushed beyond its ability to continue to run, at that moment it had used up all of the organized running behaviors that had worked for it in the past. So, just as the new brain, when it runs out of things to do, think, and feel, begins to accept some newly reorganized psychological behaviors, the old brain also begins to accept some newly reorganized physiological behaviors. But as with the new brain, there is never any guarantee that the new physiological behaviors it creates will be any better than the well-organized behaviors it has used since birth. Also, like the new brain, if it "judges" that what it creates is no better than what it has, it will keep using what it has, inadequate as this may be, as long as it can. But finally, if what it has won't work at all, as in the case of the totally exhausted runner, it must take a chance and use a new physiological behavior in the hope that it can continue to keep running and stay alive.

Perhaps in the past the runner's old brain had reorganized and provided him with some new and stronger running behaviors. Maybe it had "figured out" how to pump blood at a faster rate or metabolize waste products less poisonously, but this time none of those previously created effective behaviors worked. As it continued to reorganize, in "desperation" it came up with a new behavior that it tried in "good faith" but which proved fatal. The physiological behavior that caused his death was probably a newly created electrical signal that he generated to try to stimulate his heart into pumping more blood. This signal was so "strong," or so different from normal, that it caused the ventricles of his heart to fibrillate. This is a newly created fatal arrhythmia that causes the heart to beat so fast that it becomes totally inefficient and can't pump blood. Ventricular fibrillation, one of the two causes of sudden death (cerebral hemorrhage is the other), is always fatal in a few minutes unless it can be stopped. So, although the old brain let the new brain down, it was trying as creatively as it could to keep up with the new brain's excessive demands.

Is the death of the runner psychosomatic? I would say emphatically yes. It was the new brain (the psyche) that drove the old brain (the soma) to accept a fatal reorganization. Here we have a sudden, consciously motivated death, not usually considered psychosomatic, because most psychosomatic diseases are chronic and we are not aware of the new brain's pushing the old. Yet, there is no doubt that it fits all the criteria for such such a disease perfectly, and Alan's heart attack was the same process in slow motion.

Alan had been fantasizing for years about strangling J.B., with no awareness that this new-brain thinking behavior was having a powerful effect on his old brain. Of course, the old brain knows nothing about strangling; in actuality it knows nothing at all about anything that the mind may desire. But it does "know" that if the mind gives the body an instruction, it has to get the body to carry it out as long as the instruction persists. When Alan's new brain pondered strangling, his old brain was immediately alerted—probably through receiving some new-brain electrical and chemical hormone messages —to get his body ready for a life-and-death physical struggle. The new brain sent this strong alert because it knew that tough old J.B. was not going to take being strangled without a fight.

But Alan had no intention of actually going through with the attack. He knew it was all fantasy. Still, the more he indulged it, the more get-ready-for-a-big-fight hormone messengers he poured into his old brain. The old brain does not know fantasy or reality; all it knows is to act on the hormones sent by the new brain and get the body ready for what it "believes" is an impending fight. It quickly takes care of business, and it keeps taking care of business as long as the get-ready hormones keep coming in Alan's case he was ready to strangle for years. And then on top of all this body preparedness, in his distress he sent a super-strong strangle-his-son message on the fatal day the Porsche was scraped.

Most physiologists believe that our bodies have not yet evolved to the point where we can handle chronic physiological tensions year after year and still stay healthy. Physically we are still too close to what we were only a few thousand years ago when, if we had the idea of strangling, we went ahead and started to strangle. We won or lost, but it was soon over and we could relax. Chronic tension, produced by long-term fantasy messages from new brain to old, is a product of the complications of civilization and it can, and usually does, make us sick.

Perhaps the most common sickness associated with this kind of angering, the basic feeling behavior that is keeping Alan tensed up for strangling, is heart disease. As he remained chronically ready for a big fight, his old brain raised his blood pressure and increased his heart rate to ensure that his body would have enough blood for the fight. It also pumped clotting chemicals into his bloodstream so that if he was wounded he would not bleed to death. There is no harm if this goes on for a short time, but if it goes on for years, and still no fight occurs, the cardiovascular system starts to wear out prematurely. It is like driving your car beyond the red line on the tachometer and wondering why the motor fails.

But even more happens. I believe that the old brain, in some automatic way, "senses" that this unrelenting state of physical tension—the body's constant readiness for a fight that never happens—is dangerous to good health. In order to maintain the integrity of the body, the old brain, acting automatically (but in a sense "desperately") to preserve the health of the body, alerts the immune system as if the chronic, never-ending tension were a foreign invader. As it now searches for the "invader," the immune system also reorganizes and become creative. This additional creativity in Alan's case, and in the case of most other psychosomatic diseases, often becomes destructive. It is a crazy kind of self-destructiveness; coronary artery disease, for example, is analogous to a psychosis of the body.

As the cardiovascular system is tensed for years on end, the blood rushing through the arteries begins to erode the artery walls and produce rough spots. The excess clotting elements already circulating are trapped by these rough spots and begin to form small clots at these sites. The immune system, "seeing" a clot that normally would not be there, somehow (no one yet knows why) becomes "crazily" creative and attacks the clot as if it were a foreign body. This quickly causes the clot to become inflamed, and the inflammation enlarges it just like a scab on a skin wound is always larger than the initial blood clot. As time passes, the clot continues to enlarge through the repetition of this process until the clot obstructs the flow of blood through the artery. Alan suffered his heart attack when clots blocked one or more of the small but high-blood-flow arteries that fed his heart.

There are two possible causes of an acute heart attack, and both are related to diminished blood flow to the heart. First, as the heart receives less nourishment and becomes tired, there is a tendency for it to pump with decreased efficiency. As it does, it tries to compensate for this loss in efficiency by beating in more creative ways called "arrhythmias." But if these creative arrhythmias produce less blood flow, as they often do, the sudden reduction of blood flow through the coronary arteries causes what is known as a heart attack and ultimately causes some damage to the muscles of the heart. If the patient is alive when he reaches the hospital, modern treatment to stabilize the blood flow usually prevents an immediate fatality. In most cases these patients are given bypass surgery to increase the blood flow, and today these procedures are quite successful.

The second cause of a heart attack is a sudden clot completely blocking a coronary artery. Such an attack is usually fatal, but it happens so quickly that the heart muscle is not damaged. The heart will often quickly turn to a reorganized electrical behavior and begin fibrillating, which is probably what happened to the marathon runner. Fibrillation is usually fatal in minutes unless it occurs in an ambulance or in a hospital, where it can sometimes be treated. Fortunately for Alan, he had the first kind and has now had bypass surgery. This operation is very popular and has great value, partly because the blood supply is increased, but also because the patient now believes that with this dramatic help, he is in greater control of his life.

Given a choice, however, most of us would rather keep better control of our lives than have a heart attack and then hope that bypass surgery will keep us going. And it may be that more Americans are taking better control of their lives, because the American Medical Association reported in 1982 that fatal heart attacks during the 1970s were reduced 25 percent from the 1960s. No one knows exactly why this dramatic decrease took place, but it seems somewhat related to the nationwide increase in physical fitness that has made many of us much more diet- and exercise-conscious than previously.

My belief is that this may be more of an indirect than a direct relationship, in that good diet and aerobic exercise give those who practice them a much greater sense of control over their lives. If

Alan continues to work for J.B., he would be wise to follow such a program, because if he could grow to believe in it, he might be able to take J.B.'s antics less seriously. If he learned some control theory and began to understand how important it was for him to relax, and that physical fitness could provide the relaxation he needed, he might stop having the chest pains that may presage another heart attack.

There are many other psychosomatic diseases, and most, if not all, involve some reorganization of the immune system that drives it to attack normal tissue in an inadvertent effort to help the old brain carry out chronic hard-to-satisfy instructions from a new brain that, like Alan's, has lost control. In the case of these diseases, not only is the immune system's "help" not needed, it is disastrous. This attack on our own normal tissue by our immune system has caused medicine to label these diseases autoimmune, or self-induced. Although in different diseases it may attack different tissues or organs, the immune system always seems to reorganize in a crazy way that causes it to misread normal tissue as foreign tissue, and then attack and destroy it as if it were foreign.

Why its creativity takes this form, and why it attacks one tissue and not another, are questions still unanswered. When normal joints are attacked, the psychosomatic disease is called rheumatoid arthritis; the spinal column, spondylitis; the gastrointestinal tract, peptic ulcers, ileitis, or colitis. If it attacks the sheaths of the nerves, it is multiple sclerosis; the kidneys, glomerulonephritis; the skin, eczema. There are many other, more obscure autoimmune diseases, but these are among the most common. And what I believe is common to almost all of them is a life, like Alan's, that is chronically out of control.

There is also the strong probability that the creativity of the old brain as it reorganizes causes us to become stronger and healthier, as it should if reorganization is random. Certainly there are many examples of people who live long and healthy lives under what seem to be markedly adverse circumstances. Because we tend to pay close attention only to sickness, these healthy people have not received much attention, but my belief is that, despite their circumstances, they manage to keep their lives under good control.

Even in sickness, however, there is always the possibility that the old brain will come up with a newly reorganized behavior that will reverse what seemed a hopeless disease process. There are over 100 recorded cases of "miracle" cures of late-stage, "hopeless" cancer patients. It is likely that these cancer victims' immune systems reorganized in such a beneficial way that they were able to act beyond their normal capabilities and eliminate the cancer. Reorganization can be miraculous, but it is not a miracle; it is a normal process in all living creatures.

In the brief time that most doctors spend discussing how well or badly people are living their lives, it is not easy to discover what in the patient's life is out of control. Before and even after his heart attack, Alan never felt right in complaining to his busy doctor about his high-paying job, so he said nothing. And it would have taken a skilled counselor to get him to reveal his strangle-the-boss fantasies, which might have led the counselor to help him to realize the danger of these thoughts and guide him to a better way to handle his life.

In fact, it is quite characteristic of psychosomatic-disease sufferers that they tend to keep a stiff upper lip while they simmer inside with angering or some other controlling feeling behavior. If Alan had been a griper or complainer, he might have gained enough control through these feeling behaviors to protect his heart. But even if he had wanted to complain, he was making so much money that he would have found it difficult to get people to take him seriously and sympathize. I have had some personal experience with severe arthritics who, in superficial conversation, claim that nothing is seriously wrong with their lives except for the disruption caused by their disease. They seem to accept the destruction going on in their joints with a kind of calm resignation as if there were little they could do —it is all up to the doctor. What Norman Cousins's book proved was how little the doctor can do, and how much an arthritic can do for himself.

But if you understand control theory, this is exactly what you expect. People like Alan do not deal with their frustrations with the usual psychological new-brain feeling behaviors like angering, depressing, or complaining. For reasons known only to themselves, and of which even they may not be aware, they have chosen not to attempt to regain or keep control of their lives in the way most of us do. Instead, even with their disabling illness, they display such stoic cheer in their approach to the world that it is hard to suspect that there is probably something seriously wrong in their lives.

While appearing to ignore their frustrations, their new brain is sending their old brain powerful "help" signals that lead to their disease. But unaware of the turmoil in their old brain, they remain remarkably upbeat throughout their ordeals.

Sometimes, after they become ill, they learn to use their illness to gain control over others. I do not believe that this was in their minds prior to their getting sick, but it could account for their cheerfulness —they are getting some payoff from pain and disability. This behavior not only tends to fool physicians, but puzzles anyone who does not know control theory. Physicians, especially, find it hard to believe that these seemingly mentally "healthy," cheerful patients could have anything wrong psychologically. And the patients are almost always supportive of this stance. They hasten to agree with any doctor who treats them as unfortunate victims of serious, completely physical diseases.

Keep in mind that these patients have a major investment in not choosing a feeling behavior to deal with their frustrations, because they are trying, for reasons known only to them, not to become aware that their lives are out of control. So in a sense, physicians and patients join hands in the denial of the cause of the illness, and in doing so, keep an important, if not the most important, element of treatment (taking more effective control of their lives) out of the treatment picture. I am not claiming that good medical care is unnecessary, but medical care without better need-fulfilling behaviors will do little more than reduce the symptoms.

CANCER

As mysterious and frightening as cancer is to most of us, a great deal is already known about what causes it. Cancer researchers believe that for a cancer to become clinically observable, two steps have to happen in sequence. First, a cell and, because cancer cells multiply rapidly, soon a group of cells reorganize and begin to follow their own genetic programs. There is much speculation as to why this happens. External agents such as dioxin, radiation, and some viruses have all been incriminated, and there is some new evidence that internal agents such as a cancer-causing gene (an oncogene) may play an important part in this first step. *There is no evidence that this initial change is in any way psychologically caused.*

In contrast to normal cells, which will multiply only a given number of times and then stop, cancer cells seem to be programmed for rapid and unlimited multiplication. They grow quickly and wildly and feed on normal body tissue. If unchecked, they will destroy the body by their overwhelming demands for sustenance. But we are rarely aware of this initial step, because usually this growth is quickly and completely checked by our immune systems, which, if functioning normally, seek out and destroy these "foreign" cells before we are aware of their existence.

For the cancer cells to multiply to the extent that we have discoverable disease, it is necessary that the next step in the sequence occur. The immune system, for as yet unknown reasons, fails to function normally. It either does not find the cancer cells, or, if it finds them, does not destroy them. Much of our modern treatment of cancer is aimed at augmenting the immune system to get it to function normally or even better. Normal functioning may not be sufficient to destroy a stubborn, fast-growing cancer.

It is common knowledge that some people, informed that they have cancer, seem to lose the will to live, and die much more quickly than others with even more advanced disease. It seems as if this new-brain knowledge causes some disruption in the immune system's normal old-brain instructions to fight the cancerous foreign invader. If we don't know that we have cancer, the old brain will still fight, even if it is fighting a losing battle. When patients are told they have cancer, some may just give up and say, "This is too much for me to handle."

The will to live is a new-brain behavior that may transmit "activate-the-immune-system" hormones to the old brain the way Alan transmitted "activate-the-fighting-system" hormones to his old brain. What cancer sufferers who give up seem to do is just the opposite of what Alan did: In giving up, they stop sending activating hormones, and the old brain and the immune system fail to seek a creative body solution to their problem. The behavior of giving up, "What's the use of fighting anymore? I'm beaten," is often chosen when we are told we have cancer, the most dreaded of all diseases.

Life is not a static process. In the normal give-and-take of living, the old brain is constantly looking for creative new ways to help us to become healthier and better able to deal with disease. Cancer is a disease for which we need all the physiological creativity we can muster, and where we need this most is in the immune system. It is already not functioning as well as it should, and when we reduce or turn off its ability to be creative by sending it "give-up" hormones, we have little chance against cancer. We need all the new-brain resistance to giving up that we can transmit to the old brain so it will keep our immune systems as active and creative as possible.

When we become aware that we have *any* serious illness, we are always hard pressed to retain control over our lives. We need all the help we can get at this point from everyone around us to retain the control that seems to be slipping away. But most important, we do not need to be put in any situation that is difficult for us to deal with. Every added difficulty is another obstacle, and tired and discouraged as we often are, the last things we need are more obstacles. For example, if I suspect that I may be suffering from a serious illness such as cancer, I believe that I would not want to be told any more than is necessary for me to get good medical treatment. I want to be told that there is a good chance I will get well, because there may be. I don't want to see that my doctor is discouraged, but that she will try her best for me. After that, I do not want to know anything more, because I want to maintain as much control over my life as I can.

On my own, all I have going for me is my old brain and its immune system, and I know that the more I am in control of my life, the better the relationship will be between my new brain and my old. And the better this relationship is, the more my old brain will "fight" creatively for my life. This fight may be as important to my survival, or at least to the quality of my remaining life, as anything my doctor can do for me.

Unfortunately, the modern medical practice of keeping still-functioning cancer patients in bed in large, frightening, impersonal hospitals is probably not sensible treatment. It is convenient for the doctor and hospital, but because much of the fight against cancer must come from within, it makes sense to keep our old brain as functional as possible. Anything that can be done to help sick people maintain control over their lives is probably an essential part of any good (old-brain-supportive) treatment plan. Most physicians recognize that this is true, but they are overwhelmed and intimidated by the whole thrust of scientific medicine with its awesome treatments and huge apparatus. It's as though medical treatment has become bigger than both the doctors and the patients. The needs of the patient have become subordinate to the "needs" of treatment.

Everything done for (but really as much to) sick people in a modern hospital takes control away from them and puts it into outside hands. At some point, many patients begin to give up because the little they are able to do gets them so little of the control they desire that continuing to fight is not worth it. Unlike Alan, they need to send *fighting* messenger hormones from their new brain to their old, and when they give up, they seem to stop sending these lifesaving messages. The foundation of all good medical treatment, whatever the disease, should be to do as much as possible to help those who are sick maintain and even regain as much control over their lives as their disability allows.

13
Addicting Drugs— *"Chemical Control" of Our Lives*

Take a moment to recall the last time you felt really wonderful. Wouldn't it be great if you could experience that same feeling right now? Unfortunately, you can't. To re-create that feeling, you must do something that gives you a powerful sense of control—fall in love, get a big promotion, win a big match, or escape from behind the iron curtain. Any sudden increase in love, power, fun, or freedom is always accompanied by a burst of pure pleasure, usually followed by a period of enjoyable activity.

I have explained that our feelings are generated in two ways. *Pure, short-lived,* but extremely intense feelings occur whenever we are aware of a rapid increase or decrease in the difference between what we want and what we have. For example, we suffer pure pain when we hear that our good jobs are in jeopardy, and enjoy a burst of pure pleasure when we find out that the rumor was false. However, the main source of our feelings, good and bad, is the feeling component of long-term behaviors. For example, we choose to depress for months as the best way to deal with losing a good job, or we choose the constant joy that goes with exciting, satisfying work.

The way we have evolved is that good feelings, both pure and long-term, are *always* a part of any effective, need-fulfilling behavior, like playing a good game of bridge or eating a delicious meal. Thus, we assume we are in control of our lives when we feel good—and except for one important exception, we are. *The exception is when we choose to ingest, sniff, or inject addicting drugs. When drugs like heroin, alcohol, cocaine, and, on occasion, even marijuana reach our brain, we may, for a short time, feel ecstatic. The quick, intense pleasure that we experience feels very much like the pure, intense pleasure we feel when we suddenly take control of our lives. When we feel this drug-induced burst of pleasure, we almost always fail to realize that even though we may feel ecstatic, our lives are always seriously out of control. If we continue to use any addicting drug, no matter how good we feel, we will always lose more and more control of our lives.*

While good feelings are associated with effective control, I believe that control came first. You may observe simple organisms, like plants, struggling hard to stay alive, or in control, despite poor soil and hostile climate, but I doubt they have any feelings. Somehow, as higher animals struggled to fulfill their needs, feelings evolved: good feelings to reward them for succeeding in the struggle, and bad feelings to warn them that needs were not being satisfied. And, of course, good feelings must be balanced by bad feelings or we would not recognize the difference between them. Knowing that bad feelings will be replaced by good feelings is also a powerful incentive to look for ways to regain control. We need the promise of the "pot of gold" at the end of our emotional "rainbow" to keep us moving in the right direction. When we have that pot in sight, or in hand, we have every reason to believe we are in effective control of our lives.

Another difference between us and all other creatures is that we tend to be aware of the passage of time, and we relate this awareness to how well we are in control of our lives. "Time flies" when we are satisfied and drags when we are not. When you are bored—for example, when your plane is delayed and you have to spend six hours wandering around an airport—you are not in control of your life and the hands of the airport clocks seem frozen. When you are in control, as when you are enjoying a wonderful vacation, the days fly by. You do all you can to prolong the experience, perhaps staying up all night with newfound friends, but still the clock moves with a vengeance, as if it has a personal vendetta to deprive you of as much vacation as it can.

When we are deeply involved intellectually, time flies. When I work on a project like this book, I can sit down in the early afternoon, and before I know it, it's dark outside. I don't feel any particular emotion—mostly my behavior is thinking—but still, as I make progress, time races by. So far as I know, there is no drug that provides this experience. The main addicting drugs, which I will introduce next, all give us a sense of control by providing a variety of pleasures, and, because we feel so good, we tend to pay little attention to time. To do this, they act on the control system in the following five ways.*

Action One: Exemplified by the Opiates—Common Examples Are Codeine, Percodan, Morphine, and Heroin

All the opiates act on the control system directly to make us feel good. They imitate the recently discovered natural opiatelike chemicals secreted by our old brain, which provide most, if not all, the pure pleasure we feel when we suddenly take control in the real world. A golfer jumping for joy when he makes a winning putt is an example of how some people act when they experience the sudden secretion of a natural opiate.

The same feeling, perhaps even more powerful, is produced by an injection of heroin, especially if it is a large dose. Anyone using these drugs on a regular basis will become addicted, and while "high," will pay no attention to time. But when the addict runs short of the drug, time stands still, and few people are in less control of their lives than heroin addicts without access to their drug.

Action Two: Common Examples Are Marijuana and LSD

Marijuana acts on our sensory cameras by making the world appear easier and more pleasurable to deal with. It is a drug that seems to act as a mild pleasure filter in the back of the sensory camera so that what we perceive looks better, sounds better, tastes better, and feels

---

*This is not a book on drugs. I discuss them briefly to explain how they affect us and how, as control systems, we deal with them. For more information, I refer the reader to the classic *Licit and Illicit Drugs,* by Edward M. Brecher and the editors of *Consumer Reports* (Mount Vernon, N.Y.: Consumer Union, 1972).

better, and to this extent it is addicting. LSD also acts on our cameras, but in a more powerful, unpredictable, and not always pleasurable way, so that people seeking control do not regularly use LSD. Drugs like LSD are used by people seeking new sensory experiences—perhaps a trip into a new world. It is common that while looking for the ultimate limits of experience, an LSD user perceives the world as so altered and distorted that he hallucinates. When this happens, he may become terror-stricken and correctly conclude that he has completely lost control. For this reason it is the rare person who becomes addicted to LSD. Its action is too unpredictable.

Action Three: Alcohol

More than any other drug, alcohol acts to give the user a quick and powerful sense of control. The good feeling that accompanies its use is how the user experiences this drug-induced "increase" in control. Unlike heroin and marijuana, which tend to render users passive, alcohol often leads its users to do something active to increase the sense of control the drug has already provided. Under its influence, and actually losing control, alcoholics may act as if they believe that whatever they do will increase the control they falsely believe they have. This action is unique; no other drug acts to increase a sense of control that is actually being lost.

Action Four: Common Examples Are Caffeine, Nicotine, and Cocaine

Cocaine and its weaker analogues—such as caffeine, nicotine, Dexedrine, and Methedrine—also give a sense of control, but in a different way. Their main actions are to energize the behavioral system so much that cocaine users, for example, can act for a while as if nothing is beyond their capabilities. Unlike alcohol, these drugs may for a short time actually provide the user with an increased ability to take control of his life. Obviously nicotine and caffeine are much less powerful than cocaine or Methedrine, but they, too, are mild energizers, and also seem to work well together. To verify this, ask anyone who uses both to skip the cigarette or start the day with a cup of decaffeinated coffee.

Action Five: Common Examples Are Barbiturates, Valium, and Quaaludes

Unlike many of the previously mentioned drugs, these are mainly prescribed by physicians in an attempt to help tense patients relax and to assist patients who have trouble sleeping. They all act to sedate the behavioral system, and in sufficient doses will produce a sleeplike state that is not nearly as restful as normal sleep. They do, however, produce a sense of pleasurable rest by reducing the urgency to behave in ways that may reduce our use of feeling behaviors like anxietying. All of these drugs are addictive if used frequently.

All regular users of addicting drugs can be said to be both psychologically and physically addicted. They are psychologically addicted because they become well aware of the pleasure the drugs provide and they want to experience it as often and as long as possible. But they are also physically addicted in that the old brain accepts the drugs and integrates them into the normal body chemistry. Although we have no awareness of this because we have no direct awareness of any old-brain processes, the old brain "learns" that these drugs are beneficial to its functioning. We become aware that this has happened only when we try to stop taking the drugs. Then the old brain sends the new brain a pain message that we interpret consciously as a thirst for the drug. This is exactly analogous to thirst for water or hunger for food.

It is this double "benefit" (mental and physical) that makes these drugs so addicting. But as the user increases the dosage in an effort to increase the pleasure, the old brain, unable to "use" so much drug, can no longer function satisfactorily, and the drug in effect becomes a painful poison. Unfortunately, as the user becomes poisoned by the drug, he tends to take more and more in a desperate attempt to feel better, producing the vicious, disabling, and at times even lethal action of these drugs.

If we stop taking a drug such as morphine, cocaine, or Valium, it can take a very long time—up to several years—for the old brain to go back to its normal predrug functioning and "forget" the drug. During this interval we have little ability to feel good without the drug, because the old brain is inhibited from secreting the natural pleasure drugs that it normally secretes when we take effective control. This is a normal physiological process that always occurs when any natural drug or chemical is abundantly and regularly provided from the outside. Gradually the old brain resumes its normal function, but for a long time the ex-user does not have the ability to feel natural pleasure and must struggle through a miserable period of joylessness as he waits for his old brain to begin secreting the natural pleasure drugs that we all need if we are to feel good.

This is why addicts complain so much about not having their drug: They don't yet have the ability to experience the pleasures of normal living that nonusers take for granted. Alcohol is, of course, the exception because it is not a natural pleasure drug. What it does is chemically provide a sense of control that the user cannot distinguish from effective need satisfaction. The intense pleasure alcoholics experience is from their own natural pleasure drugs like the endorphins that are always secreted when we suddenly gain the sense that we are in control. Therefore, when an alcoholic stops drinking and is able to satisfy his needs without alcohol, he has no difficulty feeling good—he has never interrupted this natural process.

The new brain, however, has an elephantlike memory for any addicting drug; nicotine, for example, may remain in our picture albums forever. Therefore, although there may come a time when we no longer need the drug physically, we may never rid ourselves of the psychological longing for the drug unless what it provided is replaced by new effective behaviors. If we start to use the drug again, its chemical presence will quickly reactivate the old brain's "memory," and again driven by both a physical and a mental craving, we quickly become readdicted and once more lose the ability to secrete our natural pleasure drugs.

Stronger drugs like alcohol, cocaine, and Valium are also easily integrated into old-brain functioning and are perceived by the old brain as highly "beneficial" in small amounts. In the large amounts in which they are frequently used, they poison the old brain and we become physically sick. But if we stop taking the drug, harmful as it was in the amounts we took it, the old brain continues for a long time, maybe for years, to send "thirst" messages to the new brain for the drug. It seems to have no way to "learn" that in large doses the drug is harmful; it "remembers" only the beneficial effects of the small doses, so, no matter how poisonous, our old brain does not stop sending the "get-me-some-drug" messages to the new brain until it completely "forgets." Therefore, if you want to quit any addicting drug, you have to depend on your new brain to come up with an effective need-satisfying behavior, such as succeeding at your work or reestablishing old family ties. The old brain, even if it has been repeatedly poisoned, will continue to "crave" the drug. And the stronger the drug, the longer this craving will last.

Marijuana seems to be a drug that, in the small amounts most users use it, is very easily integrated into old-brain functioning. It differs, however, from most other addicting drugs in that when we stop using it, the old brain gives it up very easily. We seem not to get the strong old-brain "thirst" for it that we do for the other drugs. In small doses, therefore, it is more psychologically than physically addicting. In large doses, however, the old brain may grow to depend on it as it does all other drugs, and it will also be physically addicting. In very large doses, it, too, will poison the old brain and lead to disturbed functioning similar to the perceptual disturbances caused by LSD. Many people who use marijuana in large quantities will change to alcohol or another, stronger drug because marijuana, even in large quantities, will not give them the sense of control for which they are searching.

It should be obvious to anyone who understands control theory that addicting drugs, because they adversely affect both the old and new brains, are serious obstacles to taking effective control of our lives unless used in small, well-controlled, social doses. Giving opium to starving children to prevent the pangs of hunger, a common practice in England in the time of Dickens, was hardly healthy; the first mild infection that came along was usually fatal to these victims of poverty. We have little starvation now, but more drug use because with affluence we have become more aware that pleasure is possible. Addicts seek it incessantly and don't hesitate to use drugs if they can't get pleasure easily any other way. Even if you don't use drugs to excess, it is valuable, because of their widespread use, to know how they affect those around you. The following information is not intended to be a treatise on drug rehabilitation. It may, however, be of great value if you have to cope with drug users when they are under the influence and to get you started if they ask you for help to stop using.

ALCOHOL

The most dangerous and debilitating of all the common drugs is alcohol, partly because of the way it acts upon us, but mostly because its heavy use is so socially accepted that we tend to disregard the well-known fact that when it is used in large amounts, it almost always leads to disaster for the user.

Alcohol is an extremely simple compound, but no one has yet discovered how it works in the body to give almost all users a powerful belief that they are in control of their lives when actually they are not. This effect is cumulative: The more they drink, the greater the sense of control they experience. I have many friends and colleagues, now in Alcoholics Anonymous, who drank for years, and they confirm that this is the major effect. The picture that they "successfully" pursued was drinking until they felt in total control, which means until they were drunk. But actually, the more alcohol they consumed, the less control they had, so the common characteristic of every drunken alcoholic is the vast difference between the amount of control he actually has (almost none) and the amount of control he believes he has (total).

It does not seem to matter which of the several needs is not fulfilled; alcohol gives the user the false sense that it is. It makes the lonely sociable; the powerless powerful; the gloomy fun-filled; and the imprisoned less confined. And since our society is filled with people who are unsatisfied with the way that they are choosing to live their lives, many use alcohol in huge quantities. As mentioned earlier, unlike heroin or cocaine, it does not give pleasure directly, but from the satisfying sense of control, which probably causes a concurrent liberation of their own natural pleasure chemicals—the internal opiates.

For the user, whether the pleasure is direct or indirect is only a technical point; the pleasure felt is immediate and intense. The technical point is important, however, in the rehabilitation process because the alcoholic never loses his ability to secrete his natural pleasure drugs. Once he stops drinking and regains control, he can feel good almost immediately, so he has great incentive to stop drinking if he can retain control without alcohol. He does not have to wait the long, pleasureless interval while his own natural pleasure drugs are reactivated, an interval that almost always occurs when a direct pleasure drug like heroin or Valium is withdrawn.

As the years go by, even the most obtuse drinker begins to become aware that the "control" he feels when drunk has no substance in fact. He cannot escape from the sickness and disability that are a part of his life, drunk and sober. He cannot fool himself into believing his needs are satisfied when everyone around him turns away and he is left alone. Still, he does not quit, and may even drink more because he has taken all except alcohol out of his picture album. So he drinks alone, depending totally on the drug and even giving up trying to do the things he used to do incompetently when he believed alcohol made him competent. His continued use of alcohol, common among the residents of any city's skid row, is less to get pleasure and more to become unconscious. Only with loss of consciousness can he escape from the painful sense that, even drunk, he is still far from in control.

The most insidious action of alcohol is that the user has no perception that he has lost control until the drug begins to wear off. Without the drug, he feels a huge burst of the pure pain that always accompanies the immediate loss of control. So as soon as he can, he drinks again, each time fooling himself into believing that he has finally gained control. He also believes that anything he does while under the influence is enhancing that control. This crazy belief that what he does is good for him and, unfortunately, for those around him (remember that he thinks he is in control and does not realize he is drunk) leads to the most destructive aspect of alcohol—violence. Almost all violent crimes, especially the wife and child beating and the incestuous relationships that are so much a part of our culture, are a direct consequence of drinking. The countless, but less premeditated, tragedies of drunken driving, boating, or flying far outnumber the accidents that occur when the operators are sober. Alcohol consumption is the prime cause of violence, intentional or unintentional, in our society, and it is more often than not the "motivator" for sexual abuse by men of women and children.

There is a common scenario of a drinking man—we'll call him

Mack—whose marriage is rapidly deteriorating. Each day as the alcohol takes effect, he believes that he is in control and can now do anything he wants, and that his wife—we'll call her Kay—will not only go along with it but will like it and like him as he does it. Perhaps he just makes a simple demand that she go out and get him some more beer, or a more complicated demand that she have sex in a way that she does not like, or at least not when he is drunk. She may refuse to get the beer or participate enthusiastically in the sex. His false sense of control is as repugnant to her as his drunkenness. She may have started this evening like many others by asking him to drink less—which he bitterly resents. All day long he had looked forward to his evening beer and to the control he "regains" with it.

To Mack, sobriety is the misery and pain of an out-of-control life. Kay's "nagging" represents all the control he does not have, and alcohol represents all he longs for. Because alcohol is the greatest of all rationalizers, Mack, when drunk, thinks that anything he does is justified. Having lost all ability to judge what he does with any accuracy, he "knows" he is in control; no one has a right to dispute his authority, and if they do, he is going to do what he "believes necessary," with no thought that what he does may be horribly violent. When Kay refuses to get him more beer, he beats her because she has no right to challenge a man who is in control. Drunk, he is the captain of the family ship, with the right to put down any mutiny—and he does.

Kay, not knowing control theory, does not know what is going on. She cannot possibly grasp the fact that he believes he is in control, because it is so obvious to her that he is not. She believes that she is doing him a favor by refusing to get him beer, and expects he will have some ability to realize this, but, of course, he hasn't. The alcohol has given him "confidence" that whatever he does is effective, and he may beat her severely, believing it his duty as a husband to straighten her out.

All this takes place slowly. In the beginning, when Mack got a little tipsy, it was fun to be with him because he gained confidence in himself. And with a better sense of humor and the mild feeling of power the alcohol gave him, he related better to Kay. If he had never drunk past that level, as social drinkers do not, the sense of control that the alcohol gave him would have made him more attractive and easier to get along with. When we have confidence, we are better for having it, and this is the seemingly sensible rationale for using alcohol.

The problem that all drinkers face is to maintain the delicate balance between just enough and too much. But as any drinker gains confidence, he also tends to lose the ability to stop at the point where this mild confidence is attractive and helpful. He is tempted to take another drink, especially when he is a little out of control from a hard day or a brush with his wife or kids. First Mack went a little past that level; then a lot; and finally, instead of trying to work out problems, he drank to work them out "chemically." The vicious drinking cycle was established. He only feels in control when he is drunk, because when he is sober, Kay does not miss an opportunity to tell him in a thousand ways how dreadful he has become to live with. Theirs is the typical alcoholic marriage: She is in control when he is sober; he is in control when drunk. Without help, neither will be able to patch up the differences between them.

Kay stays with him for the usual reasons—love, loyalty, security, children—but one reason common to most wives of alcoholics is that as time passes, she has more and more control over him when he is sober. This compensates somewhat for the violent control he takes when he is drunk. If she cannot learn what is going on, all she can look forward to is more beatings and less sobriety. As long as she does not realize that drinking gives him a sense of control, she has no way to deal effectively with him. She will continue to badger him when he is sober, and he will drink more and more to regain control. But if she can manage to stay alive, she will "win." The poisonous effect of the alcohol will eventually make him so sick that he will surrender to her care. He will lose the physical stamina that he needs to keep drinking in quantity, and she will be left with a shell of a man—a burned-out, sick drunk.

If Kay wants to take effective control of her life and marriage, there is much she can do to put what is explained here into practice. First, she must learn that Mack drinks to gain the control that he has lost. And when he is drunk, he feels "justified" in doing anything to regain his lost control, including violence. She must make a plan to leave the house when he starts drinking, and if she has children, take them with her, and not return until he is sober. If on some occasions she can't leave, she must, to protect herself and her children, not thwart him. Even a tiny crying baby may be seen by him as a threat to his drunken control, and to him it may make "sense" to beat an infant.

She should also learn that there is no way that she can, by herself, reform an alcoholic. When he is sober, he may listen as she tells him about the terror and confusion he creates when he is drunk, but all this does is cause him to further lose control and yearn for more alcohol. Her good intentions—and his when sober—unfortunately compound the problem. Mack has lost control of his life, but Kay is so intimately involved in this loss that she cannot help him. It is impossible. He must stop drinking, and in my work with alcoholics I have learned that he will not stop until he gets into an Alcoholics Anonymous program that will help him begin to regain control of his life without alcohol. Kay must learn the hard lesson that she can control only her own life; she cannot control Mack's. If she continues to try, she may be killed.

If she wants to begin to control her life, she must decide whether or not she wants to control Mack badly enough to continue her life of accepting drunken beatings and listening to guilty promises to stop. If she decides that this is not what she wants, she must tell him while he is sober that she cannot and will not continue to live with him as they are. If she understands what I have just explained, she will realize that life with Mack will get worse, not better. As a condition of her staying with him, he must go to AA. To deal with her problems, which she must admit to him that she has, too, she will get involved with Alanon, the AA program to help families of alcoholics. *In fact, she should tell him that she will go to Alanon whether he goes to AA or not.*

What she will learn in Alanon—a program that, like AA, follows control theory—is how to live with him in a way in which they both feel as if they are in control of their lives and their marriage. If she can't learn this, her only chance is to get divorced. If she is strong, but not damning of his drinking or of him, and tells him that they can't stay together while he continues to drink, and if there is anything left of their marriage, he will go to AA. There he will learn that he has lost control of his life, but can regain it without the need for alcohol. He will change the picture in his album from alcohol to AA. She will change the picture in her album from controlling him to caring without control, and they will have a chance. There is no other; alcohol is too powerful. AA is the only program that I know of that helps alcoholics consistently and without cost. But even AA is not the total answer. It is the beginning, the chance to get sober. While sober, the alcoholic must regain enough control over his life to satisfy his needs. AA, by itself, cannot satisfy his needs, but it is a way—probably the best way we have available—to get the process started.

Alcohol is so much a part of our culture that it is sometimes difficult for a nondrinker to gain social acceptance. Anyone who does not drink has to be strong enough to find friends who accept him as a nondrinker. This is not hard for successful adults; but for teen-agers, because they have such a pressing need for acceptance as they make the transition into adulthood, not to drink is to risk being left out. Besides, most see and experience drinking in their homes, and sometimes a little drunkenness is treated by the family more as a joke than as a potentially serious problem.

I believe that alcohol will always be an integral, accepted, even glorified part of our culture, while other drugs will not, because alcohol is supportive of the cultural ideal—taking control of your life. The fact that alcohol is the single most destructive force in our culture that causes people to lose control is not recognized and will not be recognized, because of how it acts. The culture, or at least the culture presented by the mass media, sees it as a positive force, which it may be if it is used in delicate moderation. Supported by the media, our culture *falsely* assumes that "real" men and women will not exceed the very fine line between enhancing and losing control. Alcohol is the get-things-done, take-control drug, and to deal with it well is a sign of strength and maturity. Because it enhances the sense of control, we welcome it instead of fearing it as we should.

The advertised image of beer links it with hard, exciting work and athletic accomplishment. People who are really in control of their lives drink a lot of beer on TV and never lose control. If you believe the ads, the work is always done well; the drinking is never on the job or during the game; the parties are always fun; and no one ever gets into an accident driving home. Alcohol is advertised as the drug that happy and successful people use, and they never lose control when they use it. So when a young person begins to drink, he or she rarely considers how fine the line is between moderation and drunkenness—just one too many and a life may be irreparably damaged or lost. And, of course, the young user never feels out of control, because the more he uses, the more in control he thinks he is. Long after he is a confirmed alcoholic, he continues to "believe" he is just like the people in the ads.

The way a parent can help a child deal with this most insidious and dangerous drug is to stay on good terms with the child and, if the parent does drink, to do it in moderation as a model of how to handle alcohol. Talking to a son or daughter and explaining the effect of alcohol and the fine line between moderation and excess is also wise. Trying to persuade a son or daughter to go to AA is, to me, a must for any parent who knows that the child has a drinking problem. Don't be fooled into thinking a child is too young to be alcoholic; children as young as ten years are regular attenders of AA meetings. Parents of alcoholics should attend Alanon, and brothers and sisters of young alcoholics should attend Alateen, a special program for teen-agers who have any family members attending AA. But the most effective thing we can do is to try to raise our children so that they are enough in control of their lives that a chemical sense of control is less needed. In a later chapter I will summarize how parents might best use knowledge of control theory to raise more effective children.

Desperate parents as well as other family members should also be aware that "curing" alcoholism and abuse of other drugs—especially cocaine—is now big business. The daily newspapers are filled with ads offering hope that is likely not a reality. Many of these (often ineffective) programs are unbelievably expensive, and since most of them are covered by medical insurance, their widespread use has greatly increased the cost of this expensive insurance for all of us. Anyone thinking of getting involved with a profit-making drug program should investigate very carefully what is being offered for the money. Many are no more than custodial: Personnel is untrained; the doctor is more on the letterhead than an active participant; and the addicting drugs that they are supposed to be treating are "available" for a price. What is mostly "sold" is temporary relief for the family by getting the addict out of the house, and if you buy this, you are compounding the problem, not treating it.

There are also many legitimate low-cost programs available that can be located through the Alcoholism Council listed in the white (not yellow) pages of your local phone book. But regardless of cost, before you enroll anyone in a program, especially a live-in program,

you should get the names of at least three people who have com-
pleted the program and have been drug-free for a year. You should
talk to these people; they will not only be willing to talk to you, they
will want to talk to you. This is the only way you can find out what
you need to know about any program. If anyone offering a program
is not willing or able to provide you with these names, have nothing
to do with that program.

14

Other Common Addicting Drugs, Legal and Illegal

MARIJUANA

No matter what I write about marijuana, many will disagree. If I call it a "dangerous drug," many users will point out that it hasn't harmed them. How do they know? You can't use and not use at the same time, so you have no way of knowing how much better or worse you would be without the drug. But if I call it a "mild pleasure drug," many nonusers and the antimarijuana lobby will criticize me and show me "research" proving it causes everything from psychosis to birth defects. Fortunately, my purpose is not to resolve this controversy but to try to make some sense out of this drug's action; to explain how this particular drug "helps" people believe that with it they are in better control of their lives.

Any drug that causes pleasure or "kills" time is a dangerous drug, and marijuana is in that category. It is also a potentially addicting drug, but it has "flaws" that make it much less addicting than alcohol and most of the other pleasure drugs. Marijuana does not give much of a sense of control. Nor does it energize, sedate, or produce much pure pleasure. It is more widely used than all drugs, except alcohol, but it is less abused, because, like caffeine and nicotine, its effect is not particularly enhanced by high doses.

Its major effect is to make the world seem easier to control by causing whatever we deal with to appear more pleasant. Unlike an alcohol user, a marijuana user is more "tolerant" of the world. He does not have the urge to take control by action and becomes a passive, bemused observer of the struggles of those around him. Since our "get up and go" culture lauds action and frowns upon passive observation or any passive pleasures, those with power in our competitive culture consider marijuana more dangerous than alcohol because a marijuana user tends to drop out rather than compete. Alcoholics may get drunk, sick, and disabled, but for a long time they are competitive, and to that extent the culture supports their efforts. Marijuana is an anticulture drug because it renders its users passive and accepting of the status quo. Chronic users have little motivation to pursue the work ethic of our culture.

Those who must do boring work argue that marijuana makes the work less tedious and their drab jobs more endurable. If used frequently, however, it will impair both the workers' ability and desire to do a good job. People whose lives are seriously out of control will find little satisfaction in marijuana; it can't make an unloving spouse loving or an unsatisfying job satisfying. When those who use it find this out, they often turn to stronger, more "controlling" drugs, especially alcohol, because it is legal and accepted. Those whose lives are under relatively good control may stay with marijuana, and even prefer it to alcohol, but like social drinkers they tend not to use it excessively.

Even in small amounts, marijuana tends to reduce incentive and motivation to struggle hard, and its users often settle for less than their potential. Though they may recognize this effect, under its influence they do not care to do much about it. This is what worries parents whose children smoke marijuana, and it is a legitimate worry. The problem is, how can a parent persuade a child to stop using or, even better, never start using this drug? A good relationship with the child is probably the parent's best weapon. No parent can completely control the child's activity, but it is reasonable for parents to insist that children do not smoke it in their house. Most children will respect the wishes of a parent whom they love and respect, and will adhere to this rule. And because it is a drug that children like to use at home, they may thus use less.

Parents should avoid using their good relationship with their children to persuade them to replace "dangerous" marijuana with "safe" alcohol. The effort should be to try to get them to live a drug-free life, not to get them to move on to what, for them, may be an even more dangerous drug. But I have no great words of wisdom here. Children who feel they are in control of their lives will not use any drug to excess. If you have a good relationship with your child, and if the child is successful in what he or she does and has learned that hard work leads to success and pleasure, you need not worry if the child uses marijuana or alcohol in moderation. Moderation is measured by how well the child is in control of his or her life. If the child is not in control, is not happy, has few friends, few or no active interests, and does not do well in school, that unhappy child is likely to begin using pleasure drugs, usually beginning with alcohol and/or marijuana. These are the unhappy facts of life in the 1980s.

HEROIN

For centuries, users of opium and its stronger derivatives, like morphine and heroin, have suspected that there is a special quality to these intensely pleasurable drugs. Then, in 1975, scientists discovered what this special quality is: These drugs mimic a natural heroinlike chemical that is secreted in our bodies whenever we feel pleasure. While many people find the idea that we secrete heroin in our bodies disturbing and hard to accept, the facts are clear that we do.

Therefore, whether we like it or not, when we gain control of any situation, we feel good because our bodies have secreted their own "natural" heroin, giving us a small shot of pure chemical pleasure. The addict uses large doses of heroin, probably far beyond what we normally secrete even under the best of circumstances, in an effort not only to mimic but to exceed natural pleasure experiences.

Addicts are not interested in doing anything to gain control of their lives except to inject heroin. This is because with heroin they are "in control," supreme control, as they experience the pure pleasure that comes with "total" control. A heroin addict doesn't care if his wife won't go out for a beer or have sex with him or even if she leaves him forever. All he cares about is the feeling of heroin, and when he is high, he is withdrawn and nonhostile.

Some people can use heroin the way social drinkers use alcohol, getting the pleasure once in a while without giving up their lives for it. One large group that did this was our soldiers in Vietnam. In those dreadful circumstances, they used heroin, but few continued to use it when they came home if they were able to get their lives under good control. Most people who turn to heroin do so because their lives are very much out of control, and they quickly become addicted. Neither I nor anyone else has any wisdom for heroin addicts. They have found what they believe all people are looking for, and they are satisfied. Without heroin, as they suffer withdrawal, they are about as out of control as a human can get. But most of them are driven hard enough by the withdrawal, or the fear of it, to figure out how to get heroin. The need of the addict is so intense that even in many prisons heroin is available to addicts who have the price. Many lose their lives with impure drugs or die of illnesses associated with long-term use and the physical deprivation that accompanies it.

Some give it up through the use of powerful group programs such as Daytop Village near New York City, but most stay with it for a long time. There is reason to believe that many finally give it up on their own, because those who work with addicts report that they almost never deal with people over forty-five years old. They can't all be dead, so the solution to this mystery of where they go or what they do must be that they get tired of the "rat race" that accompanies the daily struggle to finance their habit and stop using the drug. Most researchers believe that almost all of them turn to always-available alcohol. The picture is not bright. Heroin is a life-destroying drug. Few people who become addicted to it are able to resume a normal life without the drug, either on their own or with the help of others.

THE UPPERS: CAFFEINE, NICOTINE, BENZEDRINE, METHEDRINE, COCAINE

When the German armies waged the "blitzkrieg" or "lightning war" through France and the Lowlands in 1940, the Allied forces were no match for their stamina and ferocity. The Germans fought like men possessed, and they were. Their pharmacists had synthesized Methedrine, a cheap but powerful energizing drug that allowed their soldiers to fight vigorously for weeks at a time with no sleep and little food. Just as the Indians of the high

Andes can perform prodigious feats of strength and endurance while chewing the coca leaf, from which they get cocaine and other energizers, the Germans fought like demons stoked with cheap and readily available Methedrine. Like horses doped for a race, they did not fight fairly, but fairness is a concept that has no relationship to modern war, although there may have been some sense of "fighting fair" left over from more romantic times among the Allied forces in 1940. It is doubtful that the Allies would have used these "uppers" even if they had had them, but for short-term use, before the user is drained, they do provide prodigious amounts of energy.

The "uppers," ranging from mild (caffeine and nicotine) to powerful (cocaine), are among the most addicting of all drugs. They energize the behavioral system so that it performs better—a little better for caffeine and nicotine, and a lot better for Benzedrine, Methedrine, and cocaine. But even a mild energizer like nicotine quickly becomes so much a part of our regular body chemistry that once it is accepted, the body "needs" it to function. Anyone who has smoked for the length of time that most people smoke before they consider quitting knows how much the body begins to hurt when its nicotine is removed. Mild as it is, nicotine is considered as addicting as any drug, because we use it for so long that even the old brain seems never to "forget" it. Caffeine is similar, but the effect is milder and the old brain will "forget" it much more easily and quickly than it does nicotine.

Caffeine seems to do us little physical harm, but nicotine is both directly and indirectly harmful. It seems directly linked in some way to predisposing us to heart disease, and indirectly, through the tars that we inhale when we smoke, to lung cancer. It is, however, the tars, not the nicotine, that are carcinogenic. There also may be a psychological relationship between nicotine and heart disease in that those who do not smoke are probably in better control of their lives and thus less likely to have any psychosomatic disease.

The powerful energizers are cocaine and its synthetic analogues —Methedrine, Benzedrine, and Dexedrine. In sufficient doses, these give such an unbelievable rush of energy that those who use them in large doses feel that if they wanted, they could take over the world. Feeling this way, they enjoy a temporary increase in the performance of simple physical tasks, such as fighting or having sex. If the task is complex and requires more than just energy, they probably do not perform very well. But regardless of the performance, what they do in all cases is drive their behavioral systems far beyond their normal capacity to function without rest.

All biologic systems need time for rest, renewal of the used-up chemicals, and excretion of waste products. But for users of cocaine, there is no rest. It never ceases to drive, and behavioral systems driven by it invariably start to become creative in a desperate effort to continue to perform at higher and higher levels. Ultimately, the user turns almost completely to his reorganization system and begins to think crazy thoughts and do crazy things. I believe that even the reorganization system is somehow affected by these drugs and it becomes more chaotic and biased toward weird, frightening hallucinations like worms crawling out of the skin.

These drugs, until recently, were not considered addicting, because they led to craziness, and with craziness the drug is necessarily discontinued. The user becomes so crazy he does not even know he is taking the drug, but to think that they are not addictive because of this is wrong. Cocaine may be the most addicting drug that we have, because people who are normally in good control of their lives —successful athletes, performers, and high-flying business people— seem to be so susceptible to it. They all seem to be seeking more energetic performance from their behavioral systems, and for this they seek cocaine. This is a different population from the more passive seekers of intense pleasure, who use heroin; the "go with the flow" marijuana users; or the nonperforming, but think they are performing, alcoholics.

It is possible that some people can use these drugs in moderation for the lift they provide, but because they are so addicting, this is difficult to do. Very quickly the drug takes over their lives and users lose all control, including the control they need in order to continue to use in moderation. As they become enervated by their constant activity and exhausted by their total inability to sleep, they may try heroin or alcohol in a desperate effort to get some "chemical" rest. But these drugs do not provide rest, and in the failing effort to find it, users may become addicted to them and vastly compound their problems.

Again, I have no words of wisdom except to beware of treatment programs that offer a cure for huge sums of money. Talk to some successful graduates before you mortgage the house for a promise that may not be fulfilled. Of course, these drugs have to be flushed out of the body. That's easy if the addict gets into a program where the drug is not made available to him for a price. What is difficult is to flush them from the old brain's and new brain's memory after they have long been incorporated into them. To get users to forget and start living their lives without the drug, a program must be long-term, starting with a drug-free environment for many months, maybe even a year. This must be followed by an intensive outpatient counseling program, in which the patients' blood or urine is checked regularly for the drug, for at least twice as long as the inpatient program or longer. It is wise to beware of slick ads promoting programs that promise easy or quick cures. Such cures do not exist.

Addicting drugs have legitimate medical uses, and can be an aid to taking effective control, but caution in this use is important. We live in a world where we all believe that what ails us is caused by something outside of us, so we tend to believe that the "cure" is also outside—if we are sick, the drug can cure us. But by now you have learned that most pain and sickness are related to our losing effective control of our lives, and while doctors can help, it is our responsibility to augment that help to regain the control we have lost. Knowing this, the doctor's most important responsibility becomes to avoid any treatment that will make it more difficult for us to regain control —or at least to retain the limited control we may still have. Any doctor who gives us a pleasure drug and does not make sure that we use this drug for a limited time only, while we gather ourselves together and regain control, is doing us no good and much potential harm.

THE ADDICTING DRUGS THAT DOCTORS PRESCRIBE

It is not wrong for a doctor who does not counsel to give a patient Valium, perhaps the most widely misused legal pleasure drug, if the doctor tells the patient that the Valium will not solve his problem. Even if he does not know control theory, the doctor should have some insight into the fact that the patient's life is out of control.

No doctor should ever give any patient more than one month's supply at minimal dosage, because at present the Federal Food and Drug Administration rates Valium as one of the most addicting drugs in existence. Its action is unique: It is closest to a sedative, but it also has a pure pleasure component similar to heroin. Thousands of people's lives have been ruined by indiscriminate prescription of this most dangerous of all widely prescribed drugs.

There is sense, even mercy, in a doctor's giving chemical relief to patients who are choosing to suffer because their lives are out of control—but only if at the same time they use the temporary relief the drug provides to get the counseling needed to regain control of their lives. To give any addicting drug without offering to help the patient get good counseling, and without following through to see that the patient is acting on this advice, is medicine at its worst. Doctors do not need to help people lose control of their lives; they do this well enough on their own.

The argument of many doctors who prescribe addicting drugs like Valium for anxiety and tension, Dexedrine for weight reduction, or barbiturates for insomnia is that they have no faith that counseling is more effective than the drug.* Some also see these drugs as curative and the patients as suffering from external diseases, because this ancient stimulus-response theory still governs what is taught in most medical schools. Used correctly, even addicting drugs serve an important medical purpose if that purpose is understood. A few sleeping pills to give a little rest to a distraught and sleepless person, or a little Dexedrine to lift a depressed or overweight person to the point of starting to take control, is good practice.

When a person suffers a painful, frightening heart attack, the use of morphine or one of its derivatives is usually lifesaving. Without the drug, the patient's fear would drive his old brain to the creative behavior that might lead to a fatal heart arrhythmia. But in these cases the use of the drug is limited to the attack; there is no need to keep it up after the attack is over. Used on a long-term basis, any of these drugs is harmful. Sleeping pills, usually barbiturates, are one of the most abused. They are given to people who do not have

---

*A strong argument supporting the effectiveness of counseling is made in Naomi Glasser's book *What Are You Doing?* (New York: Harper & Row, 1980).

enough control over their lives to accept that while a period of sleeplessness may be uncomfortable, it is not dangerous to health. All of us will eventually sleep enough for our needs, but if we take pills, we do not sleep normally—and to be healthy, we need normal sleep. Abnormal sleep may be more debilitating than much less of normal sleep.

Research has repeatedly shown that normal sleep entails a necessary amount of dreaming. Medications for sleeping cause us to be unconscious, but disrupt the normal and necessary nightly access to reorganization that is dreaming. We need this to resolve and bring under control the small but constant frustrations of the previous day. Without our creative dreams, we wake up hung over, still wrestling with what our dreams would have resolved. And because we are not rested, we find it even harder to cope. Now we need our normal dreaming sleep even more, but find it even harder to relax enough to go to sleep. If we then take more sleeping medication, as many do, we become addicted and dig ourselves deeper and deeper into a state of constant exhaustion. Then, to function better when awake, or to stay awake, we use too much caffeine, nicotine, or even stronger drugs, legal and illegal, and find it harder and harder both to sleep and to function while awake.

There is no drug that can produce the normal sleep we need to get the rest that gives us the energy to maintain control over our lives. In fact, there is no *long-term* benefit from any addicting drug, legal or illegal, no matter how it acts. But there is tremendous profit in both legal and illegal drugs, so they will be pushed on us from all sides as panaceas for pain, misery, exhaustion, and overweight. It is up to each of us to protect ourselves by refusing to use any addicting drug for more than a short time. We cannot depend upon anyone else to do this for us.

There are in wide use today a large number of legally prescribed antipsychotic and antidepressant drugs. It is a widely accepted medical theory that psychosis and depression are diseases caused by some chemical imbalance or disruption in the brain, just as diabetes is caused by the failure of the pancreas to produce sufficient insulin. Certainly, if we examined all psychotic and depressed people carefully, we would find that, out of the millions who "suffer," there are a few whose psychosis or depression is caused by some chemical abnormality. In these rare instances, their lives are under control; it is their old-brain chemistry that has gone haywire. This is supported by the fact that some manic-depressives—that is, some of the many people who alternate between mania and depressing—are dramatically benefited by a drug called "lithium carbonate." They seem to be people whose lives are under control when they are in the normal phase between the mood swings. These people, however, are far fewer in number than those who are given lithium in the vain hope that this chemical will cure them.

Neither I nor anyone else knows the numbers exactly, but my long experience tells me that there are probably 10,000 to 20,000 depressing people who do so because their lives are out of control for every one who is "depressed" because of a primary chemical imbalance. The figures are the same for psychotic or crazy people and for all other categories of mental abnormality except manic-depressive. But manic-depressives make up a tiny fraction of those who are mentally abnormal; and of that tiny fraction, only a fraction of those—less than half—are benefited by lithium. Nevertheless, huge quantities of antidepressant and antipsychotic drugs are prescribed in the vain hope that they will cure a nonexistent disease. Again, used in small doses as temporary relief until the patients can be counseled to regain control of their lives, these drugs have benefit; but used to cure, they promise a hope that they cannot fulfill and are a cruel delusion to the patient and the patient's family.

These drugs are not addicting. The antipsychotics drugs' actions are to paralyze the whole behavioral system so that it cannot be creative or, in these instances, crazy, but unfortunately the system also can barely behave at all. Under the influence of these strong drugs, patients are like zombies. Their ability to be spontaneous is gone, and if the dose is large, they can barely walk or talk. The most serious sign of the harmful effects of these drugs is that all joy in life is gone—they cannot even laugh. While these patients are no longer crazy, they are really not alive enough to gain the control they need to get back to any normal existence.

The antidepressant drugs are not much better if used for more than a short time. Their action is to activate our own internal, natural energizers, but to do so these strong drugs disrupt so much essential body chemistry that they are disabling to the user. For example, they interfere with vision, digestion, and normal sleep. And after a while patients who do not receive counseling, and whose best choice therefore is still to depress, will again depress so strongly that they will override even large doses of these drugs. At this point, the drugs are either so ineffective or so disabling that patients can no longer tolerate them.

No drug can fulfill our needs.* To do this, we must regain control over our lives. If we need good counseling, we should get it, but even without counseling there is much that most of us can do to regain control if we understand control theory and use it in our lives. We cannot depend on others to provide us with control, and we absolutely cannot depend on long-term use of drugs to do anything except get in the way of our regaining the need-fulfilling control that is the only answer to our problems.

---

*For a clear, well-documented, scientific explanation of the way antipsychotic and antidepressant drugs almost always damage the brain, I recommend that those involved with anyone using these drugs read *Psychiatric Drugs: Hazards to the Brain,* by Peter Roger Breggin, M.D. (New York: Springer, 1983).

15
Conflict

Can you imagine going to work on Monday and finding out that your new boss has ordered that anyone who wants to keep his job must work Saturday? That's the day your son's team plays for the championship, and he's pitching. You've waited through a long season for this big day, and your son, assuming you'll be there, talks of nothing else. As you listen to his excited chatter, you can't get up the nerve to tell him you may miss the game, and inside you feel as if you are being torn apart. What you are experiencing is the almost total loss of control that comes from the destructive effect of conflict on your control system. You have a powerful urge to do something—but what? There is no behavior that can put you in two places at the same time, so you depress all week long in an effort to soften the blow if you decide to miss the game.

It is as if your house were designed to maintain a steady 70 degrees, but with two thermostats instead of one. The first thermostat is hooked to a powerful cooling system set at 60, the second to an equally powerful furnace set at 80. Both would go full blast all day long, and the house would indeed hover at 70 as long as they did, but eventually one or both would break down from overwork. No sane engineer would design such a system; it would not make sense. But when you are in conflict, you are suffering from the living equivalent of such a faulty design. The way we are built, there is nothing to prevent us from wanting to satisfy two totally conflicting pictures at the same time, fully aware that it is not possible.

In another example, Jeff is offered a huge promotion on the basis of his moving across the country to open a Boston branch office, but his wife, Kelly, who is an only child, tells him she will not leave her aged parents on the West Coast. When he tells this to his boss, he is given three months to make up his mind. If he turns down this opportunity, he doesn't think he will ever again be considered for anything this good, and he is eager to make the move.

To express this conflict in control-theory terms, Jeff has a picture in his head of moving to Boston and being his own boss, but he also has a picture of a loved wife who will not consider such a move at this time. She told him when they married that she would not leave San Francisco as long as her parents were alive. She is perfectly satisfied with what he earns now and has faith that if he stays put, things will still somehow work out.

Jeff is caught between satisfying his needs for power and freedom and his need for love. He can't talk to Kelly about how torn apart he feels, because, not sharing his conflict, she is not sympathetic. He continues to talk to his boss about the problem, but his boss counters with how many times he and his wife have moved so that he could get to where he is. If Jeff isn't going to go, his boss urges him to make the decision quickly so they can look for someone else.

To consider another conflict, let's look at Helen. Unlike Jeff, her conflicts are not between conflicting needs but between two aspects of the same need. She is torn between her love for Bill, the man she has lived with for months, and her love for her two children. Bill no longer wants to share her with her children and he has given her an ultimatum: Send them back to their father (who wants them) or he will move out. If she wants both (and having close friends who have both, she does not feel that what she wants is unreasonable), what can she do?

Most serious conflicts evolve from our attempts to control others who will not accept our control, because what we want does not satisfy them. If Kelly would go to Boston, Jeff would do all he could to make it possible for her to spend time with her parents—even move them to Boston. He is willing to be more than reasonable and will extend himself to see that her life is disrupted as little as possible, but she will not discuss the move. She does point out that she is the beneficiary of a substantial insurance policy, and when her father, who is in his eighties, dies, they will be financially independent. She refuses to see that he does not want her father's money but the power and self-esteem he will get from the new job.

For the short time he has lived with her, Helen has insulated Bill from her children in every way that she can, but he is still adamant. He wants her, but no children that are not theirs. He admits they are good children and is willing to have them for a few weeks a year, but not on a permanent basis. He claims he is not selfish, just knows himself and his limitations. Helen begs him to try it for a while longer, but he refuses. He tries to be reasonable, telling her it would not be fair to anyone for him to pretend to accept her children when he feels he can't.

Like the two conflicting thermostats on the wall, Jeff and Helen continue to experience a substantial difference between what each wants and is able to get. They are in what is best defined as a true conflict because neither of them can come up with a single behavior that can satisfy both of their pictures. Therefore, like the furnace or air-conditioner, their behavioral systems are going full blast all the time. Still, no matter what they do, there is always a difference between what they have and one or the other picture that they want.

But remember, as long as we drive our behavioral systems, they never stop producing behaviors; and when we are in conflict, no matter what we do, there is always a difference between what we want and what we have. As it attempts to reduce this difference, the behavioral system continues trying to come up with a satisfactory behavior; it has no ability to recognize that the task is impossible. This is why, when we are in conflict, no matter how much we realize there is nothing we can do, we feel a continuous urge to behave. As it desperately searches for a satisfactory behavior, the behavioral system becomes more and more creative. Jeff has begun to reorganize physically through the common behavior (but new to him) of "chest paining." He has consulted physicians, but none can find anything wrong with his heart. Helen has begun to reorganize with compulsive housecleaning and has also chosen to become obsessive in the discipline of her children in a vain attempt to prove to Bill that they will be no problem. After working all day, she cleans half the night. She is drinking twenty cups of coffee a day to keep going, and taking Valium in the early-morning hours in an effort to get some sleep. Caught between conflicting desires, both Helen and Jeff have lost control of their lives.

Conflict is among the most common causes of long-term severe suffering, because nowhere do we lose more control than when we are in a true conflict. Jeff may push himself from chest paining to true heart disease, and Helen may turn to drugs far stronger than caffeine and Valium, but if neither Kelly nor Bill budge, the conflict will remain. True conflicts like these are not common. Much more frequently we tend to get ourselves into situations that seem to us to be true conflicts, but are not.

In these more common situations, best called "false conflicts," there is always a single behavior that will resolve the "conflict," but this is also a behavior that the person who complains of "conflict" is rarely willing to use. For example, Gert wants to be a size 10, but she also doesn't like to leave the dinner table hungry. She is willing to skip breakfast and eat a tiny lunch, but at night, after a hard day's work, she wants a full meal and eats one. She is thirty pounds over what she would like to weigh and complains of her "conflict" every time she shops for clothes and every night when she sits down to dinner. She believes she is caught between conflicting desires, when in fact with some effort she could have both.

This is a false conflict because if Gert were willing to run four to five miles a day, she could be a size 10 and still eat a substantial dinner. Besides burning calories, running also seems to make people less hungry, so food becomes less important. The problem with this "perfect" solution is that running four miles a day is hard and takes a lot of time. Many people would rather blame being overweight on their "conflict" than do the hard work that would allow them to have almost all the food they want.

False conflicts abound. We all know people who agonize about how much they would like to go to college but "can't" because they have to work, or how much they would like to get out of the house and go to work but "can't" because of the children. There is also the common complaint of many that they are stuck in a loveless marriage because they have no way to support themselves if they leave. These are all difficult situations, but none is a true conflict. In every case, if the "conflicted" complainers were willing to figure out a tough course of action and put it into practice, they would have a good chance to get most, if not all, of what they want.

In every false conflict there is an obvious hard-work choice that the "conflicted" person does not want to face. It is not easy to work full-time and go to college, but millions do. And many more figure out how to take care of a house and family and work full-time. When confronted with the hard-work alternative, some argue that they don't have the physical stamina. But they will never know unless they try. We all have a lot more strength than we realize if we can get involved in doing what we want to do.

Staying in a loveless marriage for security or because the children need a mother or father, or some variation on this theme, is another common false conflict. If you are willing to do the hard work that making a change will require, there is almost always a way. Assuming you have done all you can to find love in the marriage, choosing to stand pat is almost always tantamount to choosing a life of self-imposed misery. Even staying with a man or woman who won't marry you and trying to convince yourself that he or she is committed is usually little more than unwillingness to make the effort to find someone who wants you enough to marry you. Unless your head is deep in the sand, you are well aware that today even marriage is not a strong commitment; living together is hardly any commitment at all.

We should also be aware that people often use the complaint of conflict to control us. For example, Jack complains (to Gwen and sometimes his wife) that he is caught between his loyalty to his wife and family and his mad, passionate desire for Gwen, the other woman. Jack, however, is not in conflict at all; he is using the screen of conflict to control Gwen, and maybe also his wife, so he can continue to "have his cake and eat it, too." If Gwen (or his wife) learns basic control theory, she will stop buying into his conflict, and then Jack may be faced with a real conflict. As long as the others accept the story of his "torment," he has them under good control.

Because most of us do not understand how different a true conflict is from a false conflict, we tend to deal with both of these situations badly. What we do is exactly the opposite of what is effective: We treat true conflicts as if hard work will resolve them (it won't) and false conflicts as if there is nothing we can do when there almost always is. For example, Jeff, who is in a true conflict, believes that if he works hard on a persuasion program, he can talk Kelly into going to Boston with him. But if she won't go, he is helpless; he cannot force her to change the picture in her head, which is to stay in San Francisco.

What makes a true conflict so disastrous is not only the fact that there is no solution but that *there is no respite from trying to find a solution.* Both Jeff and Helen continue to try for the impossible because their behavioral systems are being continuously driven by a strong signal. In Jeff's head, he wants Kelly and the move; in Helen's case, she wants Bill and her kids. There is always a large difference between one or the other picture they want and what they have. The only way they can save themselves from the misery and self-destruction they are already choosing is to learn that in the case of a true conflict the best behavior is to consciously, and with complete awareness of what one is doing, choose to be passive—do nothing to attempt to resolve the conflict.

While doing nothing active is simple to advise, it is terribly difficult to practice. Doing nothing, while certainly a legitimate behavior, is also the most passive, and therefore the most difficult to choose when the urge to behave is powerful. The only way that anyone in conflict might be able to do nothing would be if she or he understood the control-theory basis of conflict that I have just explained. With this understanding, doing nothing is a logical behavior —in fact, the only behavior that makes any sense when we are in true conflict. Jeff cannot be in San Francisco and Boston at the same time, and Helen cannot have both Bill and the children, so why try? We may be up against a stone wall, but we don't have to bloody our heads against it unless we choose to.

To better understand why doing nothing is the best choice, picture yourself in the middle of a large room with a door on the wall to your left and another on the wall to your right. Behind one door is a large pot of gold; behind the other is the lover of your dreams. Both will wait for you quite a while. (In most conflicts there is more time than you think; the urgency is more in your head than in the situation itself.) If you try to force yourself to decide, as you move toward one door or the other, you will find yourself pulled back to the center of the room by the invisible string that is your desire not to lose what is behind the other door. You strain first one way and then the other, expending a lot of energy but getting nowhere. Wouldn't it be more sensible, since there is no immediate need to choose, to sit down and wait as comfortably as you can in the middle? If, while you are patiently waiting, the situation changes, as any situation may in time, you might be more able to make a choice. If you wait and a choice does seem to present itself, you will be much less exhausted and more able to deal with what you chose.

If in the end either Kelly or Bill relents, Jeff and Helen, who have waited patiently, will be better able to work things out than if they were exhausted from being miserable, sick, tired, alcoholic, or crazy. When waiting is possible, the longer you wait before you make a decision, the more likely it is that time and events over which you have little control may help you make up your mind. The world never stands still. Things tend to happen that no one can predict and the conflict unbalances. If, while Jeff waits, he continues to work hard and is gracious to all concerned, Kelly's aged parents may tell Kelly that she should go with Jeff, or the company may decide to offer him something else close to home. The boss may be replaced or get sick and suggest that Jeff take his job. Another company in San Francisco may find out that he is a topnotch worker and make him a better offer. Any or all of these events over which Jeff has little control will resolve the conflict. What he has control over is to wait and do a good job while waiting.

Helen's calm but resolute love for both her children and Bill may cause him to relent. Or her former husband may change his mind and refuse to take the kids. It is unlikely that her situation can remain the way it is for very long. As long as Bill only threatens but gives no final ultimatum, she has to assume that, even with her kids, he may need her more than he has expressed so far. If she continues to love him but makes no move to get rid of her children, there is a good chance that things will work out for her. She has control over her life, so she can wait. We should never underestimate the value of doing nothing *as effectively as we can* when we are in true conflict.

The problem with waiting is that there is usually a lot of outside pressure on us to *do* something. If we discuss our dilemmas with others—and most of us do—they usually urge us to make a move. We must keep in mind that it is *only to us* that our conflicting pictures are equal, so the pressure friends put on us to act is always from their much less conflicted standpoint, never ours. We tend, of course, to resist this pressure, but this uses valuable energy. We would be better off without their advice, but to avoid this advice, we have to stop asking them what to do. If all we want is sympathy and reassurance, then talking about our predicament is helpful. But it is foolish to look to others for solutions—they have none.

Because waiting is so hard, and the urge to move so strong, a good way to make the waiting easier is to try to spend as much energy as you can satisfying yourself in an unconflicted area. Since none of us can do more than one thing at a time, Helen might satisfy her urge to "do something" by working hard on her job, spending more fun time with her kids, exercising and getting into good shape, and doing some of the gourmet cooking that she has always wanted to do. Do anything that moves you in any satisfying direction that is not involved with the conflict and you will be in more control of your life. And the more you are in control, the less torn-apart you will feel even if the conflict takes a very long time to resolve.

If you find that the urge to do something active is so strong that doing nothing is impossible, then you can put time to work for you instead of against you, as it seems to be working now. Tell yourself that you will try either one side or the other for a specific length of time and then see how things work out. This gives you an element of control that you just don't have while you are waiting and doing nothing. For example, Jeff might decide that he will go to Boston by himself for six months and see what happens. He may or may not tell Kelly about the six-month time element, depending on his judgment of what she may or may not do if she knows. In his mind, however, it is a six-month trial, and during that time a lot could happen to resolve the conflict.

Helen could tell Bill that she has made up her mind that she is not going to give up her kids. She will continue to treat him with a lot of warmth and no complaints, but she can't accept his conditions. Instead of waiting for him to give her an ultimatum, she gives him one. She has decided to give him six months to make up his mind, but whether or not she tells him about the time limit is up to her. She takes a chance that he will leave, but in this way she gains a little more control over the situation.

If you decide to make an arbitrary move for a period of time, you still have to pick which way to go. You might take a piece of paper, divide it in half, and head each column with a choice. In Jeff's case, one column would be headed "Boston" and the other "San Francisco." Write down a Boston reason and then a San Francisco reason and go back and forth listing reasons until you can't think of any more. Whichever side has the most reasons, go that way for the time you have chosen. Few conflicts are exactly equal, and this way you may find which picture is the best to try. If, however, making this decision becomes another conflict, this solution is not for you. It would be better to do nothing and wait.

Difficult as it is to do nothing when we are truly conflicted, the opposite occurs when we are in a false conflict—here we find it easy to do very little except complain. It is easier to moan about how we lack willpower while lapping up a hot fudge sundae than to run the four miles a day that could make them possible. Seeking sympathy because your kids need you so much that you "can't" go back to college may mean you would rather talk about what you want than work to get it. In time, most true conflicts resolve or move toward resolution, but false conflicts seem to get worse. It will be a lot easier to start running when you are ten pounds overweight than thirty. And if you want more love, you have a better chance of finding it when you are thirty years old than when you are forty-five.

If you believe you are conflicted, it is important to learn how to determine whether the conflict you are struggling with is true or false. To do this, take a look at the conflicting pictures you want and try your best to figure out if there is a single behavior (consider the hard ones, too) that will satisfy both. If you take a long, honest look and find that there are none, then you are in true conflict, and rather than choose to tear yourself up, attempt the passive waiting strategies suggested in this chapter. If, however, you are in a false conflict, face the fact that what you want is obtainable only through hard work and start working. Both hoping and complaining are among our least effective behaviors.

Of all creatures, we are the only ones who suffer significant conflict, and therefore the only ones who have developed systems of morality as part of our attempt to resolve this conflict. Simple creatures like clams or snails have no conflict; all they want is to stay alive and reproduce. Even complicated animals like apes suffer little conflict, because they do not have our driving need for power and our long-term need for committed love. Only when behavioral scientists put apes into artificially conflicted situations that they would never encounter in real life do they turn in desperation to painful and (for them) creative behaviors like life-endangering depressing. In their natural state, animals cannot get into conflicting situations in which we, like Jeff and Helen, frequently find ourselves. By their standards, everything they do is responsible. Only humans come to King Solomon with a dispute over who is a baby's mother.

However, because we suffer conflict, and are always looking for the way out, we are almost always very concerned with morality and responsibility or how to fulfill our needs without depriving others of a chance to fulfill theirs. The problem we continually face in practice is that it is very difficult to be responsible or to make the moral choice when we are in a true conflict. Jeff considers himself moral and responsible, but who is to say whether staying in San Francisco or going to Boston is more responsible? Is Helen irresponsible if she sends her children to her former husband and settles down alone with Bill?

While it is easy for others, who are not in the conflict, to preach morality and responsibility when you turn to them for advice, what may be obvious to them is far from obvious to you. Has Kelly more responsibility to her father and mother than to her husband? Is Jeff being responsible to himself if he gives up the promotion he wants so much? If we want to take effective control of our lives, we must face the fact that there will never be a standard morality that we can depend on to guide us when we are in true conflict. In fact, the test of a true conflict is that we can make a good moral argument for either side. Therefore, *when we are in true conflict,* as much as we feel driven to turn to others, even moral authorities like judges or ministers can no better direct us than a flip of a coin.

Some might argue that when a conflict is between power and love, it is more moral to opt for love. But where would this argument be when the conflict is within the love need itself—as illustrated by Helen, who is torn between the love for her children and love for her fiancé? Should she give her children to her former husband, who wants them, and marry Bill (remember, these are his terms for marriage), or keep them and give Bill up? In this situation the advice that Helen would almost always get would be to chuck Bill; her prime responsibility is to her children. This appears to be morally sound advice, but if Helen takes it and then misses Bill, she may anger and take this anger out on her kids, or turn to drinking and neglect them; in either case they might be better off with their father.

Still, there is good rationale for the standard moral position, and that rationale is loyalty: All other things being about equal, the old should take precedence over the new.

Even Jeff is likely to be advised by many that the older loyalties of Kelly to her parents and his to Kelly should take precedence over the more recent promotion. Counter to the argument is the fact that Jeff may have been ambitious long before he met Kelly, and loyalty to his ambition should not be disregarded. But sticking to the old as long as you can is not only moral, it is also effective in that it almost always buys you more time. As I have explained, in time most conflicts tend to become resolvable, so here the loyal choice is not only a little easier, in that it usually is supported by those around you, but also turns out to be practical.

Jud gave Paul his first job more than twenty years ago, and now Paul has risen over Jud to the presidency of the company. Jud, who has a serious drinking problem, is still in middle management. Over the past five years while Paul was a vice-president, he protected Jud out of the old loyalty to the man who gave him his start. Jud is now totally incompetent, and without Paul's protection he would be fired. His drinking has come to the attention of the chairman of the board, and Paul, the new president, is in a quandary about how much longer he can protect a man who is a long-term liability to the company. There is no doubt that an old loyalty is being tested, and Jud throws himself on Paul's mercy when Paul calls him in to talk about what Jud must do—stop drinking—but never does.

You might argue that we do not owe loyalty to an incompetent drunk, but are the ethics of loyalty such that we need only be loyal to the innocent or presently competent? That would be a hard standard for judging our friends.

As long as there is no conflict, there is rarely a serious moral problem; loyalty will work well as a basis for most moral decisions. But when conflict enters the picture, whether it is within a need or between needs, there is no standard moral position that will work for the conflicted person. When you are being torn by a true conflict, you must recognize that, at that time, your morality will not work. It is this recognition that will help you to retain some control over your life and not feel as if you have lost control because you are immoral. To attempt to regain control by trying to force yourself in one direction or another through guilting and depressing will not help. Keep in mind that if there were a succinct moral solution, you would not be in the conflict in the first place. People who consider themselves moral and loyal might have advised Paul to say to Jud, "I have done all I can for you for five years, now it is up to you to sink or swim." These people, unlike Paul, have limits to their loyalty. He either has or has not reached his yet with Paul.

When you practice loyalty and it works, you are fortunate, but you should be wary of preaching it because it worked for you. It worked mostly because it gave you time, or possibly because you were not in a true conflict—you only thought you were. It is especially unpleasant to be lectured to by someone who claims that he has suffered a true conflict exactly like yours and solved it through moral willpower when in fact he was not conflicted at all and resolved nothing that was not easy to resolve.

We must face the fact that as long as we have conflicting needs, or as long as our individual needs can be satisfied in conflicting ways, we will always have true conflict. Morality may help us in time, but at any conflicted moment it may give us little relief. We must accept that no one can walk in our shoes except ourselves, and only we can decide what is best to do. What control theory teaches that can help in this most difficult of all situations is to wait, to delay the decision as long as we can. Every day of delay gives the situation time to evolve, and in its natural evolution the right or moral choice of what to do may become clear. But it will become clear only as the situation changes; if it does not change, there is no solution, easy or hard. When Saturday comes and your employer won't relent and give you time off to go to the game, whatever you choose will be a painful choice. There is no way to avoid the pain. It is the human condition —the price we pay for the complex genetic instructions that have carried us to the top rung of the evolutionary ladder.

We must be aware that there is no rule that says that the pictures in our albums must never conflict. They do more often than not. But there is also no rule that says we have to try to satisfy conflicting pictures at the same time. We must keep in mind that they are our albums, these are our pictures—we put them in and we can choose which of them we want at any time. Helen does not have to love Bill; she is choosing to love him, knowing that he rejects her children. Jeff does not have to take the Boston job; he is choosing to satisfy his need for power in this way at this time. We have some control over which pictures we want from our albums, and if we learn anything from control theory, it should be to give careful thought to wanting something that is in direct conflict with something else we want.

Conflict is an inevitable part of life and is always difficult to resolve. What may help us is to keep in mind that *we will not help ourselves or anyone else involved in a conflict if we choose to immobilize ourselves with pain or disability.* The rationale for all courses of action suggested in this chapter is that, difficult as they may be, they are more effective than misery.

16
Criticism

Take a close look at any good relationship—husband-wife, parent-child, teacher-pupil, employer-employee—and you will see that what makes the relationship work is caring, respect, and mutual goals. As important as these are, what is even more important to its success is what you won't see: criticism. Any lasting relationship, whether equal like husband-wife or unequal like teacher-pupil, has continued more because they don't criticize each other than because they share a lot in common.

By now you are well aware that to gain control over our lives, we need to get along well with those close to us. When we do, our lives are filled with pleasure. Most of us, however, experience the most difficulty getting along with those closest to us, members of our families. This is because we criticize them the most and they do the same to us. Most families live knee-deep in criticism, with little awareness of how totally destructive this is to their getting along. The more intimate the relationship—and marriage starts out as the most intimate of all relationships—the more destructive criticism is to its success.

Verbal criticism can take the form of sarcasm, ridicule, and hyperbole. Over the centuries we have developed countless ploys to put each other down. Because we are so relieved that it is not happening to us, criticism is the source of much humor. "The Bickersons," about a couple that bickered and criticized without mercy, was a hit on radio for years in the 1930s. Don Rickles, a current popular comic, has made a good living criticizing defenseless celebrities whom, because of their accomplishments, he considers fair game for his barbs, and our laughter shows that we agree.

But criticism is much more than what we say; it is looking at each other with disgust, disdain, or even hatred. It can also be as much what we don't do, and make a point not to do, as it is what we do or say. When we turn away or won't talk or listen, we tell others they are worthless to us; for example, when someone is talking, to make a point of not listening, to act in his presence as if he is not there. Verbal or nonverbal criticism is rude and painful.

Not only do we criticize each other far too much, but many of us extoll the virtue of this behavior, calling what we do "constructive." What is constructive criticism to me, however, is almost always regarded by you as a put-down. If you grant that I am smarter, you lose power and tend to resent me and my help rather than listen seriously to what I offer. Only in situations where you believe that your needs will be met by bowing to my superior wisdom, and if you respect and care for me as a person, will you listen to me when I criticize you. Young children, students, and newly hired workers may take constructive criticism in the spirit it is offered, but even they, as they assert their need for power by asking for more equality, will grow resentful of too much unsolicited help. This is why modern managers use seminars and workshops to teach new techniques: People will accept instruction from an occasional outside expert much more readily than from someone they know. "A prophet is without honor in his own country" because there he is seen more as a competitor than a teacher.

Therefore, because of our pressing need for power, even thoughtful and gentle criticism between equals or people striving for equality will not work. As we attempt, constructively or not, to "improve" the people we need, both we and they lose, rather than gain, more and more control over our lives. Still, destructive as this is, we are well aware of what we are doing when we criticize. Until you make control theory an integral part of your life, you may, for example, find it hard to accept that you choose to depress or to headache, but there is not one of you who could convince anyone, including yourself, that you do not choose to criticize those with whom you live and work. Almost all of us pay a bitter price in lost relationships because we constantly let those around us know that what is good for them is to perform the way we picture them in our albums.

You may recall that Susan, who told my wife about her husband, Dave, leaving her, was highly critical of him for what he "did" to her. It is unlikely that this was the first time she had criticized him. My guess, based on the many marriages I have seen fail, is that not only Dave but Susan, too, was highly dissatisfied with their marriage long before he left. I would guess that both of them engaged in a great deal of personal and perhaps bitter criticism of each other long before the break. Whatever else the woman for whom Dave left Susan did, it is likely that early in their relationship she was as accepting of him as Susan was critical. It is doubtful that she is still noncritical now that they are married. Indeed, if Dave should make overtures to Susan to return, my guess would be that this new marriage has reached a level of criticism that may now exceed what he had with Susan.

I do not want to imply that Susan was wrong to criticize Dave. She did what all of us do who do not know control theory. She was trying what she knew best to correct what she believed was wrong with "her" marriage. Dave was not perfect—none of us are—but he probably would have been a much better husband if she had used a more effective behavior than criticizing him for his flaws. Before I go into what she might have done that would have been more effective, let me try to explain why criticism is so destructive to relationships.

Control theory teaches that any relationship—for example, Dave and Susan's marriage—is really two relationships. Dave's marriage is a picture in his head, and Susan's a picture in hers. The success of their marriage depends on keeping the marriage they have in the real world close to these pictures in their heads. When either Dave or Susan became aware that there was a substantial difference between the marriage he or she wanted and the marriage he or she had, they had no choice but to attempt to reduce this difference. To do this, each chose the only behavior most married people know—criticizing the other for not living up to "my" marriage, the picture in my head. Driven by our need for power, we choose to criticize in an attempt to force the other party to accept our view of the relationship.

If Dave had taken Susan's criticism "in the spirit in which it was offered," and changed his ways "as he should have," there would have been no problem. He didn't, because what she wanted was not what he wanted; no husband and wife have the same marriage in their albums. When her criticism failed to change him, she angered, depressed, and withdrew, and both their marriages got worse. As these painful feeling behaviors failed to control Dave, whom she felt was slipping away, her increased criticism probably was the final blow to an already shaky marriage. What makes criticism so destructive is that *there is nothing else we do that will so suddenly and painfully make the criticized parties so acutely aware that there are huge differences between them.* Faced with this difference, few marriages survive. All do not end in divorce—many couples continue to live together—but the marriage is effectively over.

The best way to explain why criticism leads to this sudden huge difference that almost always leads to destructive feeling behaviors is to carry this example further and, for the sake of illustration, make it somewhat extreme. Suppose, while they still had a semblance of a marriage, Dave had talked a reluctant Susan into a winter skiing weekend. He loves to ski; she likes it only when conditions are perfect, which they rarely are. He promised that he had checked things out carefully—the season was right for good weather and the accommodations were supposed to be first-class. When they arrived, it was great for a day and then a blizzard snowed them in for a week. The accommodations were okay for skiing, but inadequate for being snowed in. They got a little cabin fever, one thing led to another, and she may have said, "This always happens—your stupid plans always go wrong. How could I be such an idiot as to let you plan anything? The only thing you'll ever plan well is my funeral!"

Just writing this hypothetical outburst is painful to me, but in my profession this is mild compared to what I have frequently heard. I am sure that as you think through your own experiences with criticism, you can match or exceed the discomfort of this example on both the giving and receiving end.

Dave, too, was hardly enjoying the week's imprisonment, and now, as Susan impugned his competence in every area, they had difficulty avoiding blows. They didn't speak to each other for a week —and later, when Dave told the "other woman" what Susan "did" to him, she assured him she would have been delighted to be snowed in. They would have made love for a week and had a marvelous time.

It does not take too many incidents like this to push a failing marriage over the brink.

When people are important to us, we continually compare them with the pictures we have of them in our albums. Ordinarily, if we get along well, the pictures we want are not far from what we have. If at times they frustrate us, we can avoid a lot of misery if we don't criticize. For example, if Susan asks Dave to stop at the store on his way home and he forgets, as he often does, she might ask him if he would make a special trip now as she needs the tomato sauce for tonight's pasta. He's tired, doesn't want to go to the store, and hates being reminded that he is forgetful, but because there was no criticism in her reasonable request, he grumbles and asks her if she really needs it. She says she does, and he goes. If either had said something critical, they might have had a blowup.

Criticism, therefore, is much more than just finding the world to be different from the way we want it. It is the world turning against us and telling us that what we want is senseless, stupid, and/or without value. For example, if I ask you to do me a favor, I may choose to be unhappy if you refuse, but if you tell me I am a fool for asking, or that what I want is stupid, it is likely I will lose all control. What I will almost always do in a desperate effort to regain control is anger, because angering is the behavior we all tend to choose when we feel the world is suddenly and (usually) unexpectedly out of control. Nothing that we encounter leads to a greater and quicker loss of control than to be criticized. And, equally, it is harder to regain control when we are criticized than in any other situation. *In my opinion, it is by far the single most destructive behavior we use as we attempt to control our lives.*

Tired as he was, Dave had no problem with Susan's asking him to go back to the store, because there was nothing in this reasonable request to put him down. It is much different from what happened in the ski lodge, when he was blamed for everything, including the blizzard. People who have studied control theory extensively believe that almost all the synapses in the brain—literally billions of them —are involved in the process of comparing the pictures. When we are criticized, the sudden huge difference in the pictures occurring in all these places makes it feel as if the whole brain is exploding in pure pain. Simultaneously, a huge signal is generated, which we feel as an immediate and overwhelming urge to behave. This urge is so strong that even our usual angering often seems insufficient, and we quickly turn to our creative systems for new behaviors, which are often more violent or painful than we have ever chosen before. If the person being criticized is under the influence of alcohol (see chapter 12), the potential for violence is greatly increased.

Some sort of personal put-down, similar to the blizzard example, is, I believe, involved in most violent behavior directed at others, or at ourselves, that occurs within families and among friends. It is well known that regardless of how unsafe our streets may be, more than 80 percent of all homicides are committed by people who know each other well. When severe criticism occurs, the painful explosion in the brain and the huge concurrent signal to behave drives too many of us to irrational angering in an attempt to regain control at any cost. Caesar fought heroically until Brutus, his beloved friend, struck. Then, impaled by criticism as much as by the blade, Caesar gave up. If we can become aware of the extent to which criticism is always associated with severe loss of control, we will make an effort to learn to deal more effectively with frustration in our relationships. Criticism is a luxury I believe none of us can afford.

Everyone is familiar with at least one couple who got along together before they married, maybe even lived together amicably for several years, but whose relationship mysteriously deteriorated after the marriage. The solution to the mystery is that many husbands or wives regard the marriage license as a license to criticize. This same license seems to be an unfortunate part of most long-term close relationships, as if the length of the relationship had made it strong enough to survive critical correction. This is exactly the opposite of what we should do. If criticism is ever effective, it is in the beginning of a relationship when the person being criticized may not feel equal to the criticizer and may accept some constructive correction. As any relationship matures, the parties involved tend to move toward a feeling of equality, and criticism is resented more and more. I believe it is from the long-term custom of criticizing those close to us that the saying "familiarity breeds contempt" has come into our culture. Unfortunately, as we grow more and more familiar, we believe that it is not only a right but a duty to tell people close to us, constructively of course, how badly they are doing and how much better off they would be if they did it "our" way.

Perhaps the most insidious form of criticism is self-criticism. If you criticize me, I can usually get away from you. But where can I go if I criticize myself? In my album I always picture myself, whatever I may do, as competent. It does not matter to me that you may think my behavior is incompetent. Like a decision to roll in the cacti, it is my best present effort to fulfill my needs. As I look at how I deal with the world to satisfy these pictures, I realize that I am often unable to get what I want for myself. My guess is that Susan, now that Dave has left and married someone else, spends part of her time reviling herself for not doing more to preserve the marriage. What she is doing is punishing herself for what she may have done wrong, and the more she does this, the less competent she will be to find the new relationships she needs. She may have done many things wrong in her marriage (Dave did as many or more than she did), but what effective purpose does her self-criticism serve? If it taught her to be more competent in her next relationship, it would serve a purpose, but angering and depressing do little more than sap her strength.

The more we flagellate ourselves with brutal self-criticism, the more we increase the difference between what we see and what we want for ourselves. To deal with this increase, we usually choose to depress, use alcohol, or contemplate suicide as we move toward choosing creative behaviors. If we want to keep control over our lives, we must not only learn to avoid criticizing others, we must equally avoid criticizing ourselves. I live by a helpful little motto, "I won't criticize myself—there are more than enough people willing to do this for me."

If, however, I see my wife or child doing something wrong, am I supposed to stand by and say nothing? How are they, especially children, to learn if no one makes the effort to point out what they are doing wrong and show them how to correct it? Of course, I have to say something, but what I say to children up to age twelve or thirteen will be different from how I will deal with older children and adults. Young children still look to parents for instruction. They know that they need guidance, and they are not yet engaged in the power struggle that they will join shortly. All I need to do is tell or show them a better way and pay little attention to what they had been doing that was wrong. I can also use this constructive approach with adults if they view me as a teacher or are not in competition with me.

If I attempt to use this same "constructive" approach with some- one who is in any sort of a power struggle with me (as are most of the teen-agers and adults who are close to me) that person will construe even mild correction as criticism. For example, as good as my intentions are, when I tell my grown son that he would be better off flying to San Francisco than driving, what he hears is a personal put-down. He hears me "accusing" him of inadequacy or bad judgment and becomes frustrated so quickly that he tends not to listen to the constructive reasons for my opinion. As adults, we are so competitive, so busy maintaining our power, that we rarely listen to what is often sound advice. The basic flaw of criticism, therefore, is not that it isn't well intended, but that its intentions are almost never realized. Instead of helping people to function together more effectively, it almost always drives a wedge between them.

What I would like to suggest is a way to correct people—especially those close to us—that will not drive them away. In fact, if we do it properly, we may even bring them closer to us. For example, when Susan was snowed in, to maintain some control she looked around for someone to blame. There were only two people possible: herself and Dave. She chose to blame Dave and did it in a devastatingly critical way, driving nail after nail into the coffin of their marriage. Control theory would suggest that she say to Dave, "This is going to be a rough week if we are going to be snowed in. I know you don't like it and neither do I, so how can we make the most of this time?"

This way she does not blame him and she does not cause him to lose control. But she is still dissatisfied, so she could also say, "Even though I know it is not your fault, I still find myself getting mad at you. Maybe we should talk about the fact that there are things I like to do and things you like to do, and they are not always the same things. You like to go to the snow a lot more than I do, so when you want to go skiing, let's talk it over and figure out what I could do when you are gone. You really have more fun by yourself."

She could use the time while they are stuck in the cabin to work out a plan for the future instead of working on the destruction of their marriage.

The general rule that I am suggesting she follow is that when you want to correct someone, do it by saying, "Let's take a look and see what is and is not working for me, for you, and for both of us. This means take a good look at my album, your album, and the situation." You may not be able to agree on exactly what the situation really is, but you do know whether it is working for you, and the other party knows the same. Then go ahead and try to work out a plan that will work better for both of you than what you have now.

For example, your employee is not doing the job and you want better performance. Following the above, you do not criticize, but you call him in and say, "I want to take a look at what we are both doing in this situation to see where it is working and where it isn't." Of course he will tense up, but you stick to the situation and go through what both of you did on a recent day (yesterday is best), step by step. Point out what you think you did and ask him to point out what he thinks he did. If you don't agree, then talk about where you see things differently, but don't get involved with whether or not what you don't agree on is good or bad. The most important thing is to move on until you agree on something you both could do that might be better. Then work out a plan to try it, set a schedule to check, and, if necessary, revise the plan. Listen to him—you may learn a new procedure that is valuable. He is unlikely to say that everything he does is good; more likely, he will point to the areas that need improving. If he sees nothing that needs improving, then take only one area and explain that this is an area in which you believe he could show improvement, and point out what you both might do that would work in this area.

This last suggestion is close to constructive criticism, but you did not do this until you gave him a chance to find a weakness himself, and an employee who sees no weakness when you see a lot is strong enough for you to get the process started in this way. As soon as he sees that you are more interested in finding a better way than in criticizing, he will begin to find other flaws, because he will get the idea that you are trying to build him up, not tear him down. The real key is to make a joint evaluation of the situation and try cooperatively to correct it so that it works better for both parties. If you do this both with your family and in your work, you will find that your life becomes much better. This way, not only does no one lose control, but both have a chance to get even more. Following this method, there is little need to criticize.

Reward and punishment, the external motivators our culture reveres, are so closely related to criticism that it seems sensible to discuss them here. Like criticism, both are products of stimulus-response psychology and would have little utility in a world that followed control theory. A control-theory world would be well aware that our only motivator is the pictures we pursue from our albums, and that what happens outside of us does not cause us to do what we do. Reward and punishment are based on the false idea that people can be forced or persuaded from the outside to do what they do not want to do. Remember, even the piglet stopped climbing the slide and chose to go without food rather than do what did not satisfy some important internal purpose. Most of the institutions in our society attempt to motivate with reward and punishment, and this is an important reason why many are breaking down, especially our schools, heavy industries, and our families.

Praise, on the other hand, is a good motivator because it is spontaneous, varies with the performance, and always satisfies our need to belong. If it is not spontaneous and does not vary with the performance, then it is in the category of reward and has much less value. What is wrong with both reward and punishment is that they interfere with the basic operating premise of the individual's control system: *They threaten its control.* If I punish you to get you to do what I want, then I am your controller, and you will resist because you lose some control. But even if I reward you, as much as you may like the reward, you know that it was because you did what I wanted, and you may still resent my control. Certainly we would rather be rewarded than punished, but if my reward is seen as less for you and more for me, you will choose to resent it. Even with my reward in hand, you have surrendered a degree of control to me and you don't like it. This is well illustrated in some labor-management negotiations, especially in the coal-mining industry. Strikes are almost always long, even though the basic wage issues are not far apart. Coal miners do a hard, dangerous job and they strike as much for power and recognition as for money.

We are all motivated by the basic needs and feel good when we fulfill them. For you to rejoice with me is wonderful—the best praise I can imagine. But for you to get me to do anything you want, you have to show me how it satisfies me. Most of us work hard for money because we want the control that money buys, but the picture of money is already in our heads when we go to work. If you can persuade me that there are other rewards for working hard, I may work for these as much as for money, but first I must put these rewards into my album—you cannot put them in for me. A boss who gives spontaneous praise for good work may get more work from his employees than one who pays well but never praises.

Stimulus-response psychology works on the premise that the rewarder or the punisher knows what the responder wants, how much of it he wants, and how often he wants it. None of us knows enough about the pictures in another person's head to guess many of these correctly on any consistent basis. This is why most "stimulators" eventually resort to punishment: They know that none of us (masochists excluded) has a picture of being hurt as a need-satisfying picture. Pain, therefore, is a strong motivator for getting us to do simple manual tasks for a while. If the task is complex, however, the person threatened with punishment will figure out a way to mess up the work and avoid blame. Slaves dig ditches, they don't program computers. In time, however, no matter how great the pain, most of us will refuse consciously (you can kill me) or unconsciously (through getting sick or crazy) to do what does not satisfy us. Therefore, for complex tasks and creative work, no one in his or her right mind would advocate a chain gang as a good way to do the job.

Our stimulus-response management approach to production has been significantly outperformed by the Japanese, who use control theory management based on a great deal of communication with workers and continually upgrading the work to keep it as need-satisfying as possible. They depend neither on rigid rewards nor on threats of layoffs to motivate people to do the complex jobs demanded by modern technology. Ultimately any system that depends exclusively on external motivation will break down. Nowhere do we see this breakdown more clearly than in our public educational system. Schools are rife with criticism, failure, and the rigid rewards and punishments of grades.

So far all the remedies suggested for the schools are based almost exclusively on S-R psychology—longer school days, harder subjects, tougher grading standards, and increased failure for nonperformers. We hear little of the need to persuade students that learning is need-fulfilling, so that they will put the idea of education, and the hard work necessary to learn, into their picture albums. Control-theory education is possible. It is successfully practiced in a few schools and in quite a few industries, but it will never become widespread until it becomes a part of our culture. It is paradoxical that as much as they practice control theory in business management, Japanese schools are much more dominated by S-R psychology than ours. The intense competition to succeed and the punitive disgrace of not succeeding are so powerful in their schools that the whole nation has become concerned with the rash of suicides among students who have failed to achieve the high standards of the pictures in their heads.

17

Taking Control of Your Life

Using Susan, who had marriage difficulties, as an example, I would like to explain how we can put control theory to work in our lives when, like Susan, we find ourselves losing control of any situation. If she had known control theory, as soon as she became dissatisfied with her marriage, she would have taken an honest look at the behaviors she was choosing for dealing with her frustrations. She would have seen that she was engaging in a lot of criticism of both Dave and herself. She would have become aware that, except for short bursts of angering, she was almost always depressing as she desperately tried to get more love and attention from Dave. As soon as she realized that she was choosing her misery, she would have asked herself the important control-theory question *"Is the criticizing and misery I am now choosing helping me to get what I want?"*

The answer to this basic question, *which must be asked by anyone who wants to regain control of her life,* is always *no.* Choosing long-term pain or criticism is not going to get us what we want now or ever. Control theory not only gives us the ability to recognize that we choose our behavior and that we may be making bad choices, but also clearly states that as much as we may want someone to change, all we can do is attempt to gain better control over our own lives. We have no power to make others do, think, or feel anything that they believe does not satisfy them.

So, as much as Susan wanted Dave to change, she would have

known that all she could do was change the way *she* was choosing to live her life. If what she then chose to do became more satisfying to Dave than what she had been doing, it is likely he would have become more loving. If what she did was satisfying to her but Dave remained withdrawn, she might have come to the conclusion that she did not need him and filed for divorce. But whatever she decided, she would have been aware that her efforts were directed at controlling herself, not Dave or anyone else.

As soon as she realized that misery was a bad choice, she would also have become aware that better choices are almost always available. This realization is always encouraging, but, before she tried to find a better behavior, she would first have taken a look at the marriage pictures in her head. Mostly she would find pictures in which Dave was acting much better than he had been recently— perhaps treating her with more kindness and spending more time with her doing things they both enjoyed. Because those were the pictures she wanted, she had been spending all her energy depressing and criticizing in an effort to get Dave to be more like these ideal pictures, but it had not paid off. As she looked at him, he was far from the husband in her head.

To begin to regain control, she would stop focusing on these pictures that she couldn't achieve and try to find a few satisfying pictures in which she was doing something with Dave the way he was now. At any point, even in an unhappy marriage, there are almost always a few satisfying activities that the husband and wife, *at that time,* still share. What Susan needed to do was to search her album for those still-satisfying marriage pictures, which likely still existed. For example, as difficult as things had gotten between them over the past several years, when she had made the effort to plan a simple social evening at home with a few close friends, it was usually a success. As tense as things had been, if she stopped criticizing and complaining for a few days before the party, they almost always enjoyed a fun-filled and relaxing time.

For the past six months, however, she had paid little attention to this picture. If it crossed her mind that maybe a party would be fun, she was always ready with excuses: She was too depressed; Dave never helped; the whole burden was on her; the people she invited always had a good time but never reciprocated. She'd had no difficulty finding many "valid" reasons for paying no attention to one of the most need-satisfying and achievable marriage pictures still remaining in her head. In the past, even when there had been tension between her and Dave for weeks, at the end of one of those relaxed social evenings Dave had been loving and attentive. She knew this, but, like most people with marriage difficulties who don't know control theory, she preferred to criticize and depress rather than plan such an evening.

The important lesson to be learned here is that when you are having difficulty getting along with someone important to you, you should spend your energy on pictures that you are fairly certain you can achieve. Susan should especially have looked for old ones that used to be fun: for example, the "send him a funny greeting card" picture—he used to enjoy those cards so much. These pictures seemed inconsequential now that she was choosing to be so miserable, but she should have looked for them as they were still there. She should even have made the effort to try to figure out a few new ones that might have been satisfying even in these bad times. I know it is hard for anyone depressing strongly to do this, but it is a sensible thinking behavior over which Susan had control, and she could have chosen to try to do it. The more she reminded herself that she was choosing to depress, the more apparent it would have become that this was a better choice.

We must keep in mind that each of us has his or her own picture album. If we search through all their nooks and crannies, we find them filled with pictures that we pasted into them years ago and have not looked at for a long time. But if they are there, they are still need-satisfying. If they were not, they could not be there.

Susan, however, did not have to settle for the few pictures she had of a better life with Dave; she could have created some more. Rather than continue to depress over pictures she couldn't achieve, she could have tried to tap her creativity to see if she could figure out some new situations that might be highly satisfying to both her and Dave. She can be compared to a driver vainly spinning her car wheels in the sand; she has to stop spinning her wheels, get out, and look for another way to get going.

You can't stop wanting any picture in your head, but you can select from your pictures those that you have a good chance of satisfying. Susan needed to avoid the common trap of saying, "If I can't have this specific picture, I don't want any." To get her marriage going again, a less satisfying picture would have been better than one she couldn't achieve. She should have told herself that she had the ability to put a lot of satisfying marriage pictures in her album. Some of them she might not achieve in the foreseeable future —maybe never. There would be some, however, that, no matter how bad her marriage had become, she still had the power to achieve. She should have said to herself, "As I do this, I will feel good, Dave will feel good, and our marriage will be better."

If Susan had known control theory, she would not have stubbornly held out for six months for pictures she could not satisfy. As soon as she was dissatisfied, she would, for example, have planned a good social evening and carried out the plan. If it didn't work, she would have been out a little time and energy; but if it did, she would have made a small beginning toward regaining control of her marriage. At the end of that evening, it is likely that she would have found Dave attentive and in a good frame of mind. She could have mentioned how much she enjoyed doing this again and asked him if he could think of something else they might do together soon that he would enjoy. If he mentioned something, she would not be vague and say, "That would be nice," or even "Why haven't we done that for a while?" which might sound critical. If what he suggested was in any way acceptable to her (which at that close moment was very likely), what she would say is "Fine, let's do it," and right then discuss when, where, and how she could help make it happen.

Besides the unplanned love and affection that continually occur in any good marriage, there are the tangible shared (and unshared) experiences that must be planned on a regular basis or the relationship will deteriorate. Even in the best marriages, these events must be planned; they will not spring forth on their own. The time to plan how and when to satisfy these important pictures is not when there is anger or tension, but when there is love and closeness. As in this example, a good time is when the more dissatisfied partner has done something to recapture a little of the love and closeness that has long been absent from the relationship. In this marriage, there had not been a well-planned, tangibly satisfying event for six months, and it was during this time that Dave found another woman to provide some of what was missing. In fact, the excuse that he gave himself to stop guilting was that Susan was no fun anymore.

It is important that the reader understand that I don't believe that one or two fun parties can save a failing marriage—much more has to be done. I use this only as an example of one of many satisfying activities that one or both partners must attempt that will renew a dragging relationship. If they continue to spend their time and energy spinning old wheels that have long been stuck in the sand, they will accomplish nothing.

At this point I am sure some women reading this control-theory advice would say that what I have suggested is all the woman's responsibility. Doesn't the man have any obligation to do something to correct the situation? Why should all the burden be on the woman? The problem with this fair thinking is that it is an attempt to shift part of the burden to Dave, but we don't know whether or not he was as dissatisfied in the beginning, when the marriage might have been saved, as Susan was. If he was, of course, it was his responsibility. Certainly he should do all he can to make the marriage better, but he will do only what is satisfying to him. And if he was not dissatisfied and chose to do nothing but withdraw into his shell while Susan criticized and depressed, that was his choice.

Control theory has made it clear that there is no way that Susan or anyone could have *forced* him to make another choice. He may eventually make a better choice, but this will be when he wants to, *not when she asks him or attempts to force him by her choice of misery.* Arguing that it isn't fair, or that "I won't unless he does," is logical, but it puts the shoe on a foot that Susan can't control. Fair or not, all Susan (or any of us) can do to satisfy herself is control her own life. If she does it in a way that Dave also enjoys, he may decide to take a little more initiative in doing some things that are satisfying to her.

The other valid choice for Susan would have been to decide that if she had to take the initiative, she did not want the marriage. She could have made this clear to Dave; told him what she would and wouldn't do; and then ended the marriage if he did not do what she wanted. The problem with this direct, confrontive approach is that Dave might have said, "Let's end it." Even if he still wanted the marriage, he might have interpreted this direct approach as too controlling. If Susan had wanted to end her marriage, taking a direct controlling approach would have been almost the sure way to do it. Most men and women who take this approach, however, are bluffing. If it does not work, they are not prepared to end their marriage. What they are well prepared to do is depress, headache, or get sick rather than look for and take the initiative to put into practice some mutually satisfying pictures that remain in both their heads.

Keep in mind that when Susan met my wife, she was still trying to control Dave (and herself) with her misery. She, of course, had no idea that her misery was a chosen behavior or that it was the most satisfying choice for her at the time. But had she known control theory and been willing to accept that she was choosing her miserable behavior, she still would have found it difficult to accept that when she chose a self-denying or altruistic behavior, it was more for herself than anyone else. No matter how much she put herself out for Dave, her behavior was always for her benefit. The chances we take whenever we do something for another person are that someone else benefits a great deal; that someone else does little or no work —we do it all; or possibly that someone else is not appreciative or refuses to reciprocate. Susan had every "right" to hope or expect that Dave would be appreciative and helpful, *but she has no control over what he chooses to do.*

For example, if Dave got drunk and abusive when Susan planned a pleasant social evening, this would have been his choice. An evening that started with the best of intentions would have ended disastrously. If this happened more than once, Susan would take these evenings out of her album. But until the party, she would have no way of knowing. Remember, she can only control her own life. Her happiness depends *not on what others do* but on what *she does,* and the sooner she learns this, the happier she will be.

If my wife had asked Susan, who was unhappy when they met (or even if Susan had asked herself), "What do you want?" the answer very likely would have been "I don't know." This is, of course, impossible. As much as any of us may try to deny it, we always know what is in our albums. If, however, we become discouraged because we can't get what we want, we lose less control by pretending we don't know. As her marriage began to fail, Susan knew very well that what she wanted was a better marriage. Perhaps a long vacation with Dave would have given their marriage a needed boost, but it was easier to say "I don't know" than to face what seemed so remote at this time. To take control of our lives, we must muster the strength to come to grips with what it is we want. This is because, although with effort we may block any frustration from awareness for a while, *we cannot stop ourselves from behaving as if we are fully aware of what is frustrating to us.*

In an effort to deny what they really want, people like Susan often sigh and say, "What's the difference what I want? I'll never get it." But her sighs and depressing are still her way of choosing to suffer to try to get what she denies she wants. From the standpoint of the pain she chooses, it makes no difference if she is aware of what she wants or not. If we don't have what we want, we will choose to anger or suffer just the same. Once you know control theory, you will not waste your time and energy refusing to face what you want just because it is hard to get, *because you know that you will choose to suffer just the same.*

To help us gain the courage to face what we want, we must keep in mind that, except for breathing, we almost always have more than one picture in our heads to satisfy any need. And if we don't have enough, we can add more. So, rather than to depress because Dave wouldn't take her on a trip, she should look for a picture that is close to what she wants that is possible for her to get. For example, there is no good reason that she could not have taken the trip without him. As soon as she got this idea, she could have come to grips with the fact that Dave was not an indispensable traveling companion. She could have gone with a friend and had a good time. Getting away from Dave would have given both a well-needed rest from each other.

As Susan learns control theory, she will still continue to depress and choose other misery, but she will not choose these for as long as she has in the past. Knowing control theory does not provide instant control, but because you are aware that you are choosing your misery, you will find it almost impossible to choose it for months or years as many people do. I often choose to be miserable for an hour or two, sometimes for as long as a day, but then I say to myself, "There must be a better choice." What I keep in mind, however, is that *the better choice is always a doing behavior.* As I explained in chapter 6, we can directly and arbitrarily control only what we do. For example, Susan can hostess a social evening, but she cannot choose to feel better because she does. However, if the evening is a success, and if most of her evenings have been, she will likely choose to enjoy herself. There is nothing about a successful event that will induce us to continue to choose misery.

Susan might also have had to learn that she had to take some previously important pictures out of her album if she wished to stay married to Dave. The main picture that most long-married people have to remove is the picture of the couple doing everything together. Getting married does not suddenly make all the pictures in the albums of the couple correspond. We marry wisely when we and our spouses share a great many pictures, but as a marriage matures, there are bound to be important pictures that are not shared and must be satisfied separately or the marriage will suffer.

As we have already learned, Dave likes to ski more than Susan does. What she could have done is use this knowledge to the advantage of their marriage rather than to its detriment as she tended to do. She could, for example, have watched the snow reports, and as soon as there was snow she could have taken the initiative and told Dave, "Don't miss the first snow—go skiing." She could have told him that she would be fine by herself as there were some other things she would like to do. "Let's plan it right now." If Dave had any feeling for her at all, he would make an effort to do more things with her when they were home together, because he would know that she was not out to deprive him of what he enjoyed doing alone.

I can think of quite a few pictures my wife and I share and some that we don't. If we make sure to share on a regular basis, and to encourage the other to enjoy what we don't share, we have the basis for a solid marriage. Even if we can't encourage the other to do what we don't share, the least we can do is be tolerant of the fact that we are different people with different backgrounds. If we take this sensible approach and try not to control each other into constant togetherness, we will usually be willing to share activities that are much more important to one of us than the other. I can think of several things that I do because my wife enjoys them much more than I, and I am sure there are an equal number that she does with me that mean little to her. Most people with successful marriages will do a reasonable amount just because the person they love wants to. If they don't encourage or at least tolerate what they don't share, they anger and become less tolerant.

If we have differences in marriage or any other relationship, the only way we can work them out is to negotiate a satisfactory compromise. Even a compromise is usually better for one party than the other, but if we compromise enough, the advantages tend to even out. This is why we negotiate before we compromise, to make sure we get our fair share. It is sad to hear intelligent people, who are suffering from differences between them, say that there is no sense talking. Talking—or, more accurately, negotiating—is all we have to work out our differences. People too often choose to suffer, complain, criticize, fight, get sick, act crazy, or use drugs, all in an attempt to control someone else (or themselves), rather than work out their differences through negotiation.

If you are in any personal difficulty, it is almost always because you have not been able to figure out a way to negotiate differences with someone important to you in fulfilling your needs. It is the only way we have; if we can't avail ourselves of it, there are no alternatives. When people deride counseling as ineffective, what they are saying is that they do not want to negotiate—they want to control. As I explained in chapter 2, *when you attempt to use power, you almost always lose belonging,* so we all must be willing to sacrifice a little power to satisfy other needs. How we do it and how much we do it is what negotiation is all about. The reason Susan looked into her album for some pictures she and Dave could still share— and found the social evening—is that this sharing may make it possible to negotiate and reach other compromises that may save the marriage. We can live with differences; no marriage is without them. But if we refuse to negotiate when these differences become extreme, we lose any chance to salvage the marriage.

Do the Susans and Daves of the world need professional counseling when they lose control of their marriage or any other part of their lives? The answer is clear: If they try to work it out on their own and can't, they should see a good counselor. But a good counselor is not one who accepts that their misery happens to them; or that if they talk about misery past or present, this will help them to make better choices. Good counseling focuses on what they are choosing to do now. Is it getting them what they want? Since it never is (or they wouldn't be there), a good counselor negotiates a plan with one or both of them to do something better. The plan is always a way for them to satisfy important pictures in their heads within their marriage. The plan may also be to find new pictures that are mutually satisfying if what they have seems insufficient.

Good counseling does not poke excessively into their past, and when the past is discussed, it is always related to the present. If they have had a traumatic past, they should be able to share it with the counselor so that she has some idea of when their lives went out of control. But it is the counselor's job to help whoever comes—Susan, Dave, or both—to understand that, as bad as things were, what went on then may have little or no bearing on what is going on now.

The greatest value of discussing the past is not for its misery but for the strengths it may provide that can be used now. In a sense, Susan was looking into her past when she searched her album for marriage pictures that once worked well for both her and Dave. There is no sense looking for something new if something old that was satisfying can be used again. Many people, however, try to avoid a difficult present by believing that the terrible things that happened to them are still overwhelming and that unless these past events can be brought to a satisfactory resolution, they will not get "well."

Susan may claim that her problems with Dave are just like the problems she had with her father. She may have had serious problems with her father, but to blame her marriage difficulties on that is a fallacy. She is not married to her father, and if she depresses with Dave as she did with him, she is choosing the same ineffective behavior now as she did then. Once she knows control theory (which counselors who use it also teach to their clients), she will quickly learn that just because she made a bad choice then, she does not have to continue making it now. As she begins to make better choices now, her life with her father will soon be forgotten. We live now and must satisfy ourselves now. We can't go back into our pasts actually or verbally and satisfy conditions that no longer exist.

It is unfortunate that many professional counselors, who do not know control theory, encourage clients to live in the past rather than teach them what they need to know to deal with the present regardless of the past. Clients should be wary of counselors who support them in their efforts to control important people in their present lives by attempting to impress them with how much they suffered in the past. Dave could easily get turned off to Susan if, supported by what she had "learned" in counseling, she continually confronted him with how much he was like her father and how difficult this was for her. If her father is dead, this puts Dave in a totally out-of-control, no-win position that will persuade him more to withdraw than to attempt to work out their differences.

Miserable things have happened to us all. Many people have been through the tortures of concentration camps and gone ahead and lived their lives. They have figured out that they must satisfy their needs now without attempting to do so by controlling others with what they have suffered and continue to choose to suffer. The only satisfaction we can get with and from others is what they choose to give us. Anytime we try to force them to give us what we want by attempting to control them with suffering, past or present, we will fail. If, as we often do when we fail, we choose additional suffering, we engage in a futile losing effort. Keep in mind that to satisfy the pictures in our heads, *we will choose to suffer pain beyond belief.* If, however, we learn that our misery is a choice, *and that better choices are almost always available,* we will make an active effort, by ourselves or with help, to choose more effective behaviors.

When we learn control theory, we must be humble enough to accept the fact that try as we will (and suffer as we will), there is no way we can actually control even a small portion of the world around us. There are many times when no matter what we do, think, or feel, we cannot satisfy ourselves the way we would like. But the fact that we can't have complete control, or even a large amount of control, does not mean that we have no control. We always have some control over what we do and think. If we can figure out something that will satisfy us even a little, we are infinitely better off than if we had wasted our efforts choosing misery in an effort to control more than is possible right now.

As we regain some small degree of control, we gain confidence that we can gain more. If Susan figures out what she can do that she and Dave will enjoy, and then goes ahead and does it, she will gain some control over a situation that before was out of control. If Dave enjoys it also and moves closer to her, she can begin the delicate process of negotiating some of the pictures that they do not share. If, together, they can work out some compromises and put them into practice, she will stop choosing misery and he will stop withdrawing. If she does these things without thinking of what's fair but because they are the only sensible things she can do, and if Dave cares for her at all, they will recoup their marriage. If she does all this and he still does not want to be married to her, than she has done all she can and should look elsewhere for love.

18
Control Theory and Raising Children

We may not all agree on exactly what a well-raised child is, but most of us share some general pictures in our heads of what we would like to see our children become. We want them as young adults to be warm and loving, hardworking and financially prudent, careful about their health (we especially don't want them to use drugs), moral and law-abiding, and both caring and respectful of their friends, family, and family friends. If this were the way my children turned out, I would consider that anything I had done to help them become this way was effective parenting.

For the most part, my wife and I are satisfied with the adults our three children have become, but if we had the chance to do it over again and use the knowledge of control theory that has now become a part of our daily lives, we would do some things differently. I will not attempt to go into the specifics of what we would change, but I would like explain to parents whose children still live with them some control-theory basics of child-rearing that may help them avoid mistakes. This chapter is not intended to be a complete guide to raising children, but assuming that the reader is now familiar with control theory, it should prove useful to any parent.

One of the most important control-theory lessons we have learned is that we should try to keep the pictures of what we want our children to become as general as those described above. As soon as we try to push our children to become the specific people that they may be in our heads, we become less effective as parents. For example, the more we want them to be doctors, lawyers, engineers, army officers, ministers, married, parents, rich, famous, or any other specific picture in our heads, the more we will push them to achieve these goals for *us*. And unfortunately, nothing that we do will alienate a child more than to be pushed to be something he or she does not want to be.

To satisfy their needs, children want to pursue their own goals. If this were not the case, we would still be in caves, mindlessly doing exactly as our parents wished. Progress has been made because children are willing to struggle for what satisfies them regardless of their parents. Too many parents attempt to mold their children to the parents' pictures, and, for them, parenting turns into a losing power struggle. Love and caring are swept aside as the parent-child relationship degenerates into angering and criticizing.

Many parents, especially those with definite pictures of what their children should become as adults, may balk at our suggestion to let children figure out the specific ways they want to live their lives. They may argue, "If I don't show him the way, he will amount to nothing. How can I stand by and take a chance with my child's life?" There is much that a good parent can do, that I will discuss shortly, to help a child succeed in the general way I described in the first paragraph of this chapter. Parents who consider this general description of a successful child insufficient, and insist that their children's success is dependent upon their becoming exactly what the parents want, will be more of a hindrance than a help.

Ask yourself, "Am I living the life I want to live, or is it the life my parents picked out for me?" My guess is that it's much more yours than theirs, and I also guess that what you are now doing is satisfying. But if it isn't, I still do not believe that you are spending much time regretting that you did not follow your parents' guidance. I also guess that even if the life you chose is working out well, your parents hindered you along the way and did not accept that your choice was sensible until it became apparent to everyone that it was.

The only specific picture that my wife and I adhere to strongly with our grown children is that we like them to be at our house on some of the holidays and, while there, to make an effort to get along well with each other. We also have the picture that they be on good terms with us and with each other. Past that, as much as we can, we try to keep in our heads the general picture of their doing with their lives what they think is best and succeeding. With the help of control theory, we have finally begun to appreciate that they are going to live according to their pictures, not ours. But whatever we can do to persuade them to keep a picture in their heads of staying on good terms with us and with each other, we will try to do.

How responsible are we for the way our children turn out? For example, is it mostly our fault if a child chooses to behave in an aberrant manner, like Tim, the pot-smoking, nonstudent of chapter 3? We certainly have the responsibility to make an effort to learn what to do that will make it less likely that any child of ours will turn out to be like Tim at sixteen. Most children give consideration to what their parents want, but if they do not agree, they, like Tim, do what they think is best. What we can do is raise them in a way that makes it less likely that they will be irresponsible, unhappy adults. Tim's parents do not realize that much of his present self-destructive behavior is his way of resisting their pressure that he start now to prepare to become a lawyer by doing well in school. His way of resisting is detrimental to him, but there is no doubt that it has worked. They no longer aspire for him to be a lawyer. They would be satisfied now if he would just pass in school, stop smoking pot, and turn off his stereo on school nights at a decent hour.

In chapter 3 I suggested that Tim's father make an effort to rebuild his rapidly deteriorating relationship with Tim because if he doesn't, there will be little he can do to help Tim change. Without a good relationship, our effect upon one another is either nonexistent or destructive. Nowhere is this more important than when you raise a child, so it is fundamental to all child-raising that you try to keep yourself as a loving person in your child's head. This is never easy to do, especially if you follow the "commonsense" fallacy that if your child is misbehaving, all you have to do is show more concern, stop being permissive, and "make" him behave. The more you try to make him behave, the more he resists, and very soon you and he are hardly on speaking terms. All of us know parents who are neither unconcerned nor permissive, yet whose children are behaving like Tim or worse and the parents can't *make them change* even with punishment and threats. What these parents have to learn is patience. It is a slow, difficult task to rebuild the tenuous relationship that always exists between a parent and a resistant child like Tim, but unless this relationship is improved, nothing we do will work.

Part of the way Tim resists the continuing pressure from his parents is to begin to remove them from his head as need-satisfying people. As he does, he will pay little attention to what they want and even less to what they do. In this situation most parents tend to make the mistake of pushing harder, with the unfortunate result that a child like Tim takes them more and more out of his head. If, at the end of this vicious cycle, Tim has taken his parents completely out of his head, as many Tims do, he will no longer pay any attention to what they want. If they finally learn a better way to deal with him, it may be too late because he has replaced them with other pictures; now he is attempting to satisfy his need to belong with drugs and rock music. This is why in chapter 3 I suggested that Tim's father invite him to go fishing—this is a picture they still shared in their albums. If the trip is successful and Tim begins to put his father back into his album as a need-satisfying person, then the necessary ground has been prepared to go further.

If, after a few fishing trips, the relationship with his father becomes more secure, they may eventually settle on the plan that if Tim does better in school, he may use the family car. This or any other plan must be worked out in a way that does not frustrate Tim severely if he does not follow through. Frustration can be a valuable learning experience for Tim (or anyone) if he can learn to deal with it effectively, but Tim has a long way to go before he can handle much frustration. If, after a few weeks, Tim is no longer carrying out the plan and slacks off in school, his father should take the car away—but when he does, he should make sure that Tim knows exactly what he can do to get it back. Tim does not have a great many patient behaviors, so if the car is taken away for too long, he will look at it as "forever" and may quickly revert to his old ways, reject his parents, and they are back to square one. The plan must make it possible for him to get the car back in a reasonable time, such as two weeks. This will seem hard, but still possible, and he will keep his father in his head as a fair person whom he needs and with whom he will continue to plan.

In general, what I am going to suggest in the rest of this chapter about raising children assumes that the parent continues to make an effort to maintain a good relationship. While these suggestions apply to children of all ages, including Tim at sixteen, they are directed more to small children. If Tim's parents had used the control theory that is suggested in this chapter, they might have prevented the problems they are now now having with him.

Before twelve or thirteen years of age, most children are fairly easy to get along with. If not, at least the parents still see them as small and don't worry that their disobedience is going to ruin their lives. They may not obey us as much as we'd like, or perhaps they are mean to sisters or brothers, but in important matters, like avoiding danger, protecting their health, and going to school, they still listen to us because they have a powerful need to belong, and we are the ones they most count upon to satisfy this need. But children, even quite disobedient ones, tend to take their parents for granted. They sense how much we love them and they believe (correctly) that we will put up with a lot of bad treatment from them and still continue to stand by them if they need our help. I can't explain why we have such strong love for our children, but we do, they know it, and they will take advantage of it to control us if we let them. But we cannot be effective parents if they control us, any more than they can be effective children if we are too much in control of them.

It is during this time, the thirteen-year grace period, that we must learn how to deal with them effectively, and the earlier we start applying the principles of control theory, the easier the process of child-raising should be. If they stop loving us—and eventually they might if we try too hard to control them—persuading them to change if they are self-destructive becomes much more difficult. Even after all the hostility between Tim and his father, they still had some love for each other, so the situation was hopeful.

The main problem that confronts parents in raising children is how they can live amicably with each other and still satisfy their own pictures. When there are differences, as there almost always are— for example, when we want them to do homework and they want to watch television—the parents are almost always much more dissatisfied than the children, so it is more up to us than our children to figure out a way to resolve these differences. But driven by our need for power, we rarely think of resolving differences with our children—we want to control them. After all, isn't it "natural" for us to control our children "for their own good"? Nothing in this chapter suggests that we not intervene in our children's lives—that we leave them alone to do as they wish. We should not abdicate our role as parents, and few children, short of maturity, would want us to. Children welcome parental control if they love their parents, but they don't want to be totally controlled. At almost any age, they want parents to grant them the power to do what they consider reasonable with their lives.

The question is not whether to control, but rather what is reasonable and how much control a parent should try to exert. The answer to this question depends a lot on what the child wants. If you believe what he wants is irresponsible, you need to exert more control than if his pictures are more acceptable. A child who wants to travel around the city by hitchhiking instead of riding his bike or taking a bus is a child who needs control. This is why it is so important to have a good relationship with your child: so that he will both tell you what he wants and accept some control from you if what he wants is, in your judgment, irresponsible. If, at any age, what he wants is far from what you want, but you have a good relationship, you can usually negotiate the differences and work out a compromise you can both accept. In Tim's case the trouble was that before he and his father went fishing, the relationship had deteriorated to the point where negotiation and compromise were no longer possible.

Because all of us, young and old, have such a strong need for power, negotiation and compromise are the only ways that both parent and child can fulfill this need and still get along with each other. Almost all the difficulties we run into as we raise children are due to our failure to understand that these are the only effective behaviors we have when children do not do as we like (or we do not do as they like). Parents who do not negotiate but try to force their children to fulfill the parents' pictures, regardless of what the children may want, always find themselves angering or bribing to try to gain some control. Children who love you will almost always compromise and accept reasonable control if you take the time to negotiate differences: explain why you want what you want and listen to their reasons for what they want. But they will resist bitterly any authority figure who will neither negotiate nor compromise.

Like all of us, they will try to satisfy their own pictures, and if they have to fight parents who won't compromise, they will do that, too. As I have explained, this fighting may take the form of direct angering, but since children, compared to parents, have little actual power, their fighting usually takes a more indirect form, such as withdrawal, depressing, disobedience, psychosomatic illness, and/or drug use. What Tim chose to do to satisfy himself is typical of children whose parents have spent little time trying to find out what their children want and negotiating differences when they arose.

Although successful parenting is a complex task, some of the complexity can be removed by reducing how we deal with children to one basic axiom:

> *Try as hard as possible to teach, show, and help your children to gain effective control of their lives.*

This means that, as much as you can, never do anything to or for a child that will cause the child to lose control. All the irresponsible behaviors children choose when growing up are their attempts to regain control of their lives. If they blame their parents for this loss —as, right or wrong, they frequently do—the relationship between them and their parents suffers, which in turn causes even more loss of control. When Tim did not succeed in school, he lost control. When his parents pushed, he blamed them for his problems and refused to accept his own inadequacy. When he took to smoking pot and withdrawing into his room to listen to music, this was his self-destructive way to try to regain control. This probably would not have happened if his parents had kept in mind that what we should try to do with our children from the time they are born is help them to gain and maintain effective control of their lives. The way they raised Tim, he was not in control until he "took over" his life at age sixteen.

To help our children gain control of their lives, we should be aware that as we raise them, all of us employ four separate and easily understood procedures. Everything we do with our children, simple or complex, can be related to one of these simple, clear-cut procedures. Once you learn them, which you should find very easy to do, you will then mostly use the ones that are effective and reduce to a minimum the procedures you use that are ineffective. These four procedures are as follows:

Doing things for them. For example, feeding them when they are young or taking them into our business when they are grown.

Doing things to them. For example, if they don't do as we want, punishing them when they are little or disowning them when they are grown.

Doing things with them. For example, playing with them when they are small or discussing mutual interests like sports and music with them when they are grown.

Leaving them alone. For example, letting them cry out a temper tantrum when they are two years old or saying nothing but wishing them well and making plans to keep in close touch when, at age eighteen, they tell us that they are going to strike out on their own.

I believe very strongly that many of us tend to do too much *for* them if what we want is for our children to be in control of their lives when they are grown. This is especially true when they are small: We carry them and dress them when they could walk or dress themselves. We do it because we love them and because it is easier and quicker to do it for them than to wait while they do it themselves. But another reason we do many things *for* them is to control them. We hope that they will appreciate what we do and pay attention to what we want as they grow. We also do far too much *to* them, like yell at them and punish them when they do not do what we want.

We do not do enough purely *with* them without concurrently doing *for* them or *to* them. For example, we go for a walk with a young child because we both want to go, but when she gets tired and complains, we carry her home. Then, because we are tired from carrying her, we may yell at her because of what we decided to do (carry her) when she complained of being too tired to walk. What started out as a good *with*-her experience deteriorated into a do-*for*-her-and-*to*-her experience—which did not help her to be in control of her life. If we had been more patient, taken a rest, and insisted that she walk home even if she walked slowly, we would not have yelled at her. We also should have been smart enough not to walk so far that she was likely to lose control by getting too tired.

Children need us. They need our company, instruction, love, and support. They need to know where we are and that they can count on us for help and guidance. But they do not need us all the time. At all ages we don't leave children *alone* enough. For example, on a rainy day, when they are perfectly capable of figuring out how to entertain themselves, as soon as they complain, we start doing *for* them and *to* them. Too often, we start to play with them, get bored, quit, and then ask them to leave us alone. We would be better off letting them alone in the first place to figure out what to do on their own. In many situations, instead of letting them get up their own games, we get far too involved. Activities like Little League, where adult needs are being satisfied as much or more than children's, teach children to rely on others, not themselves, and that they have little or no power even in play. Play then becomes frustrating and fails to be the good learning experience that it should be. What they learn, which causes them to lose control, not gain it, is that adults make all the key decisions, and when they get older and have to make decisions, they don't know how.

When Tim was small, he was a "good" boy; the present "trouble" with him did not start until he was fourteen years old. What probably contributed to the way he is behaving now is that when he was small his parents did far too much *for* him and *to* him. They imposed a lot of their thinking on him, and because it was easy and mostly satisfying, he did what he was told and followed the rules. Even though it was not always satisfying, he did this because his parents did do a lot *for* him. If he got behind in his easy elementary-school work, his parents pitched in and helped him. If he wanted a fancy bicycle that cost a lot of money, they bought it for this "good" boy. He continued to be "good," but because too much was done for him and to him, he was not in control of his life; his parents were.

Because too much had been done for him earlier, when he got to high school he was unprepared for the many mature things that he now had to do for himself. Without confidence, and lacking good preparation, he began doing little in school, and to get him to do more, his concerned parents tried to force him to work harder. Now they stopped doing *for* him and began to do a lot *to* him. They yelled, threatened, and restricted in an attempt to control him as they had done easily when he was small by doing things *for* him. But they were powerless to help him to satisfy the strong social and sexual needs that were churning inside of him; all their doing *to* him accomplished was that he chose to withdraw and began to take them out of his head. We keep no pictures in our heads of people who do things *to* us.

When he found himself failing because he could not handle the academic demands of high school, he no longer even pretended to make an effort. His parents cut off his allowance and he lost the little control that money could buy. Now, to regain control of his life, Tim rationalized that the hard work his parents were demanding of him was more for them than for him. He stated very strongly that he did not need algebra or college-prep English, that the teachers had it in for him, that "everybody" smoked pot, and that his "music" (listening to tapes and records) and his friends (young people like himself) were all he cared about. What he was doing was regaining control over his life with the meager behaviors he had. When his parents started to apply heavy pressure, it was like beating a badly lame horse, and the impasse of chapter 3 was reached after about a year and a half of high school.

To avoid these common problems, parents should, from the time their children are small, teach them how to take control of their own lives. To do this, they should avoid doing what Tim's parents did, which was too much *for* him and *to* him in a mistaken effort to get him to do what *they* thought was right. Even with infants, we should concentrate on doing nothing for them that they can do for themselves and as much with them as we can without being overwhelming or intrusive. We should also leave them alone to deal with the world on their own for short, but increasing, periods of time, starting when they are in their cribs.

For example, when a little baby is fed, loved, cleaned, and played with, and then gets cranky, it may be best to leave him alone. Even at several months, he may be checking out his power to control his parents. If he takes control through crying or fussing, he will quickly learn that when he is uncomfortable, he can cry, gain control through misery, and get his parents to do *for* him. He fails to learn to do for himself. You are loving, not cruel, when you let a well-cared-for infant alone when he is obviously tired and you can no longer do anything helpful for him (you can't sleep for him). When he discovers he is on his own, he will cry mightily for quite a while, but very quickly he will learn to settle down and amuse himself with tiny thoughts or a crib toy, or go to sleep with no "hard feelings" toward you at all. Even in infancy there are easily learned options that can be used to replace the angering with which we are born.

Let's take a look at a charming, loving, eight-year-old boy who is a world-class dawdler. He walks around in the morning in a semi-trance and the whole family takes on the responsibility of getting him ready for school. Every morning he is in complete control as they remind him, plead with him, and eventually anger at him. To deal with this exasperating situation, his parents, who are otherwise on very good terms with him, should negotiate a plan with him in which he agrees to get ready by himself in the morning in return for the after-school privileges that he now enjoys. They should do this after dinner when everyone is relaxed, and should not stop negotiating until he fully comprehends that if he does not follow through, he will lose many of these privileges. It might be wise to write out the plan and hang this up in his room.

Then, each day that he does not get ready, they should take away an after-school privilege, such as art class, soccer, or playing with friends. There should be no harshness; they might even offer him a little help the first few mornings if he makes an effort. If he complains, they should carefully explain that when he follows through, he keeps all his privileges. All he has to do is get ready in the morning and he is in control. When he does, he should also be given a lot of love and praise, and soon this problem will be solved.

When Tim was small, he was urged to do what his parents wanted him to do: go to bed, get up, and play with these (not those) children. He did not, however, suffer from overwhelming control. In fact, he went along easily because his parents were warm and loving, but the result was that he was mostly involved in activities that his parents selected for him. They were never cruel, and most of what they wanted for him he found sensible and fun to do, so it was easy for him to cooperate. But even at five and six, he should have been learning not only to cooperate but also to *operate*—to make some decisions on his own to get what he, not they, wanted. Then, as much as is reasonable for his age, he should have been left alone to make some decisions and to carry them out.

For example, when he was six he didn't like to come in for lunch during the summer when he was outside playing. He would show up starving at about three and his mother would make him a big lunch, but then he was so full that he had trouble eating his dinner. No parent should force a child to eat, and if he didn't want to come for lunch when his mother fed his sister and herself, she should have told him to work out lunch on his own. She should have shown him where the food was and pointed out that if he fed himself, he also had to clean up. He could then have decided what to do, but, whatever it was, it would be his decision and he would be left alone to make it. If he didn't eat lunch some days, his parents should not have worried. There is no danger that boys like Tim will become malnourished if they skip an occasional meal.

When Tim was ten, he wanted an expensive stereo. Instead of buying it for him, his parents should have negotiated with him to do some work around the house to help pay for it. They also should have discussed how loudly he could play it, what time he had to turn it off for the night, and how early he could turn it on in the morning. If he failed to follow the rules, it should have been taken away until they worked out a plan with him to play it responsibly.

I don't believe that I need write more examples of how it is better to do less *for* or *to* your children. You can figure this out on your own with your child if you accept that effective behaviors are not learned unless we do things for ourselves or with someone who will show and share but not take over or impose his will upon us. We learn responsibility only by taking it, and children need to follow through to help get what they say they want. If they get in trouble, they should be allowed to suffer reasonable consequences before an adult steps in. If they get in way over their heads, we should help them to help themselves as much as we can and do as little directly for them as makes sense in the situation.

Suppose your twelve-year-old promises several neighbors that she will help out by minding their young children for about three hours a day and they count on her to do this. Then a girlfriend's family suddenly invites her to go camping for two weeks and she asks if she can go. You ask her about the child care and she begs you to go to the neighbors and get her off the hook. She is a good girl and you are tempted to do this or find someone to take her place because this has come up rather suddenly. What you should do is let her handle it. If she does it badly by just going off, you should talk to the neighbors and ask them to talk to her about it when she returns. Ask them to do this as a favor to you. If they complain to you that you should not have let her go, tell them that the contract was with her, not you. This is a rough learning experience, and no matter how she handles it, she will learn the most if she does it herself.

What makes children strong and capable as well as warm and

loving is a lot of parent involvement—a lot of the *with*-them procedure. We cannot hug, kiss, and talk with them enough. We should
also involve ourselves in playing with them, teaching them, and
especially helping them to carry out responsible plans successfully
even when they do not coincide with ours. When she was sixteen,
our daughter, who had been corresponding with a Japanese pen pal
for about two years, told us that he had invited her to come to Japan
and that she wanted to go. This was not the picture in our heads,
but we told her that if she could work out all the details and the
complicated protocol, we would help pay for the trip. We would
advise her, but she had to do everything to get ready on her own.
She did, and taking control of a complex situation and carrying it
out well was a wonderful learning experience for her.

To satisfy the strong need to belong, children should be encouraged to find friends (on their own) to play with. Finding friends at
five (assuming other children are available) is good practice for the
more complex teen-age social scene later. When they do find friends,
we should be careful to be accepting of the children they find. If the
friends they find are not the ones we'd like to see them with, we
might talk to them but not interfere too much or they will lose
control in a very delicate and important area. How to deal with
friends is very difficult, if not impossible, to teach, but it is usually
very easily learned if adults do not interfere.

It is also valuable to work with them on simple tasks where they
can see that they are making a contribution to the family. This fulfills
their need for power in a way that helps them to become effective.
The assignment of helping with younger brothers and sisters is
especially valuable, as is yard work or even pitching in on a big
project like painting the house. When we work with them, we must
be patient and not rush to do for them because they are slow.
Instruct them, and show them, but let them do their part of the task
and they will gain strength and confidence.

What makes children especially strong is for them to tackle a
creative and/or competitive skill outside of school, one that requires
work and discipline but is not adult-dominated like some highly
organized children's athletics. Music, ballet, art, woodworking, car
repairing, swimming, model building, computer programming, and
electronics are examples. The whole point of these is to help children
experience the satisfaction that comes from a challenging, nonrou-

tine activity to which they can contribute something creative of their own. The more they are able to do this on their own, or with occasional parental help but a lot of parental interest, the stronger they will be.

Nothing is more motivating than an activity in which we experience our inherent, always-present creativity. Hobbies or any *noncompetitive* activities, such as playing a musical instrument, are excellent motivators (if the child wants to play, not if she is forced) because the quiet time provided by many of these activities is when we experience creative moments. The more a child experiences her creativity, the more she will depend on it and learn to use it. In doing so, she becomes familiar with one of the strongest forces we have for maintaining effective control of our lives. (This will be explained further in chapter 20 when I discuss creative, in-control time.) Tim dabbled, but he never followed through, and his greatest effort at present is obtaining marijuana and listening to rock tapes.

What Tim lacked in his life was the confidence that comes only from accomplishment. He had never accomplished much more than being good when he was little, but being good got both him and his parents a lot of what they all wanted at the time. The trouble with being good is that it is too easy. There is no challenge, nothing creative—all you do is to follow a few simple family rules and you get taken care of. But as a child grows older, being good—which too often means that if you aren't, your parents will do things *to* you, and if you are, they will do things *for* you—doesn't work. This is because what you want at sixteen you can't get by people doing *for* you or *to* you. You can't succeed in high school or as an adult just by being good. You have to work. You can't make friends with hardworking young people if they see you as lazy, so you turn to friends who, like yourself, do little that is constructive. To have fun, you depend less upon active pursuits like team athletics or hobbies and more upon the passive pleasures of drugs and music. This does not mean that young people who are active do not use drugs or listen to rock music, but they do not depend upon them, and that is a big difference.

In a sense, even though Tim was driving his parents crazy, he was still being good. He was hanging around the house doing nothing as he had done when he was little, but now, instead of this being good, it was no good. But we can't do more unless we know how and have a picture in our heads of satisfying accomplishment. If we have never worked on our own, there will be no picture. Now, as he is getting more involved with his mother and father, who have finally learned not to do things *to* him or *for* him but *with* him, Tim is starting at sixteen to try to learn what he should have learned at six. He can do it, but he is far behind. Some Tims never catch up. They get married and then drink a lot of beer while their wives (this is typical of the wives of alcoholics) repeat the mistakes of the parents, doing a lot *to* them and *for* them, but little or nothing *with* them.

Parents need to learn that children are born without knowing how to fulfill their needs. They must learn a lot or they will never take effective control of their lives. They learn nothing by having things done to them, and very little if things are done for them. They learn a lot from adults who do things with them and encourage them to do for themselves. It is not by chance that animals throw their young out on their own when their genetic instructions tell them they have done enough. An animal that cannot learn to fend for itself will not survive, and therefore will leave no faulty descendants.

Unlike animals, we are too helpless to be thrown out when we are young; a great deal must be done for us or we won't survive. But as we mature, the care has to diminish and doing *for* must move to doing *with* and then to doing *alone*. Effective parents rejoice in the accomplishments their children achieve on their own; ineffective parents depress or anger when they find they have to do *for* adult children because they have not learned to do for themselves.

To raise effective children, we must try our best to take specific pictures of what they should become as adults out of our heads. We should keep in our heads mostly short-term pictures of our children behaving responsibly by working hard in school, helping around the house, caring for their possessions, being warm and friendly with all who are friendly to them, and being able to be by themselves and figure out something to do that is satisfying and responsible. They should also be willing and able to talk with us when we have a difference of opinion, and to negotiate a way that satisfies us both. If we have children who satisfy these general pictures, it is likely that whatever they decide to do with their lives will be acceptable to us, or, if it isn't, that they will be willing to negotiate.

But even if we do all I suggest, there will be plenty of times as our children grow when they will break rules and then challenge us to do something about it. What we ordinarily do is called "punishment" or "discipline," but control theory explains that these are not the same. Discipline is effective, punishment is not—and the difference is clear. Discipline—the control-theory way—always starts with trying to teach children to follow reasonable rules through negotiation. Punishment—the stimulus-response way—starts and finishes with trying to force children to follow the rules, even unreasonable rules, by inflicting pain if they refuse. (A reasonable rule is defined as one most children who are on good terms with their parents will follow with little protest; an unreasonable rule is one to which even usually obedient children strongly object.)

Discipline involves the sanctions of the loss of either freedom or privileges until the child is willing to negotiate. It does not use such common punishments as hitting, long-term yelling, criticizing, or attacking with sarcasm. Discipline may seem similar to punishment in the sense that the child who breaks a rule and refuses to negotiate does suffer one or the other of these mildly painful sanctions, but, unlike punishment, the child has some control over the situation. When he is sent to his room or loses a privilege, the child does not serve a sentence like no television for the rest of the day; it is only for the time it takes him to agree to work out a way to follow the rules.

Punishment is inflicting pain, physical or mental, in the hope that the rulebreaker will remember the pain and next time follow the rule. Once the pain is inflicted, the child has no way to avoid it—*it is done.* The punished child feels a deep loss of power and control, and he usually attempts to deal with this loss through choosing the painful and self-destructive feeling behavior of shaming. There is ordinarily no teaching or negotiating in the punishment way, and no attempt to make the sense of the rules a part of the procedure. If the punished child decides that the pain is worth whatever is gained by breaking the rule, then the punishment is ineffective. The most serious flaw in punishment is that it does not take into account the fact that the rulebreaker is trying to satisfy a picture in his head. Unlike discipline, there is nothing in the punishment procedure to teach him that there is likely another picture or a better behavior that would be within the rules.

Punishment is by far the most widely used of all human control procedures, and the fact that so many punished children and adults continue to be out of control is sad testimony to the ineffectiveness of this traditional stimulus-response procedure. Nowhere is this more apparent than in the failure of our overcrowded, punitive prisons, which release people who are less in control of their lives than when they went in. Probation, on the other hand, is a disciplinary procedure that is almost always effective if the probation officer is well trained and not overloaded as too many are now. In a society where control theory was practiced, only the very dangerous (still unfortunately huge numbers) would be sent to prison; the rest would be treated with strict but creative probation, where they would learn to regain control of their lives.

What control theory suggests is that we never punish any child. To deal with a very young child, under two and a half, who is too young to understand that she broke a rule, it is sensible to restrain her firmly, but not painfully, and tell her in a stern voice, "No," when for example she turns on the gas or pinches her little brother. If the tiny child loves you, the restraint, accompanied by a strong no, is sufficient. When we deal with a child of three, old enough to know that she broke a rule, we should always discipline, never punish. A three-year-old who spills her milk both for attention and to assert herself can be told that she is responsible for cleaning up the mess. If it takes her a while and she is a little messy in doing it, it is still better than doing it for her or yelling at her. If she refuses, she should be told that she can go to her room until she decides to clean it up. She should also be served her milk in a wide glass, half-full, to prevent it from happening again due to clumsiness. But even if she spills her milk by accident, she, not her mother, should correct it.

Suppose your eight-year-old does not come home for dinner and you have to scour the neighborhood to find her. She is well aware that she should have come home, so you talk to her to teach her what to do to prevent it from happening again. In this negotiation she affirms that she respects the rule and you work it out so that next time she will tell you where she is going. She also agrees that if she leaves that place for another child's house, she will call and let you know. You agree that if she is not home on time, you will call and tell her to come home.

This works for a while, but then she stops coming home, and when you call, she isn't where she said she would be. Basically she found the plan too restrictive and, to assert her power, decided not to follow it.

Now you no longer talk, but apply a sanction. You tell her that she has to stay home until she can make a plan to come home for dinner when she is playing at a friend's house. She doesn't want to stay home and she cries, but you are firm: She cannot go out after school the next day unless she has a plan. You offer to help her with the plan, but she has to have one. You do not hit her, threaten her, or yell at her, but you do insist that she stay home until she has a plan. With an eight-year-old, the plan can be as simple as just solemnly promising to come home on time from now on. It could also be that she will ask her older brother to remind her if he is near, or that she will call home and ask if she may stay a little longer, but if she may not, she will come right home.

What the plan is with a young child is not important—what is important is that she have a plan that she can put into action. If she can do it, she has responsible control and she learns the value of having it. If you punish by hitting or yelling in the hope that she will remember the pain and not do it again, she has no control. You can never take back a slap or a yell. It is done, she suffered it, and now she has even less control than she had previously. She will probably compound the problem by choosing to anger or depress in an attempt to regain control by controlling you that way.

Tim accepted the plan offered by his father that when he started to do the school work, he would gain the use of the car. It could have been a part of the disciplinary plan for his father to pay for a tutor to help him to learn to do the work, because if Tim could not do it without help, the plan would become punitive. If he began to do the work and then stopped after a few weeks, the car would again be taken away until he started studying. Tim fully accepts his commitment to this plan and his parents should not allow him to pressure them into renegotiation.

The next time you are faced with a child old enough to be disciplined, try the following four disciplinary steps and you will have a good chance to succeed not only in working out a solution to the problem but also in teaching your child to be more effective in the future.

1. Check the picture in your head of what you want from the child and make sure that what you want is also reasonably satisfying for the child. If the child is breaking a rule, be sure the rule is reasonable—which means it is one that most children will follow and one that you were willing to follow when you were a child. Work on your relationship with the child by doing something with him that you both enjoy and that has no direct bearing on the problem. (A good way to reach Tim might be to offer to listen to some of his music and let him explain it to you, but you should not try to get close by smoking or drinking with him.)

2. Try to wait until both you and the child are calmed down, and then, with as little angering as is possible for you in the situation, ask the child if he is satisfied with what he is doing or if he understands that it is against the rules.

3. If the child is not satisfied or admits that he is breaking a rule, negotiate a better way for the child to satisfy himself and you. Make sure, if you are involved in this plan, that what you do is as much *with* and as little *to* or *for* the child as possible. If the child can carry out the plan by himself, so much the better.

4. If the child claims to be satisfied with what he is doing and does not want to change, then, if you have the power, invoke a sanction that does not cause the child to lose control. The sanction is always some loss of freedom (go to your room) or loss of privileges (no ice skating) until the problem is worked out. Make sure that the child is able to change; if he needs help here, offer to instruct him or arrange for outside help, but don't do it for him. Also make sure that the loss of freedom or privileges is not for too long: Ten minutes is maximum for a five-year-old; an evening without television might be right for a ten-year-old. Whatever the restriction or loss of privileges, it should be appropriate for the child's age and long enough that the child see some sense in negotiating. It should not be so long that he gives up and does not want to try to correct the situation.

This advice could be extended to children of any age. I now associate mostly with people with grown children, and the greatest difficulty I see is that they still do too much to and for their children. They do these things partly because it is difficult for parents of grown children, whom they love, to bow gracefully out of their children's everyday lives. Since it becomes increasingly difficult to do things *with* them, the parents make the mistake of doing too much *for* them instead of just leaving them alone. If the children are "ungrateful" —as many are when they view what is done for them as an attempt to control them—they may withdraw and stay away. If they do, the parents may begin to do things *to* them, like depress, in an attempt to control them by causing them to guilt.

To keep on good terms with adult children, continue to be warm and loving, but do as little as is possible *for* them or *to* them, as much *with* them as you both enjoy, and respect them enough to be willing to leave them *alone* if this is what they want.

When children reach the middle years, their forties to sixties, things between child and parent seem to reverse. Now, with equally unsatisfactory results, the child starts to do too much to and for the parent. This was described in the case of the daughter, Phyllis, who was being controlled by her mother, Carol, that I introduced in chapter 7 and that I will discuss in much more detail in the next chapter.

19
Controlling Ourselves or Others with Pain or Misery

Most of us have people in our families very much like seventy-four-year-old, physically healthy Carol and her middle-aged daughter, Phyllis, whom I discussed in chapter 7. Carol, a "professional" depresser, controlled Phyllis with her complaints of misery. Phyllis had to be at her beck and call or Carol would withdraw into painful silence until Phyllis begged her to relent. Phyllis escaped from Carol's clutches through periodic migraining, and like many people we know, she would benefit from learning enough control theory to deal with Carol, or those like her, more effectively. But perhaps Carol, who lives a life of excruciating, self-chosen suffering, would benefit as much or more than Phyllis from this knowledge. Carol will probably never learn control theory as a theory, but if Phyllis can learn it and put it into practice with her, Carol, without realizing it, will learn enough to live a much more satisfying life. When she begins to live with less depressing, she will likely credit her improvement to vitamins or herb tea rather than to Phyllis's intervention, but what she believes is much less important than the fact that she has begun to live more effectively.

To deal with Carol, Phyllis first has to learn what to me is one of the most important axioms of control theory: *Never let anyone control you with the pain and misery he or she chooses.* This does not mean you should reject them, fight with them, abandon them, or beg them. And it certainly does not mean you should not be sympathetic and supportive for many months to someone you know who has suffered a personal tragedy. But what it does mean is that, difficult as this is at first, you should deal with long-term sufferers like Carol—who has encountered nothing more exceptional than growing old—as if they were not miserable at all.

For example, when Carol makes her regular morning call to Phyllis and, in her theatrically weak and depressing tone of voice, asks if Phyllis can come over immediately, Phyllis should not respond with her usual immediate promise to make a special trip over as soon as she can get ready. Phyllis should not ask "What's wrong?" because Carol has a list of ready answers that will quickly overwhelm Phyllis's meager "Do I really have to come right away?" defensive question. If Phyllis even hesitates, Carol will say, "I'm too weak to discuss it on the phone." Her voice will then trail off and as Phyllis yells "Mom, Mom, what is it?" Carol will just sigh and say nothing, again successfully establishing the urgency of her immediate need for Phyllis.

If, as usual, Phyllis rushes over, she will find nothing different from any previous urgent morning. Carol will go through her usual complaints and fears that no one cares about her, and add that she was so faint that she felt that if she hadn't called early, she would not have had the strength to call later. She will be a little contrite, saying she knows how busy Phyllis is and she hates to call. But she would also remind her that if she didn't call, she would not hear from Phyllis from one day to the next—which is not true.

What is true is that Carol has been depressing for over ten years, and Phyllis does not initiate inquiries as often as she did. Carol, however, calls several times a day, always with "good reason," so if Phyllis were to call her, it would seem superfluous. When Phyllis does call, Carol has also used the ploy of taking a long time to answer and then telling Phyllis that she had another of her sleepless nights and just dozed off for a moment; Phyllis's call awakened her. It does not take too many of these experiences to make Phyllis reluctant to call.

Carol is no doubt an expert depresser, but she is far from unusual. Compressing her behavior into a few paragraphs may make her seem extreme, but there are many Carols, young and old, all around us, suffering their lives away in a desperate attempt to take control of someone (or anyone) whom they believe they can control with a painful behavior. As long as they can gain some control over someone, they will continue to depress. But even if they cannot gain any control over a specific person (perhaps they live alone, or no one pays attention to them no matter how they suffer), they still may continue to depress, because they have not figured out a better behavior. Carol will continue to depress for years even if Phyllis moves away and breaks off all contact with her, because she has depressed for so long that, without some help from someone she cares about, she is unlikely to learn anything new.

Once Phyllis accepts that she cannot let Carol control her with depressing, the first thing she has to do is realize that Carol is choosing all the pain and misery about which she complains. She must never waver from her new control-theory understanding that Carol is not "depressed" but choosing to depress, or she will be unable to help Carol make some more-effective choices. This will not come easily. Carol's expertise is to act as if the most wonderful thing that could happen in her life would be to miraculously get over the "depression" that has laid her low for years. To begin to deal with her as I suggest here, Phyllis will have to accept on faith that Carol is choosing her misery. But faith will turn to understanding if what I suggest is accurate and Carol does begin to depress less. As she sees Carol begin to make more-effective choices, Phyllis will gradually begin to realize that control theory applies to long-term depressers like Carol as it does to all of us.

When she begins the difficult process of persuading Carol to make better choices, she can expect no cooperation, because Carol will view what Phyllis has begun to do as a challenge to her control, and she will not cooperate unless she believes she is gaining, not losing, control of her life. Right now, Phyllis *is* pretty much her life, so if she relinquishes some control over Phyllis, she will have to take control of some other aspects of her life that she has let slide while concentrating all her efforts on controlling Phyllis.

To start, Phyllis must begin to separate herself from Carol's control by setting regular times for her and Carol to get together. No matter what "emergency" Carol complains of, Phyllis must not run over to her apartment. She should go about this with both subtlety and determination and continue to visit regularly. Once she embarks on the plan, when Carol calls, Phyllis should make a definite appointment to see her when it is convenient to Phyllis's schedule, not Carol's.

For example, in answer to one of Carol's urgent early calls, she should say that she is planning to stop by in the late afternoon and she will be hungry as her day is too busy to take time out for lunch. She should request that Carol have a snack ready for her when she gets there at about four. When Carol pretends not to hear her, she should repeat herself, saying that after a busy day she is looking forward to the peace and quiet of Carol's place for about *forty-five minutes* before she has to go home and prepare dinner. No matter what Carol's response to this new procedure (and Phyllis should prepare herself for everything from fireworks to silence), she should repeat clearly when she is coming, how long she is staying, that she expects a snack from Carol, and hang up. If she has to hang up while Carol is talking, she should. If Carol calls back, she should answer once, repeat what she said with kindness, and then either leave the house or not answer the phone.

When Phyllis gets to Carol's house, she should be warm and caring, but she should stress how tired she is from her busy day, flop down at the table, and ask Carol to get her a cup of tea and a snack. If Carol is in bed, Phyllis should go to the bedroom, say hello, and then, repeating that she is hungry, return to the kitchen and make her own snack. She should do nothing for Carol except call to the bedroom for Carol to come out and join her. If Carol comes out and looks to be waited on, Phyllis should pay no attention and continue to eat her snack, except to suggest that if Carol wants something, she should make it and they can eat together. Phyllis should tell Carol that she was looking forward all day to one of Carol's goodies and that she is disappointed that Carol was in bed. All the while she should take the initiative and chatter about her interesting, but exhausting, day. As she talks, she should suggest a day and a time for her next visit. As Carol is healthy and ambulatory, Phyllis should try to arrange that next time they do something together away from the house.

She will get many distress calls between this time and the next. Carol will sense that she is losing control of Phyllis and may even make a trip to the local emergency room, complaining of shortness of breath, to punctuate her distress. Phyllis has to go when they call, but even there in the hospital, to begin the long process of teaching

Carol that she will not be controlled by dramatic moves like this, she should adhere to their plan to go out together.

In essence, Phyllis's plan is to move from "caring for" to "sharing with" Carol. Phyllis should insist that Carol do things for her and for herself, and back that insistence up by no longer doing for Carol as she has in the past. Each time she sees her, she should ask Carol to do something small or even fairly substantial that she can still do for Phyllis; for example, make some of her special apple cheese cake for Phyllis to take to a hospital where she volunteers. Phyllis should keep in mind that depressing is not a crippling choice unless it is treated as one. If Carol asks Phyllis to buy her something, Phyllis should counter, if it is at all feasible, by taking Carol to the store and letting her buy it for herself. If Carol has money, she should pay for what she buys. If Carol makes a fuss in a store or a restaurant, Phyllis should tell her that she will not take her out shopping for a month, or some other definite time, unless she stops fussing immediately. If she does not stop, Phyllis should cut the trip short and take her home.

The more Carol does for herself and Phyllis, the less she will depress, because as she regains control over her life, she will need less control over her daughter. Phyllis should encourage her to spend time with friends and get involved in activities, and back up these suggestions by helping Carol to make the definite plans that are necessary to get beyond talk. These should be extras in the sense that they should not take the place of time Phyllis spends with Carol, but they will become attractive to Carol when she realizes that what she is getting from Phyllis now is all she is going to get. She then has the choice of doing something enjoyable for herself or sitting home depressing. She will depress for a while before she makes a move to do something more effective, but when she finds out that she can depend on Phyllis for so much and no more, she will gradually stop depressing and make some moves. Phyllis has to be patient. This program to move Carol toward more-effective behaviors takes time, but my guess is that if Phyllis is consistent in doing what I suggest, she should see progress in less than six months.

Phyllis must be prepared to deal with the variety of new miseries that Carol will create as she becomes aware that she is losing control over Phyllis. Carol will headache, backache, and ache in any and all places that people have learned to ache. She will sick, and if she is a drinker (but not a drunk), she will drink more heavily. But if Phyllis keeps in mind the control theory she has learned, if she puts a picture in her album of herself being a good daughter but not a slave, she will get through the ordeal that Carol is putting her (and herself) through.

Above all, Phyllis should completely stop asking Carol how she feels. More than any other question, "How do you feel, Mom?" leads right into Carol's taking control. When they talk, Phyllis should ask her what she is doing or what she wants to do. She must not get involved discussing feelings with Carol unless Carol wants to talk about *good* feelings. As I explained in chapter 7, we cannot change how we feel if this component of our total behavior seems sensible —and depressing seems eminently sensible to Carol. To help Carol, Phyllis should focus on what Carol is doing and thinking, because these are components that she can change. Using control theory, old as well as young can be taught new ways, and when they learn them, they are the happier for it. I don't want to imply that this is an easy process, but it is easier than what Phyllis has been doing. For years she has chosen to escape into migraining to avoid what to her is the heavier pain of guilting when Carol's demands overwhelmed her. As she builds a different relationship with Carol, Phyllis's headaching will cease and she will have much more energy, since dealing with Carol is draining her.

While Carol is to some extent controlling her own anger at not being able to fulfill some of the pictures in her head, I would judge that most of her pain is directed at controlling Phyllis. There are, however, many people who choose a miserable behavior not so much to control others (although that is always a factor) but to control themselves, especially their angering (which frightens them) at not getting what they want from the world. More than most others, these people will find control theory hard to accept and very hard to put to work in their lives. I believe, however, that many of them could do it if they made the effort to learn how their misery keeps their angering in check. In chapter 7 I described several people besides Carol who also chose misery. The two who stand out as people who are attempting to control themselves are Terri, who washed compulsively, and Randy, the brilliant student who was afraid to go to class.

Terri has an unfulfilling marriage, as many people do. Her husband, Mr. Steady-But-Dull, has no intention of leaving her as Dave left Susan. He is satisfied being married to Terri. It is Terri who is so unsatisfied that she "has" to wash her hands compulsively fifty times a day with no awareness that this compulsive behavior is keeping her angering at her husband and her thoughts of infidelity in check. She has a picture of love and sex in her head that is not being fulfilled. She also has pictures of staying married for all the usual reasons: children, security, fear of the singles dating scene, and loyalty. But these pictures do not get her the love and the sex she desires.

She is in a false conflict—that is, a conflict that could be resolved with hard work—but her choice to wash has made her unaware of this most of the time. She says her marriage is not great but it would be better if she could get over her "compulsion." The truth is just the opposite: It is her "compulsion" that keeps her unaware of how unsatisfying her marriage is. If she is to regain control of her life, she must face the fact that the "something inside her" that compels her to wash her hands all day is that she is much more dissatisfied with her marriage than she is willing to admit to herself.

If she were able to learn about the pictures in her head, and that she is choosing, not compelled, to wash her hands, she might be able to take an honest look at the marriage she has and see how different it is from the marriage she wants. She may never be able to come to grips with the angering that she so quickly chooses when she has no effective way to satisfy the sexual urges from both of her brains, but she can learn that she has better choices to deal with her marriage than to wash her hands. Right now, as soon as she gets any awareness of the intense angering that bubbles just below the surface of her life, she washes and keeps it under crazy-clean control.

Like Susan, she must ask herself, "Is choosing to wash my hands getting me what I want from my life?" The answer, as I explained in the last chapter, is always no. In her case, however, unlike Susan's, she must also face the unhappy fact that from the sex and romance standpoint, her marriage may be seriously flawed. Susan was not dissatisfied with Dave when he was attentive, she was dissatisfied when he withdrew. Terri's husband does not withdraw. He is very much involved with her, but his involvement isn't her picture of the romantic man she wants. It is possible that he could learn to satisfy her more if she would tell him what she wants, but she has not been willing to do this so far. To her, it is totally unromantic to spell out her desires; a real lover would sense what she wants. It may be that she will never be able to convey her desires to him, but even if she could, he might still be unable to satisfy her. There are many times when, try as we may, we cannot satisfy the pictures, especially sexual pictures, in another person's head.

Theirs is a tragic but not uncommon marriage. There must, however, be better ways to handle her frustration besides handwashing, having an affair (she does flirt, which helps a little, but also frightens her because she has a stay-faithful filter in her camera), or dissolving the marriage. If she can learn control theory, she will begin to look for better ways than handwashing to deal with her frustration. For example, to satisfy her need for love, if not for sex, she could begin to do some volunteer work with teen-agers. She might find them so open and loving that she can get some vicarious satisfaction from being around them. If she finds a teen shelter or a halfway house, or gets involved with a community or church-related teen-age group, she may get love beyond her expectations as she shares with and helps the young people.

You might argue that this will not get her the sex and romance she craves, but you should again be aware that half a loaf is much better than none. If she shares vicariously or sublimates to get part of what she wants, she may be able to stop washing. She can also read romantic novels (millions of women like her have made Harlequin Books a wealthy company) or watch the daily soap operas on television. These may not work for her by themselves—they are too passive—but coupled with active involvement as a volunteer or paid worker with teen-agers, she may be able to drop her compulsion completely.

It may be that after a while as a volunteer, she will decide to go back to college to get a professional degree in counseling so she can work at a higher level. If she does, she will put so much energy into this satisfying unconflicted activity that for all practical purposes her "conflict" will be submerged. If her husband is sensible enough to listen to her successes and encourage her to go farther, it may even kindle or rekindle a little romance in their relationship.

However, as she stops handwashing and gets involved in all this activity, she may decide that she is now capable of ending her marriage, especially if she finds a man who gives her the romance she cannot get from her husband. Whether she does or not—and as many women like Terri stay as leave—now at least she has a chance to choose. As long as she was a "sick compulsive," she had no chance at all.

With the help of control theory, Terri could work to gain this understanding on her own, or she could get help. But with or without counseling, she must come to grips with the fact that although her marriage is far from the marriage in her head, choosing misery is an ineffective way to deal with this difference.

Randy, the business-school graduate student of chapter 7, was counseled, but if he'd had access to a book on control theory, it is possible that he would have been able to help himself. He was afraid to go to class his last year because he did not want to finish. If he finished, he would have to throw himself and his new skills on a world that he thought would not "give" him the high-level job that he pictured in his head. The counseling that worked with Randy was to help him to take control of his life in school, to deal with the intense "panic" and overwhelming "anxiety" that "grabbed" him when he entered any class. When he came for counseling, he was so out of control that he could not sit in a class for more than five minutes before he literally had to run out to regain a semblance of control.

This is not a book on counseling or psychotherapy, and the rich complexities of a successful counseling relationship cannot be described here. What I will explain is the essence of what went on that, following the control theory explained in this book, led Randy to regain control of his life. As soon as we got acquainted, I asked him if he wanted to graduate and get his M.B.A. degree. We spent some time establishing that, as far as both of us could judge, this was what he really wanted. I was aware that if a student was pursuing a course of study that was not the most desired picture in his head—perhaps because he was obeying a parent or studying for a lucrative but boring career—phobicking could be a way out. He insisted, however, that this was not the case—he very much wanted a career in business. Thus, it seemed sensible for us to plan what he could do to get his degree. He had to take control of the present, and we did not discuss the future extensively except to agree that if he did not graduate, the future would be less than satisfactory.

Together we made an action plan. He would tell his instructors that he was afraid to sit in class because he suffered from a phobia. We felt his teachers would be sympathetic if he told them this and also that he was being counseled for the problem, and they were. He asked their permission to sit in the back of the class near the open door and leave quietly if it became too difficult to stay. He told them he thought that in the empty hall he could pull himself together quickly so that if he left, it would be for only a few minutes. This simple plan, in which he regained some control—he could choose to come and go—of a previously out-of-control situation, worked. He almost never left class and he passed with "A" grades in both his courses.

But the plan went far beyond passing the courses. What he also discovered was that the pictures in his head demanded that he be perfect and were thus too strict. He was able to change these disabling pictures for less rigorous ones because it became apparent to him that when he told powerful (to him) people like his instructors about what he regarded as a serious flaw in himself—his phobia— they did not reject him; they valued him as a good student and went along with this reasonable plan. He now could see himself able to succeed in his field; jobs were not open only to perfect people—they were open to the less perfect like himself. He changed his picture to being less perfect so that when he looked at himself in the real world, he now saw a capable person who could talk to people in power and hold his own.

He got a good part-time job during school, stopped phobicking almost completely, and now, many years later, he experiences only short periods of discomfort in unfamiliar situations. He will never totally forget how to phobic. None of us seems able to forget these powerful behaviors. But he knows it is a choice, and that a better choice is always available if he will make the effort to figure one out. He is a big success in his career and is very much in control of his life now. To Randy, a plan to take some control of what seemed to him a totally out-of-control situation, and then to change his picture of what he had to be and still retain control, was the key.

Mary, whom I described in chapter 7, was also phobic; but unlike Randy and Terri, her phobicking was more to control others than to control herself. In this sense, she was more like Carol in that she chose to be afraid to leave the house as her means of controlling

George, her husband. Her phobicking covered up her fear that if she gave him any freedom at all, he might stray from the marriage. But unlike most people who phobic to control others, she did not so much want his love and support as she "enjoyed" exerting her power —the power of "agoraphobia" is immense. While she was not aware that this was what she was doing, she was aware that she neither loved nor respected him; she regarded him as a weakling because he was so much under her phobicking thumb. George finally got fed up with being at her disposal all day long, even at work, and left her; and because she did not need him except to use him, she had no further reason to phobic. She thought of replacing George with her daughter, but fortunately her daughter was smart enough not to rush in to take George's place. Mary decided in a matter of a few weeks to stop phobicking and start living.

If she had loved George, or if she had needed him to take care of her, she would not have stopped phobicking. When George left, she would have stayed home and starved until someone in the family or some social agency stepped in. Phobickers do not usually stop, as Mary did, because most of them are much more dependent than she was. What she got from George was someone she could push around, but as the years passed, this was no longer satisfying. When George unexpectedly showed a little spunk and left, she was "surprised" at how happy she chose to be without him.

While Mary is unusual as a phobicker, she well illustrates the control-theory point that *when our choice to be miserable does not get us what we want, and we believe that a better choice is possible, we will quickly give up our misery.* Mary differs from most phobickers in that she believed a better choice was possible—most phobickers don't. As I said in chapter 7, to her friends Mary's cure may have seemed miraculous, but Mary had some insight into why she needed George and she was lucky he left. No miracles were involved in her "cure."

In this country there are many people who behave like Mary, Terri, and Randy. They firmly believe that they are suffering from a disease, and almost all of them believe that their only hope to be "cured" is by drugs or by a counselor who accepts that they are suffering from a mental illness. As long as they believe that they are sick, and are treated and regarded as sick, they maintain control through their "disability" and get worse, not better. The problem is that almost all of the treatment offered to them either supports their "sickness" or teaches them that they are "sick" if they do not already believe it. Nowhere is this better illustrated than in the case of Richard, the insurance adjuster who "snapped" his back at work and has remained incapacitated for the past four years. He has had three back surgeries, over $150,000 in medical care, his back hurts worse than ever, and it is doubtful that he will ever return to work.

When Richard hurt his back, he chose to continue to backache long after it healed, because painful as it was, he gained a degree of control over his life that he had never experienced before. As long as he continued to backache, he was able to control many physicians representing a wide group of medical specialties, from neurosurgeons to physiatrists,* as well as a large cast of supporting medical personnel ranging from nurses to physical therapists. This huge and expensive treatment team, which probably numbers over twenty skilled people, is completely analogous to Phyllis, who by herself was Carol's whole treatment team. The reason I draw this analogy is to point out that although these teams are similar, there is one vital difference. Richard wants to control the medical team that is treating him, but they also want to be controlled by him (really by his backache). This is because a large part of their living is derived from being controlled by countless people like him. Phyllis, on the other hand, hates being controlled by Carol and will jump at a chance to learn control theory so that she can teach Carol more-effective choices and escape from her control.

If the treatment team "controlled" by Richard had embraced the control theory of this book, Richard would have had no surgery, no extensive medical care, and his medical expenses would have not amounted to more than a fraction of what has been spent and may still be spent, as Richard is far from "cured." There are many ways —like giving him Amytal and seeing him do deep knee bends to diagnose the fact that he is not physically disabled and needs to be counseled to take control of his life without backaching. But Richard's chances of getting the care he needs are remote at this time because the people he controls with his backache have a vested

---

*Physicians who specialize in the rehabilitation of the physically disabled.

interest in being controlled. It is analogous to giving an alcoholic alcohol, telling him it is good for him, and then wondering why he does not stop drinking.

Lawyers are another group of powerful and expensive people whom Richard controls with his backache. They, too, like nothing better than to be controlled by people like him, so he now has access to prestigious law offices where good lawyers treat him as if his backache were the most important thing in the world. He cannot fail to be impressed by the power he has that has moved all these people to get him $150,000 worth of treatment—and because he still hurts, they will get him more if they think they can. Financially, the sky is the limit for medical care, and the more he receives, the greater the lawyers' fees. Even if his doctors are beginning to believe that he is more in need of counseling than surgery, the lawyers will find other doctors who will offer him further surgery or expensive physical therapy.

Richard also has a sense of control over his employer and his wife and family. In short, for four years the whole world has revolved around his backache. In all this time, Richard has hardly seen a bill for all these services—the bills go to his lawyer. And as long as he continues to choose to backache, all this powerful and complicated "therapeutic" machinery continues to operate.

Even if a counselor is finally called in, she is starting with many strikes against her. She has to teach Richard to choose a better way to live his life, which means giving up the paining. But Richard by now has a vested interest in all that his paining gets for him and he is unwilling to give it up and return to his humdrum job. In the end he will get over some of his backache when the workman's-compensation insurance company finally settles his case. When he realizes that he no longer has any control through backaching, and if he has not been injured by the three surgeries or become addicted to pain-killing medication, he will figure out a way to get better. Once someone like Richard is injured in a compensable accident, through which legal and treatment teams have a vested interest in being controlled by his pain, machinery is set in motion that seems almost impossible to stop. As I worked for years with many Richards, it seemed to me that once these great medical and legal mills started to grind, it was only the sore back that was important; the fact that it was only a part of a whole man seemed incidental to the process.

In most cases, if you have controlled others or yourself through choosing pain or disability, you can expect little help from anyone who views you as sick. You will get help only from a counselor or family member who understands what you are choosing to do with your life, won't let you control him or her with it, and helps you to find the better choices that are always available. In the beginning you will bitterly resent anyone who does not support your "illness" and thus escapes from your control. People will give you this book to read and you will resent both them and the book because if you accept what is written, you will have to consider giving up the tremendous control you have gained through the painful life you have been choosing for so long.

Whenever you give up control, even painful control, it is neither easy nor quick to replace what you have "lost." Like a drug addict without drugs, there is a painful period that you will choose to suffer through as you learn to make better choices with your life. The best thing you can do is stay close to anyone who does not believe you are sick. These are your best friends and they will see you through the period of transition from pain to responsibility. It is also your responsibility, if you want to stop miserabling, to take the initiative and tell your friends, relatives, and even professional helpers that you are not sick and you do not want to be treated as sick. What you need is their help and support as you learn to work and play without pain or disability. You need laughter, not self-indulgent paining; companionship, not sympathy; and personal accomplishment, not dependence on those who earn a living from your misery.

20
Taking Control of Our Health

Health care is delivered in this country in a way that causes almost all of us to experience a marked loss of control when we go to a physician for treatment. Except in unusual circumstances, our only responsibility is to present ourselves to the physician as sick. It is then her responsibility to treat us or to direct us to treatment that will make us well or as close to well as is possible. There is little or nothing in the present system, either in theory or practice, that encourages, or even expects, the patient to participate actively in his treatment, because almost all control is removed from the patient and relegated to the physician.

But as I explained in chapter 12, most of the long-term diseases we suffer, such as heart disease or rheumatoid arthritis, are psychosomatic in origin; they are caused by our losing control over our lives. Because our present medical delivery system, which concentrates almost solely on physical causes and treatments, has nothing to do with helping us to regain control over our lives, it is generally ineffective for these diseases. It follows, therefore, that the most effective treatment for psychosomatic diseases is what we can do for ourselves to regain control, not what our doctors can do for us. For example, Alan, whom I discussed in chapter 12, suffered a heart attack and remained disabled even after coronary bypass surgery because his life was and continued to be out of control. He would have been much better off if he had depended upon his physician less and himself more.

Alan's heart attack did not come without warning. He had been examined regularly by his physician, and while he had no obvious signs of heart disease prior to the attack, he did complain of fatigue and not feeling fit. His blood pressure was on the high side of normal, and the blood chemistries that are thought to be related to heart disease were also in the high-normal range. Still, he got a "clean bill of health," accompanied by his doctor's friendly admonition to take it a little easier and keep in close touch if he developed any alarming symptoms.

His physician did not inquire into the way he was presently choosing to live his life, nor what he might do to take more effective control over a life that a little inquiry would have revealed was seriously out of control. Alan's doctor may have sensed that Alan would not have been receptive to such an inquiry, and he may not have wanted to take the time and make the effort to stray from pure medical treatment and try to teach Alan what is presently well known that may prevent a heart attack. So in a sense both Alan and his doctor unwittingly "conspired" to set the stage for his attack. Alan's mistake was to depend totally on his doctor for things that his doctor could not do—prevent his heart attack by treating him medically—and would not do—take the time to inquire into his life and prescribe a psychological, physical-exercise, and nutritional program that might slow or stop his progressive heart disease by helping him get his whole life back under control.

Had Alan been willing to take the initiative and broach the subject of a total preventive program, it is likely that his physician would have cooperated with him or referred him to a medical program that took these important health measures into account. If Alan had known control theory, he would have taken this initiative and not settled for the strict medical care that did not prevent his heart attack. If his physician did not want to cooperate in getting actively involved in such a necessary program, Alan would have taken control of his own health by initiating most of this on his own (which anyone can) and making an active effort to find a doctor who believed in these sound preventive measures. This is not to say that any one thing he might have done would have guaranteed the prevention of a heart attack, but there is much evidence that when we change the way we live our lives, we can reduce and even prevent heart disease.

To take control of our health, we have to give up the traditional idea that when we get sick our physicians can cure us. The fact that doctors do cure some (not much) serious noninfectious illnesses is helpful to our health but still does not make the he'll-cure-us approach valid. A major part of our total responsibility is to be responsible for our own health. Physicians should serve as expert consultants to supplement what we can learn by ourselves that will preserve our health. If we get sick, we should not abandon the basic premise that we, not our doctors, are responsible. As much as we are physically or mentally able, we should remain in charge of our own care, with the doctor consulting with us more actively in time of illness. What is important is that we not behave one way when well and another when sick, but that the approach continue to be the same. We are always in charge; we may accept more treatment when we are sick than when we are well, but we never turn our lives over to others. When we do, we lose control, and *if effective control is essential to health—and I believe it is*—we lose the best chance we have to get well and stay well.

We also have to face the fact that although there are exceptions, like holistic medicine, our present system could be more accurately characterized as as a sick-care system than a health-care system. This is because the present payoff for the whole system is in treating sickness; there is little or no reward, financial or psychological, for maintaining or increasing health. When you visit the huge hospitals that seem to dot all of our cities, you cannot escape the conclusion that these massive institutions exist because they "serve" a stream of sick people who are difficult or impossible to cure. If sick people were easily or quickly cured, most of these hospitals would wither away. It is my belief that most sick people are difficult to cure because they are suffering from psychosomatic disease. What is presently offered by the medical establishment removes all treatment responsibility from the patients, but in doing so removes the most important element in the treatment of these diseases: the patients' ability to control their own lives.

Neither Alan nor any of us can wait until the medical establishment begins to accept and teach all of us that responsibility for health, and even for treatment when there is illness, is more the patient's than the doctor's. If this is to take place, it must be initiated by the consumer. There is neither financial nor personal incentive (doctors and hospitals will lose power) for any major part of the medical establishment to do this now. A medical consumer who has put control theory to work in his or her life will be a person who is prepared to get this process started. Just as the American auto industry improved their product because consumers refused to buy poorly built cars and turned to imports, we must refuse to accept a medical delivery system that does not recognize that to be healthy, we must take prime responsibility for our own health. When we do, the system will slowly begin to change from sickness care to health maintainance, and our medical bills, which are astronomical under the present sick-care system, will shrink substantially. But, again, this is not the fault of the medical establishment alone; it is our fault for letting others be responsible for our lives.

If Alan had known control theory, he would have been better prepared to pay attention to the fact that he did not feel well for a long time prior to his heart attack. The reason he did not pay attention was that he was frightened. Not knowing that there was much he could do to improve his health, he tried to deny the mild but indicative symptoms like a little chest pain and occasional shortness of breath. He relied on his doctor's vague advice to "take it easy" and "keep in touch" and he tried to reassure himself that his doctor was correct (as he was) in his opinion that at the time of Alan's last examination he was not sick. But Alan was an intelligent man and he knew that there is a big difference between not being sick and being in good health. Alan was not in good health long before his heart attack; and as his once healthy coronary arteries slowly eroded and clogged, he still was not sick, by the standards of current medical practice, until the attack. If he'd had a health program to turn to while he still had fairly good coronary-artery circulation, he might have prevented his heart attack.

Actually, there are many good programs, but, it is easy to see, they are all based on the premise that we must take control of our own lives and, in doing so, our own health. In Alan's case, if he had known control theory, he would likely have done much more to take control of his out-of-control work situation. From his control-theory knowledge of criticism, he would have recognized that if he didn't do something to improve the relationship between himself and J.B., his health would be in jeopardy. He knew J.B. as well as anyone did, and in one of J.B.'s more relaxed and expansive moments Alan could have approached him and asked if they could talk. He would have prepared for this talk by writing down carefully all the very considerable contributions he was making to the success of the business, and when he got together with J.B., he would have ticked these off one by one. Then he could have asked J.B. what else he could do to make the business more successful. No matter what J.B. said, he should have written it down. Then he should have told J.B. kindly but firmly that he felt they were not getting along as well as he would like. No matter what J.B. then said—and it is doubtful that he would have said much to this obviously truthful assertion—Alan should have asked him what they could do to make their relationship better.

At this point J.B. would probably have had little to say, but if he said anything, Alan should have let him talk and listened. Alan should then have given J.B. a copy of the list and told him that if he wasn't doing what was on this list as well as J.B. wished, he would like to talk again privately, and that he had enjoyed the opportunity to get together with him. If J.B. continued to attack him in front of others, as was his practice, the next time he did, Alan would tell him that they must talk privately about the specific problem, then walk away. He would tell J.B. that these public attacks upset him, and if he is upset, he does not work efficiently. He might (though it is very unlikely) have gotten fired for this regaining-control approach, but losing a job is better than having a heart attack. Much more likely, however, J.B. would respect his polite assertiveness and begin to pick on someone else.

Just as there is nothing in control theory that says we should choose misery or get sick, there is no reason to remain passive when we are attacked. The best thing to do is defend ourselves sensibly, as I suggest. If we choose to remain psychologically passive, as Alan did, we may lose our health. Once Alan learns control theory, he will be acutely aware of when his life is out of control and he will be ready to do something sensible to remedy it. No matter how sensitive to psychological factors Alan's doctor is, he cannot solve Alan's problems for him. Sympathetic listening will help temporarily, and encouraging Alan to face his work problems is even more helpful. But the responsibility is still Alan's. He, not his doctor or J.B., is in charge of his life.

The most difficult place to retain control over your life is in a hospital, yet doing so may be vital to your recovery. You should not be passive but take an active interest in all that is being done for you. You should insist that your doctor explain all procedures and that you understand what is going on. If you disagree, you should voice your disagreement. It is not presumptuous to ask the doctor to give you a good reason for what is done that makes little sense to you. You are not in the hospital to protect tradition or the the medical establishment; you are there to find out all you can to help get yourself get well. You should be especially sensitive to getting rest and should insist that procedures be coordinated so that you are not continually disturbed. You have a right to expect that the hospital procedures serve you, not them, and it's especially important that you not acquiesce passively while angering inside. Your old brain is working hard enough to get you well; it does not need the added hormonal and chemical burden of anger or fatigue.

You should also do as much as you can for yourself. If there is any way you can help the nurses or aides with your treatment, the more you do, the more effective the treatment will be. The passivity and dependency fostered by most hospital treatment are your enemies and you must be as active as you can be. Think as much as possible in terms of what you can *do* and as little as possible about how you *feel*. Avoid talking about your feelings to those who visit, because if you see your misery is controlling them, it will be hard to stop choosing more misery even as you are getting physically better. The key again: Keep as much control as possible. Your ability to control your life even when seriously ill is your best chance for health. How to stay in control when you are acutely ill is well described in Norman Cousins's new book, *The Healing Heart,* * in which he recounts his personal battle to remain in control when he suffered a severe heart attack. You can learn much from this valuable book.

When you leave the hospital, work out a detailed recovery plan

---

*Norman Cousins, *The Healing Heart* (New York: W. W. Norton, 1983).

with your doctor and follow it. Now you have a chance to be in charge, and you should do everything you can to avail yourself of this chance. If you have to stay home, do not stay in bed unless you don't have the strength to get up. Get dressed and engage yourself in some worthwhile activity. When you get tired, go back to bed and rest or nap until you feel refreshed. Push to the limits of your physical restrictions and always ask the doctor if you can do more. Question the value of any long-term medication, and do not take any addicting drug, such as Valium, for a protracted period. Try to use as little medication as possible, because all medication has dangers. But if you are convinced that the medicine prescribed for you has value, take it faithfully for as long as it can be justified to you that you need it.

To be healthy is far different from not being sick. Health means to feel good, strong, alert, rested, mentally sharp, and physically active. Health means to look forward to challenge, both mental and physical. It means time passes quickly rather than dragging. Only you can assess your health. Doctors can only tell you that you have no observable illness, which is a far cry from health. To be healthy, you must have good control of your life; and to help you maintain this control, it is important to have a regular relaxing time each day, which I would like to call an "in-control time." It does not matter what you do—a pleasant nap, a long hot shower, a regular after-work get-together, even a hard tennis game can be very relaxing. But whatever it is that you do, for at least thirty minutes each day you should try to do exactly what you want to do.

For example, remember a time when you were playing Monopoly and had hotels all over the board? Almost every roll of the dice brought in money, and you were safe almost everywhere you landed. Even though you were the obvious winner, you went on playing, magnanimously lending money and taking over distressed property from the other players. You chose to be so relaxed, so generous, and so easy to get along with because you were in control. Your needs for power, fun, and belonging were being wonderfully met by winning this ingenious game, and if you had a cold when you started, you probably didn't even blow your nose as long as you were winning.

To be healthy, we need times like this, and one important lack in Alan's life was that he did not take this important daily in-control time. He tended to be intimidated by J.B. into working late, and then hurried home to a family that was often disgruntled because he was late. He would then anger at them because they didn't understand what he was going through with J.B. One of the important things he has to negotiate with J.B. is better working hours. He needs more time off or he never will get this daily relaxation that we all need to be healthy. Alan, being highly competitive, will probably choose to relax with a competitive game like tennis or racquetball. If so, he must play with people who are about equal to him in skill; otherwise, the pain of losing or the boredom of easy winning will take much of the benefit out of the activity. For any game to be an in-control activity, however, the game itself, regardless of winning or losing, has to be enjoyable. It is hard for any game to be consistently satisfying if we don't win our fair share.

But beyond winning, what makes any game satisfying enough for it to be an in-control activity is that we must enjoy the company of the people we play with. While learning, I played tennis for years with a man who beat me consistently, but I was so grateful that such a good player was patient enough to play with me that for a long time losing was satisfying. He was not only a scrupulously fair player who called all the lines accurately, but also the kind of person I enjoyed talking with between sets. Therefore, if our in-control time is an activity that involves others, they have to be satisfying to be with even if some days the activity does not work out well. There is no guarantee that any game—tennis, golf, or even cards—will be good, so for the game to be an in-control time, there must be a guarantee that the people with whom we play are consistently enjoyable.

Whatever the activity, the time we spend doing it has to be long enough for us to relax completely. It must also be a time when the difference between what we want and what we have is so small that we feel no urge to do anything else. As the new brain relaxes, the whole body will also relax. Even strenuous exercise can be a mentally relaxing activity if it is what we want to do at the time. There is obviously no set minimum of in-control time that is right for everyone, but my guess is that for good health we all could use a half-hour a day, and more would be better. If it is regular, however, even five minutes of complete relaxation can do wonders for a busy person, such as a mother with small children. For those lucky enough to be able to do it, a three-minute catnap can provide invaluable relaxation also.

For the in-control time to be effective, what we do must satisfy a single clear picture in our heads and never be a time when we experience any conflict. For example, if I want to play tennis, I play with nothing else in mind. If I want to sit and gaze at the TV, this is what I do and all I do. It does not have to be the same activity each day, but it must occur each day, and if it is with others, whatever the activity, they must all be people we enjoy. If we use alcohol during this time (many people like a drink to help them "unwind" when the day is over), then the situation where we drink, either home or at a bar, must be so satisfying that even if we choose not to drink, we still feel in control. Alcohol can enhance the in-control time, but if alcohol is *needed* to get the relaxed feeling of control, this would not be the healthy in-control time I am trying to describe.

Many people have asked me if sex would fulfill these requirements. The answer is that if it is satisfying to both partners, it would be an excellent in-control time. But since sexual satisfaction depends so much on so many factors that are hard to control, if I were looking for an in-control-time activity, I would not depend completely on sex; it is a wonderful extra to add to our in-control time. Few of us have too much relaxation, but we should depend on activities that are much more under our control than an intimate relationship usually is. Reading, especially before bedtime, is an example of an activity that is almost completely under our control. We can do it almost every night, and if it is satisfying, it fulfills the requirements for this time perfectly. On the other hand, while going to the theater or to concerts is very enjoyable, there are so many real frustrations attached to these complex activities, like great expense and mediocre performances, that they cannot be depended upon to provide the regular in-control time we need.

Whatever the activity or activities, they should neither depend completely on a certain person nor require a great deal of effort or expense to carry out. This means that if you play tennis or golf, you can afford to play, you can take the time to play, and you have a few regular people that you enjoy playing with. In-control time can also be a hobby that you devote yourself to regularly and that you occasionally share with others; but the hobby, not the others, must provide the satisfaction. This is why there are so many hobbies—they all provide this time easily on a regular basis.

Although I don't do it regularly, I am walking the dog more than I used to and I find this to be an excellent in-control time. I write mostly at home, and when I am tired of working, I take the hound for a walk and feel relaxed and renewed after a half-hour stroll down the same street. It is a welcome break from what I am doing, and as a willing companion the dog is perfect: She has never turned down an invitation to a walk and I don't expect that she ever will.

With this brief description, you should have no difficulty understanding what an in-control activity is, but, keep in mind, it is easy to persuade yourself that you have this kind of a time when you may not. It is more than a rest, a game, or time away from work; it is a daily time when you feel a deep sense of control because you are doing what you want to do and no one is disputing your right to do it.

It is much harder to find this time without chemicals than most of us realize. Would all of the good times you see on the television beer commercials be that good if there were no beer? Does your game—for example, bowling or poker—provide you with relaxation and the feeling of control, or does it frequently frustrate you because the ball does not go where you want it to go or the cards come up wrong too often? Are you willing to make the effort to find the good books and magazines that make reading in bed a high point of the day, a time you look forward to with pleasure?

I believe that not nearly enough of us have this in-control time now. Let's say that both you and your spouse have had a hard and unsatisfying day at work. This does not mean you have bad jobs; it means that few jobs can come close to providing eight hours of satisfying work. As the day progresses, you begin to accumulate a series of frustrations, and at the end of the day these frustrations still rankle. They are not in themselves overwhelming, but, like straws on the camel's back, as they add up, they get heavy. To relieve yourselves of these work frustrations, both of you need some time to unwind, and you are both hoping to get this time as soon as you get home. You recognize that there will be more frustrations at home, but before you deal with these, you want to unload the ones you have from work. You are well aware that there is a limit to how great a load of frustration you can carry at one time without losing control and then choosing to anger, depress, or behave in some other potentially destructive way in an attempt to regain it. We all find ourselves snapping at our spouses or kids, not because what they are doing is particularly "frustrating" but because we add what they are doing to an already heavy load of minor irritations. The whole family has a chance for a better evening together if, for example, one unwinds with tennis while the other soaks away the cares of the day in a hot tub. Here common sense is good control theory.

Effective as it is, regular in-control time has limitations: It will not relieve you of major problems. If your marriage is on the rocks, or your child is very ill, or you missed an important promotion, you will not be able to get this out of your mind because you play tennis or stop after work for a happy hour or two. You must do something active as Alan did when he talked to J.B. A good in-control activity will buy you a little time while you plan, but it is no substitute for satisfying specific pictures in your head. As explained in great detail in chapter 7, it is possible to be extremely frustrated and not sick. There are plenty of painful feeling behaviors like depressing or headaching that we can use to gain some control. But when you are depressing or headaching, you are not healthy as I defined *health* earlier in this chapter.

CREATIVE IN-CONTROL TIME

When I was doing the research for my 1976 book, *Positive Addiction,* * I became aware that inside of us, if we learn how to tap it, we have a great source of potential strength. Certain simple activities that are actually meditations, such as regular relaxed running, may enable us to tap this potential to the extent that running has helped heavy drinkers to become recovering alcoholics, lifelong migraine headachers to stop migraining, and even those suffering from progressive coronary artery disease to slow the progression. Runners, to cite just one large group of positive addicts that I studied, not only gained a great deal of physical strength and health,

*William Glasser, *Positive Addiction* (New York: Harper & Row, 1976).

which was to be expected, but significantly increased their mental strength through, I believe, gaining greater access to the constant creativity that is inside us all.

I do not want to imply that to be creative we *need* to become positively addicted; most highly creative people are not. And meditating does not guarantee that we will gain any useful creativity. Driven by the differences between the pictures in our heads and what we have, we all tap our creativity all the time, and many times with powerful results. Sitting relaxed and happy at this word processor —which, for me, takes all the drudgery out of writing—I constantly get new ideas. I gear myself to pay attention to them, and when they come, I often use them. This also happens when I am lecturing to an attentive and supportive group. New ideas constantly and surprisingly pop into my mind, some of them very useful and many of them very funny.

I believe that all of us can gain greater access to our creativity by paying attention to what it constantly provides. Most of the time, however, we are so busy that we either don't pay attention or distrust our creativity. In fact, one of the main differences between great and ordinary people may be that great people pay close attention to their innate creativity and give careful consideration to what it offers. But as we can rarely be too creative, a positive-addiction activity can add a small but important dimension to our lives that is worth considering.

Not all runners or other meditators are sufficiently relaxed and self-accepting to reach the meditative state of mind that gives them access to their creativity. They (runners especially) go after this elusive mental process as if it is an uphill race that they must win, and if they do not reach the "standard" they are striving for, they criticize themselves and push themselves in a quest for ever-increasing achievement. This may satisfy their need for power, and may even become a compulsive behavior to make up for frustrations in their lives, but it does not provide the relaxed self-acceptance that gives them the relaxed and satisfying sense of achievement that is needed for the activity to become positively addicting.

For example, a good way to tell a meditating runner from a compulsive or competitive runner is that the meditator rarely mentions her activity, because she values its creative privacy, whereas the competitive runner may talk of little else. His shoes, his times, his diet, his body-fat-to-muscle ratios are all his attempts to call attention to the importance of his running. The meditating runner may also race on occasion, but most of her runs are for the sake of running. She prefers to run alone or in the company of another noncompetitor like herself. Many runners, however, do both: They run mostly for meditation, but also race or run an occasional marathon. Recognizing the difference between the two kinds of running, they keep them separate.

The regular pleasure that can become addicting is the same pleasure you gain when you unexpectedly gain access to your creative process during a time when you are relaxed and in good control. Think of how much fun it is to brainstorm or even just relax and talk to good friends who will listen to your fantasies without putting you down. In all this pleasant activity, the main source of the pleasure is creativity. When we are thinking creatively, we may come up with a worthless or even destructive new behavior, but because there is no need to use it, it comes and goes as a passing thought. Any creative thought that passes through our awareness, however, may be valuable. If we are able to put it into practice, it may help us to gain greater control.

Getting involved in a positively addicting activity is analogous to getting an opportunity to play a slot machine without putting in money: We may win and we cannot lose. Positive addicts gain access to their creativity, which is always both pleasurable and potentially strengthening, but are under no pressure to use this access unless it seems to be helpful now or later. Keep in mind, however, that creativity is not necessarily good; all it is necessarily is new. But creativity gained through a positive addiction has a chance to be very good because, *being in good control,* we will use only creative behaviors that are constructive. Only when our lives are seriously *out of control* will we, in desperation, accept and put into practice a creative mental or physiological behavior that is crazy or causes disease.

Positive addictions do not come easily or quickly. If you start to run on a regular basis hoping to become positively addicted, you should be aware that for the first six months, at least, you have little chance to reach this desirable goal. What you will get in just a few weeks, however, is a very healthful in-control activity. Assuming that you enjoy running and run after work, it is relaxing and the small frustrations of the day quickly drift away. If you run in the morning, you will start out with a clean frustration slate, fresh and ready for work.

But if you make the effort to run regularly three times a week for at least forty-five minutes, after a minimum of six months, but sometimes not for several years, you *may* become positively addicted to this activity. There is no guarantee that you will ever become positively addicted, but if you do, what started as a good in-control activity has evolved into an even better creative in-control activity. Many good in-control activities—like a hot bath, or a social drink after work—will never become positively addicting, because they do not take enough effort or concentration. It is the effort of running and swimming, or the high concentration of a good meditation or yoga exercise, that wipes out all on your mind but what you're doing and thus sets the stage for you to reach a positive addiction. If you succeed in reaching it, it does more than sweep away minor frustrations of the day: It gives you easy access to your creativity. This in turn can provide you with a small, but still significant, amount of additional strength to help deal with any problems you may have in your life.

To understand this process, keep in mind that creativity is so vital to our survival that our creative systems never turn off. Take a close look at anything you do regularly and you will notice that you almost never do anything twice in exactly the same way. Our creative systems are continually offering us what may be improvements, and usually without awareness we try them out. If they work, as they often do, we add them to our behavior with little conscious knowledge that we have done so. But beyond this we are frequently surprised by totally unexpected flashes of creativity which also confirm that our creative systems are always active.

I believe that it is to gain access to this creativity that people have for centuries been engaged in a variety of behaviors that are called "meditations." This means that meditations can be physically active, like running or swimming; or physically inactive but mentally concentrating, like Zen; or a combination of both, like yoga. But active or inactive, they must be single-minded enough that you can do them with no distraction or they will not work.

Running, for example, is satisfying because runners start with the picture in their heads that they need more exercise. Running becomes a way to get into shape, and they put pictures in their albums of themselves running regularly at least three times a week. It takes time and effort to build endurance, but there is no skill involved; we all know how to run, and any way we do it that is comfortable is good enough. If you are in normal health and run regularly at least three times a week for about forty-five minutes, in three months you should be able to run about five miles in less than an hour. You are not going fast, but even if it takes an hour, it's twice as fast as walking. For running to be a meditation, the first thing to learn is that fast or far is not important; what is necessary is that you run easily. All you need to do is put forth enough effort so that four or five slow miles pass before you know it.

If you keep running, your endurance will slowly continue to increase, but how much you eventually gain is not important. What is important is that you see yourself as a good runner gaining in endurance to the point where the miles float easily by and you look forward to your daily run. You will never reach the pleasurable level of positive addiction if you push yourself, because this means that on many days you will be dissatisfied. An addicted runner has good endurance, but she is contented and does not compete with herself or others. As you continue to run, and believe more and more that you are achieving what you set out to do, you find yourself in almost perfect control as you move easily over the ground. Now, on a regular basis, the runner that you see in the real world is identical to the runner in your album.

Because this activity, while it takes effort, requires little or nothing from your mind, it soon becomes an easy, routine, old-brain activity that even the old brain "enjoys." If you are satisfied to run for months and months in this relaxed state of complete control, you begin to experience short periods of time when you seem to lose track of what you are doing. You find that you have covered ground that you do not remember covering. It is not that you were unconscious, but that during the easy, routine rhythm of the run your mind slipped away from what you were doing and began to wander by itself. You may also notice a train of thought or a series of thoughts that are totally different from the way you usually think. As you come out of these brief states, things around you may take on a better appearance: Trees, flowers, even sidewalks and alleys may begin to look different and more appealing.

What has happened is that for a brief period you were in the positive-addiction or meditation state of mind. You were tapping directly into your creative system. You were mostly aware of it through new thoughts, but you also noticed that for a minute or two, or even a little longer, you felt very good, even ecstatically high. Physically you may get the feeling of power and confidence. It's as if something good has been added to your being that was not there before. For some runners this may not happen while running but immediately afterward, when they are in the state of exhilarated relaxation that usually follows a satisfying workout.

When this happens—and it does not happen often or for long for even the most dedicated runners or other meditators—you begin to become aware of your own creative system. New thoughts, feelings, and even the suggestion of new behaviors filter into your awareness. Most of these are worthless, but even the brief glimpse into your own undiluted creativity seems to provide a sense of power and confidence that is almost always accompanied by a release of natural opiates that you feel as a burst of pleasure.

Easy running is now so effortless, it is as if you are doing nothing, and it is just this state of effortless achievement, where all that is active is your creative system, that is the meditative state of mind that you are trying to achieve. As simple as it is to describe, this is not an easy state to reach. The Zen masters have worked for centuries to find ways to reach this state, which they call *satori,* where for a short time you and the world are at total peace—or, in control-theory terms, where the pictures in your head and the world meld together as if they were one, and creativity is all there is.

You may never realize that you are using the additional creativity to which you now have access, but I am sure you do all the time. And as you continue to practice this creative in-control activity, the altered state of mind lasts longer, sometimes for fifteen or twenty minutes. Runners and other meditators report that when they are in this state, they get creative flashes that solve problems they were not even aware they were pondering. They admit a lot of creative garbage pops in also, but they separate the creative wheat from the chaff and admit that they even enjoy the chaff. And down the road —who knows? What seems now to be chaff may turn out to be good grain. As they continue, they find that their minds become fascinating places to visit and they look forward to these little trips into their own creativity.

Do not feel that you will live any less effectively if you do not have a regular creative in-control time. Unlike an in-control time, which I believe we all need, a creative in-control time, while good, is hardly essential. It is, however, an important control-theory concept that is well worth knowing if you are looking for ways to add strength to your life.

21
How to Start Using Control Theory

I hope you now understand my explanation of control theory, but I realize that it is a big step from *reading* what may make sense to you to *using* the ideas in your life. The key to taking this step is not to attempt to make any quick changes in your life. In the beginning, just attempt to look at people around you through a control-theory filter. As you do, the theory will start to become more alive, and what you see people doing, thinking, and feeling more understandable. Then begin to look at your own life in the same way, and with little effort you should find yourself beginning to put control theory to work in your life.

Let me give you a simple-to-understand example of what I mean when I say "Look at people around you." My wife and I attend many of the nearby university's football and basketball games. The stands are filled with people like ourselves, loyal to the home team, but there is always a small, vociferous group loyal to the opposition. All of us are attempting to satisfy our needs for power, belonging, and fun, and for this we have pictures in our heads of our team winning. When it does win, we choose to feel very good because we are now very much in control. If our team loses, most of us choose to depress for a short time to control our anger. One mildly inebriated fan, after we won a big game, offered the disconsolate losing fans a jagged broken bottle as they filed out, saying, "Here, you can use this if you want to cut your throat." We all laughed at him, but this simple situation where control is clearly tied to winning is a good place to observe the variety of feeling behaviors that we all choose when we gain or lose control of our lives. We cheer to encourage our team to greater effort and scream with joy when they do something well. But thousands of us become silent as we lapse into total depressing when our team loses in the final seconds. I cite this game example because everything is so clear-cut and understandable. There is no conflict, and if we win, we satisfy a very definite picture in our heads almost perfectly.

As you observe control theory in many obvious situations, you will naturally begin to extend this observation to your own life. If you observe yourself failing to get a promotion that you wanted, you will see yourself behaving in much the same way you did when your team lost a "crucial" game. The picture in your head was not satisfied, you were frustrated, and you chose to depress because you lost control. But unlike the game, where the picture of winning fades rapidly, the picture of the promotion persists. If you had settled for just reading the book and not observed a lot of control theory as it operates in the people around you, you would find it difficult to stop depressing and easy to blame the boss for your upset. But after you have seen others make a lot of painful choices, you become better able to see yourself choosing what you are now feeling.

You know that if the picture in your head of being promoted is not satisfied, and you do not want to change this picture, you have no option but to behave in an attempt to get the promotion you want. You also know that you are choosing your behavior just as you chose to cheer or depress at the game. You are well aware that the course of your life is determined by the pictures you want at the time, and that you will not give up trying to satisfy these pictures even though, for lack of something better, you may resort to painful or self-destructive behaviors.

As you look at people you know, first try to figure out what the important pictures in their heads are. You may not know exactly what they may be—most situations are not as transparent as a football game—but everyone is always behaving to satisfy his or her pictures, and as you observe their behavior, try to guess at what the current pictures might be. Notice how difficult it is for people to change their pictures even though what they want is impossible to obtain. Keep thinking about the pictures you want and see how many pictures you are keeping in your album that you have little or no chance to satisfy. Remember that of all the pictures, the only one that cannot be changed or removed is the picture to breathe. Ask yourself, "Am I choosing to be a slave to a picture I can't satisfy?"

Then look at the behavior of the people you are watching. You may have to guess the pictures, but you don't have to guess behaviors. Whether you know control theory or not, it is obvious that all the happy "crazy" behaviors you see at a game are chosen. What you have learned that few people who are not familiar with control theory know is that when you see misery, that, too, is a choice. Putting this new knowledge to work in your life will take a long time because you have had a lifetime of thinking that misery happens to you, and it certainly feels as if it does. But as you look through your control theory filter at your neighbor choosing to depress to control his wife; your brother, who has never succeeded financially, choosing to drink his life away; or your old aunt depressing for years in a desperate effort to control your cousin, it will gradually become apparent that these are choices. This constant, but easy and interesting, control-theory observation of the people around you choosing all the painful, self-destructive behaviors will help you to accept that you are no different from them. We are all humans choosing pain as well as pleasure as we attempt to satisfy the unrelenting instructions in our genes.

Finally, keep in mind the material in chapter 6, which explains that we have arbitrary control over what we *do*. No matter how much we depress, how painful our heads, how broken-out our skin, how clogged our coronary arteries, how much we drink, we can always change what we do and think. We can't choose to stop our heads from hurting, to elevate our mood with or without drugs, or to unclog our arteries. We can, however, choose to do something that is more satisfying than these. If we want to make the effort, we can increase our social lives, play satisfying games regularly, study for new careers, and act warm and loving with our families. Valid as the argument may be that we do not feel like trying to change our behavior, we always can. And when we do, if what we do is satisfying, we will always feel better or act in a less destructive manner.

The two important concepts to remember are:

1. Your pictures are yours. You put them in and you can exchange them, remove them, and add new pictures. You can also choose to concentrate on ones you can satisfy, and allot little time and energy to those you can't satisfy but are not yet ready to take out of your head.

2. Whether you directly choose a behavior, such as depressing, or make an indirect creative choice, such as a psychosomatic illness, you always have the option to do or think something more satisfying. You have to breathe, but that is all you absolutely must do. The rest of what you choose is up to you whether you "feel" like it or not.

If you can put these basic concepts to work in your life, first through a lot of observation, and then through personal application, you will be well on your way to taking effective control. Be patient. You have lived a long time without control theory, and change is always slow. If you understand that the pathway to practicing control theory is through the pictures in our heads and the behaviors we choose, you have made a good start. Once these are solidly within your grasp, the rest will follow.

Index